Folklore, People, and Place

Folklore, People, and Place is a contribution towards better understanding the complex interconnectivity of folklore, people, and place, across a range of different cultural and geographical contexts. The book showcases a range of international case studies from different cultural and ecological contexts showing how folklore can and does mediate human relationships with people and place.

Folklore has traditionally been connected to place, telling tales of the land and the real and imaginary beings that inhabit storied places. These storytelling traditions and practices have endured in a contemporary world, yet the role and value of folklore to people and places has changed. The book explores a broad range of international perspectives and considers how the relationship between folklore, people, and place has evolved for tourists and indigenous communities. It will showcase a range of international case studies from different cultural and ecological contexts showing how folklore can and does mediate human relationships with people and place. By exploring folklore in the context of tourism, this book engages in a critical discussion of the opportunities and challenges of using storied places in destination development. The case studies in the book provide an international perspective on the contemporary value of folklore to people and places engendering reflection on the role of folklore in sustainable tourism strategies.

This book will be of interest to students, academics, researchers in fields such as anthropology, folklore, tourism, religious studies, human geography and related disciplines. It will also be of interest to scholars and practitioners of traditional ecological knowledge.

Jack Hunter, PhD, is an Honorary Research Fellow with the Alister Hardy Religious Experience Research Centre, and a tutor with the Sophia Centre for the Study of Cosmology in Culture, University of Wales Trinity Saint David, where he is lead tutor on the MA in Ecology and Spirituality and teaches on the MA in Cultural Astronomy and Astrology.

Rachael Ironside, PhD, is a Senior Lecturer and researcher at Robert Gordon University, Scotland. Her research interests focus on the role of supernatural folklore, and how it impacts our experience and understanding of place and cultural heritage.

Routledge Advances in Tourism and Anthropology: People, Place and World
Series Editors:
Dr Catherine Palmer (University of Brighton, UK) C.Palmer3@brighton.ac.uk
Dr Jo-Anne Lester (University of Brighton, UK) J.Lester@brighton.ac.uk

To discuss any ideas for the series please contact Faye Leerink, Commissioning Editor: faye.leerink@tandf.co.uk or the Series Editors.

This series draws inspiration from anthropology's overarching aim to explore and better understand the human condition in all its fascinating diversity. It seeks to expand the intellectual landscape of anthropology and tourism in relation to how we understand the experience of being human, providing critical inquiry into the spaces, places, and lives in which tourism unfolds. Contributions to the series will consider how such spaces are embodied, imagined, constructed, experienced, memorialized and contested. The series provides a forum for cutting-edge research and innovative thinking from tourism, anthropology, and related disciplines such as philosophy, history, sociology, geography, cultural studies, architecture, the arts, and feminist studies.

Everyday Practices of Tourism Mobilities
Packing a Bag
Kaya Barry

Tourism and Indigenous Heritage in Latin America
As Observed through Mexico's Magical Village Cuetzalan
Casper Jacobsen

Tourism and Embodiment
Edited by Catherine Palmer and Hazel Andrews

Tourism Encounters and Imaginaries: The Front and Back Stage of Tourism Performance
Edited by Frances Julia Riemer

Folklore, People, and Place
International Perspectives on Tourism and Tradition in Storied Places
Edited by Jack Hunter and Rachael Ironside

For more information about this series please visit: www.routledge.com/Routledge-Advances-in-Tourism-and-Anthropology/book-series/RATA

Folklore, People, and Place
International Perspectives on Tourism and Tradition in Storied Places

Edited by Jack Hunter and Rachael Ironside

LONDON AND NEW YORK

First published 2023
by Routledge
4 Park Square, Milton Park, Abingdon, Oxon OX14 4RN

and by Routledge
605 Third Avenue, New York, NY 10158

Routledge is an imprint of the Taylor & Francis Group, an informa business

© 2023 selection and editorial matter, Jack Hunter and Rachael Ironside; individual chapters, the contributors

The right of Jack Hunter and Rachael Ironside to be identified as the authors of the editorial material, and of the authors for their individual chapters, has been asserted in accordance with sections 77 and 78 of the Copyright, Designs and Patents Act 1988.

All rights reserved. No part of this book may be reprinted or reproduced or utilised in any form or by any electronic, mechanical, or other means, now known or hereafter invented, including photocopying and recording, or in any information storage or retrieval system, without permission in writing from the publishers.

Trademark notice: Product or corporate names may be trademarks or registered trademarks, and are used only for identification and explanation without intent to infringe.

British Library Cataloguing-in-Publication Data
A catalogue record for this book is available from the British Library

ISBN: 978-1-032-31693-2 (hbk)
ISBN: 978-1-032-44831-2 (pbk)
ISBN: 978-1-003-37413-8 (ebk)

DOI: 10.4324/9781003374138

Typeset in Times New Roman
by SPi Technologies India Pvt Ltd (Straive)

Contents

List of Figures	viii
List of Contributors	ix
Acknowledgements	xii

Introduction: Mapping the Territory		1
RACHAEL IRONSIDE AND JACK HUNTER		

PART I
Re-making and Re-shaping the Past 25

1 Rebuilding the Sacred Union with Basque
Fountains and Springs 27
MARÍA MARTÍNEZ PISÓN

2 Bedecked in Ribbons and Bows: Dressed Trees as Markers of
Heritage, Hope, and Faith in Southern England 40
ETHAN DOYLE WHITE

3 "Unite and Unite, and Let Us All Unite": The Social
Role of the Calendar Custom in English Communities 55
SOPHIE PARKES-NIELD

4 "The Spik O the Place": Dialect and Its Place in the Folkloric
Cultures and Traditions of North-East Scotland 67
PETER H. REID

5 Folklore, Story, and Place: An Irish Tradition with
Vast Touristic Value 82
SHANE BRODERICK

vi *Contents*

PART II
Folklore and Indigenous Landscapes

95

6 Sacred Anishinaabeg Folklore: Okikendawt
Mnisiing, the Island of the Sacred Kettles
RENÉE E. MAZINEGIIZHIGOO-KWE BÉDARD

97

7 Break in the Reef of Time: An Indigenous Science
Approach to the Olowalu Petroglyphs on Maui
APELA COLORADO AND RYAN HURD

109

8 Creating *La Cuna del Folklore Nacional*: The Colonisation of
Indigenous Celebrations, Legends, and Landscapes in
Nicaraguan State Heritage Tourism
PAUL EDWARD MONTGOMERY RAMÍREZ

122

9 Wildness Makes This World
MATTHEW COWAN

134

10 Tasting the Intangible: Examples of
Communication from Sápmi
KAJSA G. ÅBERG AND DORIS A. CARSON

143

PART III
Reimagining Folklore in a Globalised World:
Tourism, Placemaking and Re-enchantment

155

11 A City Made of Stories: Re-enchantment and Narrative
Placemaking in Madrid
LETICIA CORTINA ARACIL

157

12 The Folklore of the Subterranean: The Spectres of the
Underground in Dudley Tourist Sites
SIAN MACFARLANE

169

13 Ghosts, Extraterrestrials, and (Re-)enchantment:
Possibilities and Challenges in Post-secular Tourism
EVA KINGSEPP

186

Contents vii

14 Mythical Park: Reflections on Folklore, Its Natural
Environment, and Tourism 199
KATJA HROBAT VIRLOGET

15 Virtually Haunted Places: Armchair Ghost Tours
Through Weird Space 214
ALICIA EDWARDS-BOON

Concluding Remarks: Exploring Further 226
RACHAEL IRONSIDE AND JACK HUNTER

Index 231

Figures

1.1	Waterfall of Toberia (Araba) (Photograph by Author)	31
2.1	Runes at Knowlton (Photograph by Author)	43
2.2	Knitted Item at Knowlton (Photograph by Author)	44
2.3	Ribbon with Note at Avebury (Photograph by Author)	45
2.4	Marc Bolan Memorial Tree (Photograph by Author)	46
2.5	Churchfield Wood Fairy Tree (Photograph by Author)	48
4.1	The Area in Scotland that Doric Is Spoken (Image: Robert Gordon University)	69
4.2	The Doric "F" Words (Image: Robert Gordon University)	70
4.3	"We Spik Doric Here" Shop Stickers (Image: The Doric Board)	78
7.1	Petroglyphs at Olowalu Are Made by Scratching Away the Patina of the Basalt (Photograph by Apela Colorado, 2021)	110
7.2	Petroglyphs with This Characteristic Filled in Triangular Torso Are Dated from AD 1650 to the Modern Era (Patterson, 2002) (Photograph by Apela Colorado, 2021)	118
9.1	The Stone on Mauri's Land that Splits at Midsummer to Release the Devil (Photograph by Mika RintaPorkkunen)	138
9.2	Wildness Makes This World, Exhibition View, 2021 (Photograph by Jenni Latva)	141
14.1	Lintver (Picture by Author)	201
14.2	Mare's Head Cadastral Boundaries (Picture by Author)	202
14.3	Storytelling Event (Picture by Author)	206

Contributors

Kajsa G. Åberg, PhD, is a tourism strategist at the regional development organisation Region Västerbotten in northern Sweden. With a doctorate in human geography, and a background in heritage studies and as an entrepreneur in tourism, Kajsa engages in initiating and strengthening connections between academia, practitioners, and public sectors.

Leticia Cortina Aracil is an independent researcher working as a guide and Humanities lecturer in the city of Madrid. Her research interests include the existential interpretation of material culture, with an emphasis on corporeality and its impact in the building of worldviews. She has published work on philosophical anthropology, mythology, and folklore.

Renée E. Mazinegiizhigoo-kwe Bédard, PhD (Anishinaabeg, Kanien'kehá ka, and French-Canadian). She is an Assistant Professor at Western University, holding a joint appointment between the Department of Gender, Sexuality and Women's Studies, and the Indigenous Studies program. Her areas of publication include Anishinaabeg motherhood, maternal philosophy, and spirituality.

Shane Broderick holds a BA (Joint Honours) in Folklore and Celtic Civilisation from University College Cork. He teaches for the Irish Pagan School and is a Fáilte Ireland accredited national tour guide.

Doris A. Carson, PhD, is an Assistant Professor at the Department of Geography, Umeå University in northern Sweden. She is a human geographer with an interest in the future of small villages and communities in sparsely populated northern peripheries.

Apela Colorado, PhD, is a traditional cultural practitioner of Oneida and Gaul ancestry. She is Founder of Worldwide Indigenous Science Network, which fosters the revitalisation, growth, and worldwide exchange of traditional knowledge. Dr Colorado is also the author of *Woman Between the Worlds* (2021). Her foundation's website is www.wisn.org.

Matthew Cowan is an artist from Aotearoa New Zealand and a doctoral candidate at the Academy of Fine Arts at the University of the Arts Helsinki, working in the realm of traditional European folk customs. His works are

x *Contributors*

photographs, videos, and installations, which play with the inherent strangeness of the continued popularity of long established folk customs in a modern world.

Alicia Edwards-Boon, PhD, recently completed her doctoral research on London ghost tourism, from the nineteenth century to the present day, at Manchester Metropolitan University. She currently holds a LA&PS Postdoctoral Fellowship at York University, Toronto. Her research interests include the supernatural, haunted space/place, Gothic tourism, and Black Diasporic Gothic.

Jack Hunter, PhD, is an Honorary Research Fellow with the Alister Hardy Religious Experience Research Centre, and a tutor with the Sophia Centre for the Study of Cosmology in Culture, University of Wales Trinity Saint David, where he is lead tutor on the MA in Ecology and Spirituality and teaches on the MA in Cultural Astronomy and Astrology.

Ryan Hurd, MA, is Lecturer in Psychology and Holistic Studies at the John F. Kennedy School of Psychology at National University. With a background in both cultural resource management and consciousness studies, Ryan is interested in topics at the intersections of culture, ecology, and the imaginal. His author website is www.Dreamstudies.org

Rachael Ironside, PhD, is a Senior Lecturer and researcher at Robert Gordon University, Scotland. Her research interests focus on the role of supernatural folklore, and how it impacts our experience and understanding of place and cultural heritage.

Eva Kingsepp, PhD, has a doctorate in Media and Communication studies. She is Associate Professor at Karlstad University, Sweden. Her main research deals with popular media and cultural memory as transmedia storytelling, with a special focus on cryptohistory and influences from occulture, fantasy, and science fiction.

Sian Macfarlane is an artist and researcher, working with photography, performance, and archive, based in the West Midlands. Her artistic work and wider research concern hidden histories and folklore customs and beliefs, exploring installation and new technologies such as AR to activate these elements. She teaches photography at Coventry University. Website: www.sianmacfarlane.com

María Martínez Pisón, PhD, a Spanish-Basque educational psychologist and Associate Professor in UOC. She also belongs to the Society of Sciences Aranzadi (Donosti), collaborating in ethnographic research. She is the creator of *"Por encima de todas las zarzas"* (Above all the brambles), a divulgation project about Basque traditional culture, folklore, and magical practices.

Sophie Parkes-Nield is a practice-based PhD candidate at the Centre for Contemporary Legend (CCL), a folklore research group based at Sheffield

Hallam University, where she is researching English calendar customs and the novel. For more information about Sophie, her writing and her research, please visit her website: www.sophieparkes.co.uk

Paul Edward Montgomery Ramírez, PhD, is an Indigenous Chorotega decolonial heritage specialist and public archaeologist. His work focuses on the use of heritage resources as tools for creating forums and economies that bring dignity for marginal peoples. At the time of writing this article, Paul Edward is an Adjunct Professor and NAGPRA (Native American Graves Protection and Repatriation Act) compliance officer at Cleveland State University.

Peter H. Reid, PhD, is a Professor at the School of Creative and Cultural Business at Robert Gordon University. His teaching and research includes the management of cultural services, heritage and storytelling, particularly in the North-East of Scotland. He delivered his professorial lecture entirely in Doric.

Katja Hrobat Virloget, PhD, works at the Department of Anthropology and Cultural Studies, Faculty of Humanities, University of Primorska. For the implementation of The Mythical park she received the Slovenian national prize, Prometheus of Science for Excellence in Communication (2020). She is co-editor of the international journal *Studia Mythologica Slavica*.

Ethan Doyle White, PhD, has a doctorate in medieval history and archaeology from University College London (UCL). His research interests include the religions of early medieval England, modern Paganism and ritual interactions with landscape, subjects on which he has published various books, edited volumes, and journal articles.

Acknowledgements

We would like to thank all our contributors who inspired and made this collection possible. It has been a pleasure to explore these extraordinary corners of the world through their stories, philosophies, and traditional cultural knowledge, and we feel privileged to have the opportunity to bring their work together. We would also like to thank the editors at Routledge who trusted us to collate this book and guided us through the process. Finally, we extend our gratitude to our spouses, family, and friends who have continually supported and encouraged our curiosity.

Introduction

Mapping the Territory

Rachael Ironside and Jack Hunter

Folklore: Tradition and Experience

There is a distinction between folklore materials and their academic study, though both are often referred to by the same word. The term "folkloristics" was proposed by folklorists in the nineteenth century in an effort to make clear the distinction between the formal *study* of folklore (including explanatory paradigms, theories, research methodologies, and so on), and the folklore materials themselves (Dundes, 1965, p. 3; Burns, 1977). Folkloristics span multiple disciplinary boundaries, including literature, linguistics, history, and anthropology, all of which are drawn on in the analysis of folklore materials (Dundes, 1996). Others prefer terms such as "folklore studies" to establish the distinction (Bronner, 2017). Folklore materials – the objects of folkloristic research – frequently include, but are not limited to "traditional ideas" (Burns, 1977, p. 109), and "speech, tales, songs, dances, and customs" (Bronner, 2017, p. 1). Alan Dundes (1934–2005) provided a very influential definition of folklore in terms of the word's etymology. "Folk," he suggests, "can refer to *any group of people whatsoever* who share at least one common factor […] Every group has its own folklore," which may consist of any number of items featured in an expansive (though not exhaustive) list, including "myths, legends, folktales, jokes, proverbs, riddles, chants, charms, blessings, curses, oaths, insults, retorts, taunts," and so on, as well as "folk costume, folk dance, folk drama […] folk art, folk belief (or superstition), folk medicine, folk instrumental music […], folk metaphors […], names (e.g. nicknames and placenames)," and much more (Dundes, 1965, pp. 2–3, emphasis in original). It is these things that constitute the "lore" in folklore.

With the emergence of scholarly approaches to analysing and interpreting the vast spectrum of folklore materials and traditions in the nineteenth and twentieth centuries came a (gradual) proliferation of different attempts at defining the field and its subject matter. Early definitions of folklore implied an assumption of the "antiquity of the material, the anonymity or collectiveness of composition, and the simplicity of the folk" (Ben-Amos, 1971, p. 4). Romantic notions of folklore suggested the existence of a golden age in the distant past, which folk stories provided fleeting glimpses of, and pointers as to how it could be restored. It is well known that the folk stories collected by

DOI: 10.4324/9781003374138-1

2   *Rachael Ironside and Jack Hunter*

the Brothers Grimm were influential in the establishment of a pan-German identity in the nineteenth century, for example, ultimately contributing to the establishment of a unified German state in 1871 (Csapo, 2005, p. 6). Dan Ben-Amos points out, however, that the criteria of anonymity and antiquity are "circumstantial and not essential to folklore" (Ben-Amos, 1971, p. 4). Folklore is not necessarily "old," indeed folklore could equally be defined as "current popular knowledge." Alan Dundes, for example, suggested that folklore could be conceived as "autobiographical ethnography – that is, it is a people's own description of themselves" (Dundes, 2007, p. 55), with individual elements of folklore constituting "units of worldview" (Dundes, 1971). Furthermore, folklore is not just a collection of beliefs disconnected from reality. More recent efforts to define folklore have shifted towards an emphasis on practice and away from beliefs. Simon Bronner, for instance, explains: "Put simply, folklore is 'traditional knowledge, put into, and drawing from, practice'" (Bronner, 2017, p. 46). Folklore is, therefore, cultural knowledge – passed down from one generation to the next.

There is also an element of folklore that is experiential in origin, emerging out of direct practical engagement with the world. This is true for traditional ideas about the weather, agriculture, horticulture and other aspects of the ecological environment and daily life – which are built up over many generations of practical experience and observation (see the next section on Traditional Ecological Knowledge) – as much as it is true for "supernatural" folklore traditions. It has been suggested that some supernatural folk traditions have been constructed around pre-cultural core experiences, such as the "Old Hag" tradition in Newfoundland, for example, which the folklorist David Hufford recognised as a particular cultural interpretation (amongst many others in the cross-cultural context) of the medically recognised sleep paralysis phenomenon (Hufford, 1982). Folklore is not, therefore, necessarily irrational or "superstitious" in nature (even when concerning the supernatural), but may in fact be "associated with accurate observations interpreted rationally" (Hufford, 1982, p. xviii). Crucially, however, this does not necessarily "suggest that all such belief has this association. Nor is this association taken as proof that the beliefs are true" (ibid.).

Folklore, then, can broadly be understood as consisting of complex systems of beliefs, ideas, experiential knowledge, traditions, techniques, crafts, customs, and stories, held and practised by contemporary people across a wide range of local contexts, which relate as often to the everyday world of plants, animals, weather, seasonal cycles, daily activities, human relationships, and so on, as they do to the supernatural world of fairies, ghosts, goblins, and other spirits.

Folklore and Place

The experiential dimension of folklore also connects traditions of belief and practice to place. Certain locations may become associated with particular traditions because of historical and legendary events that apparently took place there (Baker, 1972), or with ghosts, witches, fairies, or UFOs because of

Introduction 3

experiences repeatedly reported in those places over time (McCue, 2012, p. 91). First-hand extraordinary experiences become stories, and are passed on from one individual to another in the form of *memorates* – stories of events that are believed to be true (Honko, 1964) – which help to build up a location's reputation. Folklorist Lauri Honko explains: "Belief in the existence of spirits is founded not upon loose speculation, but upon concrete, personal experiences, the reality of which is reinforced by sensory perceptions" (1964, p. 10). Place names in Wales, for example, "show the wide spread of belief in bugbears and spirits" in the country (Richards, 1969). Some locations come to be associated with stories of miraculous healing (Kõivupuu, 2020), and rocks, wells, and springs throughout Europe are often connected to an origin story relating to the deeds of Saints, or other folkloric and pre-Christian figures (Cusack and Wilson, 2016, pp. 69–72). Key landmarks in the local environment, such as boulders deposited by ancient glaciers in unlikely places, or prehistoric standing stones, might also be explained by recourse to the activities of giants – or other supernatural entities, such as dragons or the devil – in the primordial past (Richards, 1934; Spooner, 1965; Hunter, 2022). As anthropologist Christopher Tilley points out, such narratives can contribute to a distinctive sense of place, local identity, and wider landscape, which may be understood as "a series of named locales [and] a set of relational places linked by paths, movements and narratives" (Tilley, 1994, p. 34). Stories help to explain, define, and connect places. They provide a means to establish a personal or communal sense of relationship to place. Adopting an Aristotelian perspective, sacred geographer Bernadette Brady suggests that "As an area becomes rich with cultural layers […] it will grow in its potential to influence human activity, such activity as wanting to maintain place names and taking measures to protect a storied location" (2022, p. 184).

Storied landscapes and places play an important role in many spiritual and religious traditions. We only need to think of the central significance of landscapes in the major world religions – the Holy Land for Jews, Christians, and Muslims, for example – and the monuments and locations that become sites of pilgrimage for many thousands of believers each year. Indeed, pilgrimage is a central point of connection between travel, people, culture, belief, and the land, as pilgrims move through significant locations and reflect on their participation and faith (Nolan and Sidney, 1989). Justine Digance explains that:

> Traditional religious pilgrimage is far from diminishing in popularity with age-old centres such as Rome, Jerusalem and Lourdes still attracting the faithful, with newer sites such as Medjugorje and Sri Sathya Sai Baba's palatial Ashram at Puttaparthi in India, proving to be popular pilgrimage sites today. A veritable cornucopia of secular pilgrimages [also] abound […].
>
> (Digance, 2006, p. 37)

Movement through storied landscapes is not just a hallmark of the pilgrimage traditions of the major world religions. The Aboriginal Australian

4 *Rachael Ironside and Jack Hunter*

concept of "the dreamtime" goes a long way towards demonstrating the close relationship between narrative, spirituality, and the landscape amongst indigenous communities as well. Although there are many different indigenous Australian terms that are translated into English as "dreamtime," making it a tricky concept to use accurately, there are nevertheless some defining characteristics across tribal groups that are worth mentioning in this context. Indeed, Alan Rumsey suggests that the apparent differences in defining the dreaming between groups are in fact "[...] variants of a single 'mode of orientation,' to place," in which "enduring, physical features of the lived landscape [are the] prime locus of objectification" (Rumsey, 1994, p. 126). Similar orientations to place are found in other indigenous cosmologies and are also reflected in traditional European folklore. The dreaming also refers to ancestral creation myths – the stories of how the world and the features of the landscape came to be – as well as to an "a-temporal metaphysical reality" that overlays and interpenetrates the physical environment (Hume, 2000, p. 125). In moving through the landscape, through sacred sites and mythic locations, and re-telling dreaming stories, it is possible to *participate* in the act of creation itself. Lynn Hume explains that from the "orientation" of the dreaming:

> Everything is interconnected in a vast web of sacredness. Ancestor tracks and sites, and the Dreaming stories associated with them, make up the sacred geography of Australia. The entire continent is criss-crossed by tracks that the Ancestors made on their travels [...] Those responsible must take care of the country by periodically following songlines pertaining to these myths, thus maintaining their connections to the land and keeping the land.
>
> (Hume, 2000, p. 127)

For indigenous Australians the physical features of the natural landscape offer a direct connection to the creation event and are revered and protected as sacred sites (many of which are currently under threat from government coal mining operations, despite their cultural, ecological, and spiritual significance, see Lewis and Scambary, 2016). Indigenous Australia's sacred landscapes and dreaming stories are also echoed and reflected in the folk traditions of other parts of the world, which similarly portray the image of a living mythical landscape with which we can participate. Traditional stories about place often also contain detailed ecological and environmental knowledge about the varieties of plants, animals, and other-than-human beings that inhabit the land, including their characters, properties, behaviours, and uses, as well as prescribed modes of interaction with them.

Traditional Ecological Knowledge

Traditional Ecological Knowledge (TEK) is a term that has been gaining increasing relevance and attention in academic and popular discourse since the 1980s and might be considered a branch of folklore dealing with the

Introduction 5

ecological environment. Social ecologist Fikret Berkes explains that systems of traditional ecological knowledge represent the cumulation of "experience acquired over thousands of years of direct human contact with the environment" (Berkes, 1993, p. 1), which includes "an intimate and detailed knowledge of plants, animals, and natural phenomena, the development and use of appropriate technologies for hunting, fishing, trapping, agriculture, and forestry," and so on (Bourque, Inglis and LeBlanc, 1993, p. vii). Moreover, it is argued that systems of traditional ecological knowledge represent a form of "holistic knowledge, or 'world view' which parallels the scientific discipline of ecology" (Bourque, Inglis and LeBlanc, 1993, p. vii). Traditional forms of knowledge and knowledge transmission include:

> [...] oral narratives that recount human histories; cosmological observations and modes of reckoning time; symbolic and decorative modes of communication; techniques for planting and harvesting; hunting and gathering skills; specialised understandings of local ecosystems; and the manufacture of specialised tools and technologies (e.g., flint-knapping, hide tanning, pottery-making, and concocting medicinal remedies).
>
> (Bruchac, 2014, p. 3814)

In addition to the techno-ecological-medical-scientific knowledge contained within indigenous traditions – which Western scientific approaches have often been very keen to exploit – systems of TEK are also frequently bound up in wider spiritual cosmologies, with implications and frameworks for participating in and understanding the world that far exceed those of Western science and ecology. Notably, this often includes an animistic worldview, in which the cosmos is conceived as personal and relational in nature. In Graham Harvey's words, from an animistic perspective the world is understood to be "full of persons, only some of whom are human," acknowledging the fact that "life is always lived in relationship with others" (Harvey, 2005, p. xi). These animistic and relational elements of traditional knowledge are often sidelined, or dismissed, by Western science in favour of more "practical" information (Wright, 2021). Linda Tuhiwai Smith explains:

> The arguments of different indigenous peoples based on spiritual relationships to the universe, to the landscape, to stones, rocks, insects, and other things, seen and unseen, have been difficult arguments for Western systems of knowledge to deal with or accept [...] These arguments give a partial indication of the different world views and alternative ways of coming to know, and of being, which still endure within the indigenous world. [...]
>
> (Tuhiwai Smith, 2012, p. 78)

Biologist Robin Wall Kimmerer has suggested, however, that rather than being at odds with Western scientific perspectives, traditional ecological knowledge and Western scientific ecological knowledge have many points of

6   *Rachael Ironside and Jack Hunter*

overlap and might be complementary to one another, explaining that the synergy of perspectives can be useful in a variety of different ways:

> Traditional ecological knowledge can be a source of new biological insights and potential models for conservation biology and sustainable development [...] Examination of traditional ecological knowledge explicitly brings multicultural perspectives into the core of the science curriculum, where they have generally been absent [...] Recognition of traditional ecological knowledge increases opportunities for productive partnerships between Western scientists and indigenous people [...] Traditional ecological knowledge integrates scientific and cultural concerns in a holistic manner [...]
>
> (Kimmerer, 2002, pp. 432–435)

Just as there is scope for the incorporation of TEK into scientific ecological knowledge, so too is there scope for the incorporation of other folkloric perspectives and traditions, and the ecological information they contain, which may have practical applications in the conservation of endangered ecosystems and sacred sites, as well as for cultural conservation. In a study of TEK in Northern Ghana, for example, Boafo et al. (2016) found that "diverse forms of TEK developed over generations are still being applied by communities and households in the form of taboos and totems, customs and rituals, rules and regulations, and traditional protected areas" (2016, p. 32). They conclude that it is "imperative that national, regional, and local policies aimed at identifying, documenting, and implementing potent TEK are formulated to help safeguard ecosystems and improve livelihood systems" in Ghana (ibid.).

This kind of ecological knowledge might also be referred to as ethnobiology or folk biology. Ethnobiological frameworks (of which there are many, including those of Western biology) can be either adaptive or maladaptive. Anthropologist Roy Rappaport explains that

> Nature is seen by humans through a screen of beliefs, knowledge, and purposes, and it is in terms of their images of nature, rather than of the "actual structure" of nature, that they act. Yet it is upon nature itself that they do act, and it is nature itself that acts upon them, nurturing or destroying them.
>
> (Rappaport, 1979, p. 97)

The assumptions inherent in different worldviews, then, lead to different behaviours towards and within the natural environment. For example, misconceptions about certain animal species in bodies of traditional ecological knowledge *can* lead to those animals being persecuted when encountered in the wild, with the consequence of destabilising ecosystem dynamics. As an interesting illustration of this principle, Ceríaco et al. (2011) conducted a study of contemporary folk theories of geckos (*Hemidactylus turcicus*) in Portugal (Ceríaco et al., 2011). They found, for instance, that

Introduction 7

Several locals (4%) thought that geckos feed on human blood and skin, while approximately 25% believed the gecko to be poisonous and 24% that the animal was a vector of dermatological diseases. Several stories were reported regarding the poisonous and disease vector nature of the gecko. One of the most typical stories presented by the locals (10%) related to the poisoning of an entire family by a gecko falling into a saucepan on the stove.

(Ceríaco et al., 2011, p. 5)

Folk ideas such as these have led to the active extermination of gecko populations in the region, threatening their survival. Recent research on the role of beliefs about "magical animals" in wildlife conservation efforts in Madagascar also supports the dual role played by folklore, having the potential to both protect and endanger rare species and natural habitats. In their case study, Holmes et al. describe how aye-ayes (*Daubentonia madagascariensis*) in Madagascar face similar persecution to geckos in Portugal because of their associations with witchcraft in local traditions of belief (Holmes et al., 2018).

There is, then, a complicated relationship between folklore, other bodies of traditional knowledge, and the ecological environment in which they have developed. Systems of traditional ecological knowledge undoubtedly contain valuable lessons for developing healthy human relationships with the natural world, but, as with geckos in Portugal and aye-ayes in Madagascar, some traditions may also have the inverse effect. There cannot be a one-size-fits-all approach to understanding the relationship. Every region and group has its own stories and frameworks for engagement with the world – different orientations, assumptions, and behaviours that may not necessarily adhere to those of others – and it is the differences in folk traditions between regions that contribute to the appeal of folklore tourism, as well as to the challenges in implementing it effectively.

Folklore and Tourism

Travel with the purpose of visiting places associated with folklore stories, customs, and traditions is recognised as a global phenomenon by scholars (Buchmann, 2006; Harsono, 2017; Everett and John Parakoottathil, 2018). However, despite the growing interest from tourist destinations in adopting folklore into their development strategies, scholarship in this area remains relatively limited. The term "folklore tourism" has received some attention and is often regarded as a subset of heritage and cultural tourism. Its amorphous nature, in this sense, encapsulates wider reasons to travel – literature, language, art, events, people, film – and arguably makes this area of tourism particularly difficult to define neatly. Broadly though, folklore tourism is considered to be a form of travel associated with motivations to witness and participate in folklore performances, including traditional rituals and cultural events, combined with pilgrimage to landscapes of folkloric significance (for instance, natural rivers and mountains connected to folktales, or sites of

8 *Rachael Ironside and Jack Hunter*

religious worship and practice, see Harsono, 2017). More recently, scholars have also recognised the role of supernatural folktales and storytelling as a form of folklore-based tourism incorporating wider terminology, such as "paranormal tourism" (Houran et al., 2020), "ghost tourism" (Hanks, 2016), and "mythical tourism" (Buchmann, 2006). As such, folklore tourism is multifaceted, encompassing a wide-range of visitor experiences from folklore-inspired events (such as the Robin Hood Festival, see Everett and John Parakoottathil, 2018), to supernatural trails and walks (such as ghost tours in Gettysburg, see Thompson, 2010), to immersion in the food and drink culture of a nation (Yunxia, 2019). In this book, we consider folklore tourism in its widest sense, as a form of travel to places associated with folkloric tradition, custom, and storytelling.

While pilgrimage to places of religious, spiritual, and cultural significance (many of which are also connected to folklore) has a long history, the emergence of folklore tourism is considered a relatively recent development. Through the late nineteenth and much of the twentieth centuries, rapid modernisation, urbanisation, and rationalisation contributed to a movement away from spiritual and esoteric thinking towards more scientific, secular ways of approaching the world. This is the process of "disenchantment" that Max Weber recognised in his lecture on *Science as a Vocation*, and which he described as being characterised by:

> […] the knowledge or belief that, *if only one wanted to*, one could find out any time; that there are in principle no *mysterious, incalculable powers at work*, but rather that one could in principle master everything through *calculation*.
>
> (1946, p. 7)

As such, folklore stories, customs, and their landscapes, particularly in Euro-American countries, encountered a de-prioritisation in mainstream culture in favour of modernisation and rationalisation. For some countries, a movement away from superstition and traditional customs was considered a necessary step towards progress and the opportunity to change global perceptions of national identity (see Light, 2007).

However, despite Max Weber's assertion that modernisation equated with the end of religious and spiritual thinking, the mid-to-late twentieth century witnessed a profound re-emergence of alternative, non-secular beliefs and contemporary hyper-real popular cultures (Bowman, 2000; Possamai and Lee, 2011). More recent perspectives have suggested that, rather than returning after a period of absence, this esoteric dimension of Western thought never really left in the first place, and its traces can be seen threaded right throughout the modern history of mainstream science, technology, media, social science, and culture (Josephson-Storm, 2017; Noakes, 2020; Natale and Pasulka, 2020; Espirito Santo and Hunter, 2021).

The growth of folklore tourism gained momentum towards the end of the 1900s as destinations around the world sought to establish new ways of engaging local and visiting communities. In part, this "folklorisation" of place was spurred on by local government and destination marketing organisations (DMO's) who, in an effort to harness the economic potential of tourism (which was seeing significant growth in the 1970s), sought to capitalise upon the culture and traditions of a region to draw visitors in. This was a top-down approach to folklore tourism, which led to the development of physical and cultural infrastructure, as well as the rebranding and identity shaping of particular destinations. On 4 April 1975, for instance, key stakeholders in Germany met to establish the "German Fairy Tale Route" celebrating the country's rich tradition of folk literature. Heinrich Fischer, first director of the newly established consortium, founded the route to attract tourists to the area on the premise that "folk literature, after a period of partial submersion in floods of printed social criticism, appeared to experience the beginnings of a renaissance" (Hemme, 2005, p. 71). In other countries, government-backed projects also sought to celebrate and preserve local traditions and culture through tourism initiatives. For example, the Bomas of Kenya opened in 1973 as a cultural museum and performing arts venue, and still to this day invites tourists to celebrate the cultural heritage of the nation through traditional dance and performance (Bruner, 2001).

Folklore tourism has also been unplanned, even accidental, emerging from the bottom up. The rise of popular media – including television, film, and latterly the internet – has played a key role in popularising places and their associated folklore narratives (Hill, 2010). The emergence of Dracula tourism in Romania from the 1970s onwards, for example, provides a compelling illustration of the media's role in popularising a destination based on its associated stories. While Bram Stoker's classic book *Dracula* was published in 1897, it was only during the second part of the twentieth century – amongst a plethora of Dracula-based films, television programmes, and books (including the best-selling *In Search of Dracula*, 1972) – that Romania was "put on the map" for tourists seeking an experience with the vampire myth and its associated folklore. This was despite a general reluctance to embrace the Dracula narrative from Romanian authorities (Light, 2007). Similarly, in Roswell, New Mexico, USA, the first tourist attractions and events promoting the Roswell Incident of 1947 emerged in 1991. Publication of the book *The Roswell Incident* in 1980 renewed interest in the story (which had been all but dismissed by the mainstream at that point) and led to the development of the International UFO Museum and Research Centre (IUFOMRC), later followed by the first UFO festival in 1997, which attracted over 47,000 people (Meehan, 2008). Similarly, at Rendlesham Forest in Suffolk, UK, Forestry England have recently established a UFO walking trail. Their website explains how the "trail will stimulate your imagination, taking you through forest, heathland and wetlands and some of the areas connected to the UFO sighting in December 1980" (Forestry England, 2022).

Consequently, we can say that tourism in storied places has evolved from a combination of deliberate top-down economic strategies in tandem with bottom-up public interest in locations associated with folklore and extraordinary experiences. For destinations, embracing folklore as a tourism asset has led to significant economic benefits. In Scotland, for instance, the visitor economy surrounding "Nessie" was worth over £41 million to the Scottish economy in 2018 (The Press and Journal, 2018). As such, folklore has become a valuable resource for placemaking. In the past 50 years, folklore has not only featured in tourism itineraries, but places have become tourist destinations explicitly *because of* the folklore associated with them. Contemporary examples include Salem, Massachusetts, promoted as "The Witch City"; York, England, hailed as the "Most Haunted City in the World" in 2014; and Roswell, New Mexico, where the local tourist information website hosts the tagline "We Believe," in connection with its popular UFO folklore.

Why Do People Take Part in Folklore Tourism?

The growth and success of folklore tourism over the past 50 years suggests a healthy demand amongst travellers globally. But, *why*? In heritage and cultural tourism scholarship, understanding why people consume cultural experiences has long been an object of study. Motivations including a desire to learn (Falk, Ballantyne, Packer, and Benckendorff, 2012; Richards, 1996), culture seeking (Correia, Kozak, and Ferradeira, 2013), escapism (Özel and Kozak, 2012), and identity construction (Bond and Falk, 2013) are of key importance. Research into the reasons behind participation in folklore tourism is somewhat more limited, although given the close connection between folklore, heritage, and cultural tourism there are likely many motivational similarities. Recent research suggests in particular that seeking out "excitement, joy, and surprise" (Pharino, Peare and Pryce, 2018) and a general sense of curiosity about folklore and the paranormal (Obradović et al., 2021) are central motivations.

Ironside (2018) argues that some forms of contemporary folklore tourism (such as ghost tourism) may have their roots in cultural practices such as legend-tripping. As Bill Ellis (1996) defines it, legend-tripping is the practice of visiting places where something uncanny has occurred with the intention of experiencing something supernatural. Places such as abandoned buildings, cemeteries, and bridges often become popular sites for legend-tripping because of the folklore and legends attached to them. The Mothman of Point Pleasant, West Virginia, popularised by the Fortean writer John A. Keel's famous book *The Mothman Prophecies*, is an interesting case in point. A whole industry has built up around the sightings of the enigmatic cryptid, including the establishment of a Mothman Museum and the erection of a steel statue of the winged humanoid, which has become a popular tourist attraction in itself (Sherwood, 2013). While legend-tripping is often considered an activity undertaken by youths who travel to locations to test the veracity and credibility of a legend (Bird, 1994), the experiential dimensions of legend-tripping – the desire to "escape from the mundane" (Ironside, 2018, p. 97) and the "conscious suspension of reality in the interest of fun" (Holly and Cordy, 2007, p. 346) – may resonate with the motivations of most contemporary tourists. Like legend-tripping, folklore tourism offers participatory experiences for visitors. As Everett and John Parakoottathil (2018) observe in their study of the Robin Hood Festival in Nottingham, this participation may be explicit and involve visitors taking part in performance and role-playing as a form of everyday escapism. Alternatively, participation may be subtle or implicit. On ghost tours, audience participation may be limited, yet the audience is invited through storytelling to suspend rationality and engage with the *possibility* of seeing a ghost (Krisjanous and Carruthers, 2018). Both situations – events that take place in liminal spaces between the ordinary and the extraordinary, the real and the imaginary – provide opportunities for contemplation and the enchantment of place.

Tourists may also seek opportunities for alternative forms of knowledge-acquisition and education through folklore experiences. Folklore stories are deeply embedded in the culture, heritage, and environment of local communities, and yet can often offer something more than historical or scientific fact alone (Hopper et al., 2019; Paphitis, 2013). In her study of haunted heritage in the UK, Michele Hanks (2011) explores the role of ghost stories in the presentation of difficult history. As she argues, ghosts may act as a form of social memory – constituting a mythico-history (Malkki, 1995) – that offers a blend of historical fact, interpretation, and myth, to provide a back-stage glance into places and their people. Despite the obvious commercial agenda of most ghost tourism, entertainment is interwoven with history to encourage engagement with place at a deeper level (Garcia, 2012; Gentry, 2007; Holloway, 2010). The incorporation of humour, and the "nip and bite" of playfulness common in ghost walk narratives (Thompson, 2010), enables the presentation of dark heritage in a way that authorised heritage alone may find difficult to achieve. As such, tourists may actively seek out folklore stories as an alternative form of heritage or dark tourism.[1]

In their study of the push-pull motivations for ghost tourism in Spain, Dancausa, Hernández, and Pérez (2020) also identified the search for novelty and emotional experience (push motivation), as well as the organisation of the tour (pull motivation), to be important motivating factors. Others have noted the desire for thrilling or scary experiences (Holloway, 2010; Garcia, 2012), an interest in pursuing ontological and spiritual questions (Eaton, 2015; Ironside, 2018), and the inherent draw of atmospheric and spooky places (Ironside, 2018; Thompson, 2010).

Arguably, the desire for an *experience* – whether that be novelty, emotion, thrill, learning, or escapism – is especially important to the folklore tourist. By providing the opportunity for this, folklore tourism appeals to the contemporary consumer who, as Pine and Gilmore (1999) observed over two decades ago, are seeking more memorable and meaningful interactions in an experience economy. Others have observed that forms of folklore tourism, like paranormal tourism, may indeed be driving a shift from an experience economy to an "enchantment economy" (Houran et al., 2020).

Problems with Folklore and Tourism

The potential for folklore to offer tourists the opportunity to learn about, reflect on, and experience place through particular cultural lenses is undoubtedly beneficial. Furthermore, the economic impacts and opportunities provided through placemaking initiatives have helped to reinvigorate destinations – both rural and urban – through the celebration and commercialisation of folklore. However, the "folklorisation" of place can present complex challenges for local communities, visitors, and the surrounding natural and heritage environment.

In her study of ghost tours in Edinburgh and Toledo, Garcia (2012) observed the tensions that exist between the presentation of ghost tours as an educational experience and the need to entertain for the purposes of commoditisation and appealing to consumer interests. Unlike historical fact, folklore often relies on the interpretation (and re-interpretation) of multiple narratives – as such, one story may take many forms depending on the context and storyteller. The separation between "fact" and "fiction" is, therefore, more fluid with folklore and can lead to the fragmentation of historical and personal narratives (Goldstein, Grider, and Thomas, 2007). Like dark tourism, the tendency to trivialise, or glorify, certain aspects of dark heritage, such as gore, human suffering, and misery may also be prominent in the interests of providing an "entertaining" experience for tourists (Garcia, 2012). For local communities this can be problematic. On one hand, folklore may provide a tool to present the difficult heritage of a place, while at the same time shaping the tourist gaze so that visitors come to see and understand a place in ways that are not fully authentic, or sympathetic, to the local culture and community. In Transylvania, for example, the promotion of Dracula tourism was initially met with strong resistance from local communities. The connection to Vlad Tepes, who for many was a national hero, was considered culturally insensitive and disparate from the heritage narratives the region wished to portray for itself (Light, 2007).

For local communities, the use of folklore may also contribute to a sense of "otherness" and a disconnection between authentic local culture and that constructed through the tourist gaze. Performing folklore customs (through traditional dance, song, storytelling, or dress) has the potential to reinforce cultural stereotypes that may be distinct from the contemporary lives of local people (Lőrincz, 2021). Furthermore, the appropriation of folklore customs for tourism purposes, such as in the form of souvenirs and other consumable trinkets, may devalue their meaning and importance for the community (Viken, 2022). As recognised by George (2010) and Lőrincz (2021), this disconnect is heightened when there is a lack of consultation between local communities and those developing folklore-based tourism strategies. The co-creation of tourism resources is, therefore, vitally important in maintaining a sense of authenticity for tourists and ownership for local people.

High-volume tourism to places associated with folklore also raises challenges for local communities and the natural environment. As Ironside and

Introduction   13

Massie (2020) discuss, the high volume of visitors to the Fairy Glen located on the Isle of Skye, Scotland, presents environmental challenges. The performance of spiritual practices to appease the fairies (such as creating stone circles and spirals), as well as removing stones and other natural souvenirs, has led to dramatic changes to the landscape and ecology. Local communities are also impacted by the volume of traffic on the narrow, single-track roads and the "invasion" of land once enjoyed more peacefully by those living in, and around, the Glen. Similar issues of souvenir collecting and vandalism have been reported in both natural habitats, such as the Fortingall Yew Tree, Scotland (The Scotsman, 2019), and heritage sites, such as Loon Lake Cemetery, USA, known by legend as a "witches cemetery" (Waskul and Waskul, 2016).

The use of folklore in tourism, therefore, raises questions about the balance between the economic, socio-cultural, and environmental value of places and people. In some instances, this may lead to a conflict between local "identity vs. economy" (Tunbridge 1994). The issue of appropriation is also apparent here. As Obradović and colleagues point out in relation to the potential for paranormal tourism in Serbia, "It is important to ensure that during the development of this type of tourism […] the customs and rituals of the local population are not endangered, but preserved" (Obradović et al., 2021, pp. 229–230). Local people must be at the centre of folklore tourism. The difference between "placemaking" (a top-down approach led by governments and agencies) and "placemaking" (a bottom-up approach led by communities) is perhaps an important distinction here. As Ironside and Massie (2020) suggest, a folklore-centric gaze that shifts the tourist focus from the *consumption of folklore in landscapes* to a *relational approach with folklore* that considers the people, environment, and heritage of a place as part of a "living" landscape may be especially beneficial.

Folklore-Centric Tourism and Environmental Education

In recent years, the sciences have been at the forefront of climate education and ecological knowledge exchange, but research increasingly suggests that narrative approaches to ecological learning – through myth and storytelling, for example – are often more effective than purely fact-based approaches, especially with children and young people (Holm et al., 2015; Hallam, 2019; Hopper et al., 2019). Education about ecology and the environment is paramount to developing solutions to, and resilience against, further climate change and ecological degradation, and is essential for establishing a sense of connection to the natural world, leading to "a stronger commitment to nature," which in turn "could lead to higher human interest in environmental protection" (Restall and Conrad, 2015, p. 1). Storytelling has been shown to be a very effective way to engage people with their environment and local ecology in meaningful and fulfilling ways (Hopper et al., 2019). For instance, we may be encouraged to preserve certain sites and natural landscapes because of the stories and folk-traditions that are attached to them. A brief survey of newspaper reports from the last 25 years reveals that the power of

14 *Rachael Ironside and Jack Hunter*

the association between natural landscape features and folk-traditions is still very much alive. Take, for instance, the role of the elves or Huldufólk in Iceland (The Guardian, 2013), or the fairies in Ireland (The Irish Times, 1999), in influencing planning body decisions about roads and other construction projects. The association of certain rocks, trees, or bushes with stories of the fairies, then, can lead to very real changes in human behaviour, especially in the direction of pro-environmental action. Research by Kim et al. on Korean nature proverbs found a similarly beneficial role in that they can be particularly "meaningful for communicating ecological principles and natural resource management practices" (Kim et al., 2017, p. 14). They suggest that proverbs have the potential to enhance ecoliteracy, even amongst urban populations:

> environmental educators can use proverbs or folklore sources as a bridge for unifying traditional ecological wisdom and cultural expressions with modern scientific and systems-based learning of sustainability.
>
> (Kim et al., 2017, p. 14)

Recent moves to recognise the legal personhood of environmental features, such as rivers, mountains, and entire ecosystems, in order to ensure their protection might also be understood in this context (The Guardian, 2017) – a recognition that the landscape and its features are not merely resources to be plundered for human consumption but have an intrinsic value in their own right and with which we can participate and interact. Thinking about landscapes and ecosystems in this way – as many indigenous traditions do (cf. Nelson and Shilling, 2018; Yunkaporta, 2019), and as the folklore suggests our ancient ancestors likely did too (see Taylor, ; Shapland,), has the potential to transform the way that we relate to, and behave within, them.

As Ironside and Massie define it, a "folklore-centric" approach is a relational approach, and in this way it resonates with perspectives contained within systems of traditional ecological knowledge. Robin Wall Kimmerer emphasises three key elements of traditional ecological knowledge that could have important implications for folklore tourism. She explains how TEK is founded upon notions of animacy, reciprocity, and ceremony. The element of animacy suggests an understanding that we live in a "world of being, full of unseen energies that animate everything" (Kimmerer, 2013, p. 49). Reciprocity calls for the establishment of mutually beneficial relationships between people, place, and the other-than-human beings that constitute them, and the development of what Kimmerer refers to as "cultures of gratitude." She explains:

> In such cultures, people have a responsibility not only to be grateful for the gifts provided by Mother Earth, they are also responsible for playing a positive and active role in the well-being of the land. They are called not to be passive consumers, but to sustain the land that sustains them.
>
> (Kimmerer, 2011, p. 257)

Introduction 15

Finally, ceremony serves as a means to establish mutually beneficial relationships between the human and non-human worlds. Ceremonies "are a form of reciprocity that renews bonds between land and people and focuses intention, attention, and action on behalf of the natural world, which is inclusive of the spiritual world" (Kimmerer, 2018, p. 31). A folklore-centric tourism that draws on local traditional knowledge, insights, and perspectives to encourage respectful participation with place could be an important strategy for the simultaneous preservation of traditional intangible cultural knowledge, ancient monuments, and natural ecological habitats.

This Book

The chapters collected together in this book have been selected in order to give as broad a perspective on the cross-cultural context as possible. As we have already seen, folklore is universal to human groups, and so the potential scope of a book like this is near-infinite. We acknowledge that the full cross-cultural context is not addressed by all of the chapters, for example, we do not have chapters on the rich varieties of African, Australian, or Asian folklore traditions, but we hope that what we have drawn together in this volume will contribute to opportunities for more inclusive, global studies in this area in the near future.

Part I: Re-making and Re-shaping the Past

Part I begins our exploration of the relationship between folklore, people, and place by considering different attempts to rediscover lost traditions of connection to the natural world, and to preserve fragile remnants of ancient ways of living in, and with, the land. We explore how connections between folklore, people, and place serve to enliven heritage for local and visiting communities. Chapters in this section investigate forms of intangible heritage in particular places that are remembered, preserved, but also reimagined through contemporary folklore initiatives. In her chapter, María Martínez Pisón describes Basque folkloric traditions of fairies, gods, and goddesses, and a plethora of sacred wells and springs that are far removed from mainstream tourist routes in the region. Martínez Pisón describes projects that are being developed to help protect these locations for future generations, and to encourage a re-engagement with them by tourists and locals, with an aim to establish a renewed sense of connection to natural sacred sites. Next, Ethan Doyle White's chapter, "Bedecked in Ribbons and Bows," investigates the Southern English tradition of dressing rag trees. A practice that initially emerged as a folk-remedy for certain ailments in the nineteenth century, but which took on new meanings in the 1990s and 2000s. During the COVID-19 lockdowns, the practice transformed again into a means of bringing socially isolated communities together. Sophie Parkes-Nield then goes on to discuss the role of calendar customs in establishing both a sense of community and a community's sense of connection to place. This is achieved through the

16 *Rachael Ironside and Jack Hunter*

presentation of three case studies of different traditions, some of which are generations old, while others are much more recent in origin. While such customs undoubtedly draw tourists into communities, they do so in different ways. Next we explore how folklore is embedded in the languages and dialects of different regions. In the two case studies examined here – Scotland, presented by Peter H. Reid, and Ireland, by Shane Broderick – folklore and language contribute to the distinctive identity of place and community. In Reid's chapter the identity of the North-East of Scotland is explored, with a particular emphasis on the role of the Doric dialect in encapsulating the culture and traditions of the region. This sense of uniqueness is considered in relation to its value as a form of placemaking and heritage consumption. In Broderick's chapter, we explore the long oral and written traditions of Ireland – myths, stories, monuments, and place names – and consider their potential for the creation of touristic experiences that conserve and protect natural, cultural, and intangible heritage simultaneously. The chapters in this section suggest that the act of remembering ancestral, forgotten, or hidden folklore holds potential for the re-discovery, re-animation, and re-enchantment of landscapes. Together, the chapters in this section offer a rich perspective on the role of folklore in remaking and reshaping the past in an increasingly globalised world, exploring challenges and opportunities for people and place.

Part II: Folklore and Indigenous Landscapes

Part II looks to the folklore of indigenous peoples in Canada, Hawaii, and Nicaragua to provide case-studies of indigenous folklore traditions and their close entanglement with the natural environment. In her chapter, Renée Bédard describes the folklore of Okikendawt, the Island of the Kettle Pots, in northern Ontario, home of the Dokis First Nation. Anishnaabe tradition and folklore binds the people who have lived in this region for thousands of years to elements of the landscape understood as ancestors and relations – a perspective that provides a powerful framework for engagement with place that is bound up with ethical and behavioural guidelines known as *bebaamaadiziwin*. Apela Colorado and Ryan Hurd then explore an alternative to the usual touristic approach to the petroglyphs of Olowalu, on the island of Maui, by presenting them in the context of indigenous science and traditional folklore, which invite a deeper participation with sacred places than many standard tours allow for. Of particular interest at Olowalu are the unusual acoustic phenomena that occur when percussive instruments are played there, providing an embodied sense of connection to place, if only people would take the time to participate when they visit. Paul Edward Montgomery Ramírez's chapter takes us next to Nicaragua to explore the tensions that have arisen from the appropriation of indigenous folklore for state tourism purposes, highlighting the complexities that can arise through the politicisation of folklore. Ramírez describes the establishment of La Cuna del Folklore Nacional (the cradle of national folklore) in the Masaya region, a top-down effort to

Introduction 17

attract tourists to the region that draws on, and transforms, indigenous Chorotega folkloric traditions. Matthew Cowan's chapter then goes on to describe the processes and outcomes of an art project based around Helsinki in Finland to discover hidden places and local folklore through semi-ethnographic interviews, exploring the very personal reasons why people come to develop a distinctive sense of connection to particular places, as well as to the sense that certain places are "wild". Finally, Kajsa Åberg and Doris Carson's chapter turns to consider the role of local food consumption and storytelling in Västerbotten, a region in the far north of Sweden, where indigenous Sami cuisine has become a booming tourist attraction. The overarching themes of the chapters in this section highlight the struggles of indigenous peoples to maintain their traditions in the face of colonial oppression and highlight the very different orientation to the world that underlies indigenous approaches to tourism, travel, and place. Taken together these chapters offer a range of insights into potentials for the decolonisation of tourism, and for a shift in the perception of indigenous landscapes for visiting tourists through the reclamation and enhanced representation of traditional stories of people and place by indigenous communities.

Part III: Reimagining Folklore in a Globalised World: Tourism, Placemaking, and Re-Enchantment

In Part III, we turn our focus to investigate how folklore has been reimagined in a globalised world. As we have explored, folklore can be an asset for places that seek to attract new, and existing, audiences and create experiences that engage tourists with place and community. For some destinations, folklore has become the primary identity of a place, such as Salem, Massachusetts, or Transylvania, Romania, at least from the perspective of tourists. For others, folklore is an evolving form of tourism presenting new opportunities and challenges. The chapters that follow address some of these issues in both natural and urban environments. In Madrid, Leticia Cortina Aracil considers folklore in the city from the perspective of a tour guide. By considering the changing demographic and physical landscape of Madrid, Leticia explains how places hidden by the process of modernisation can be enlivened through storytelling, fostering a sense of re-enchantment for visitors. In Sian Macfarlane's chapter, we are taken underground to the subterranean landscape of Dudley, England. In these mysterious underground places, Sian explores the relationship between the industrial, the rural, and the folkloric. While the rich folklore traditions of Dudley are currently underutilised, Sian argues that the subterranean landscape provides a unique opportunity to connect visitors to the socio-cultural history of the region and its relationship with the natural resources so important to its industrial past. In the third chapter, Eva Kingsepp draws upon her case study in Sweden to explore the tensions between the traditional, secular worldview still prominent in Sweden and the movement towards embracing forms of paranormal tourism by the regional tourism board in Värmland. Through her discussion, Eva highlights

18 *Rachael Ironside and Jack Hunter*

how some forms of paranormal tourism are deemed more acceptable than others and examines the role of the media in developing social perceptions. In the final two chapters, Katja Virloget and Alicia Edwards-Boon draw upon case studies to investigate how the use of technology can play a role in engaging people with places of folklore. In the natural landscape of the Mythical Park, Slovakia, Katja identifies key challenges and opportunities presented after the creation of a new folklore trail available via a GSM mobile app, or in written form. As she acknowledges, the development of a new tourism product using folklore raises concerns about the petrification, banalisation, and misinterpretation of heritage, reinforcing the vital importance of co-creation between community and developers. In the urban landscape of Manchester, Chester, and Liverpool, Alicia introduces the armchair ghost tourist through an examination of virtual Ghost Bus tours. Alicia argues that, much like in-person ghost tours, digital alternatives perform a role in the production of supernatural and weird spaces. Indeed, virtual forms of folklore tourism may offer more inclusive opportunities to engage with place, providing access to global tourism without the restrictions of traditional travel.

Collectively, each of the chapters in Part III considers the relationship between folklore and place from the perspective of new and evolving tourism experiences. Despite geographical differences, similar opportunities to connect and re-enchant people with place through folklore emerge whether this is through traditional storytelling in-place, or new digital and virtual technologies. In developing folklore tourism, the intra-history of a place, the hidden, and sometimes forgotten, landscapes and stories are given a platform to be remembered and celebrated. However, these opportunities are also recognised in light of the inherent challenges of commercialising folklore. As the chapters in this section address, using folklore as a tool for placemaking raises important questions about how to manage the creation of folklore experiences in a way that is true to the heritage, culture, and tradition of local communities and landscapes.

Note

1 Dark Tourism as defined by Stone (2006) involved travel to "sites associated with death, suffering and the seemingly macabre" (p. 146).

References

Baker, R.L. (1972). 'The Role of Folk Legends in Place-Name Research.' *The Journal of American Folklore*, 85 (338), pp. 367–373.
Ben-Amos, D. (1971). 'Toward a Definition of Folklore in Context.' *The Journal of American Folklore*, 84 (331), pp. 3–15.
Berkes, F. (1993). 'Traditional Ecological Knowledge in Perspective.' In J.T. Inglis (ed.), *Traditional Ecological Knowledge: Concepts and Cases*. Ottawa: International Program on Traditional Ecological Knowledge, pp. 1–10.
Bird, E., (1994). 'Playing with Fear: Interpreting the Adolescent Legend Trip.' *Western Folklore*, 53 (3), pp. 191–209.

Boafo, Y.A., Saito, O., Kato, S., Kamiyama, C., Takeuchi, K. and Nakahara, M. (2016). 'The Role of Traditional Ecological Knowledge in Ecosystem Services Management: The Case of Four Rural Communities in Northern Ghana.' *International Journal of Biodiversity Science, Ecosystem Services & Management*, 12 (1–2), pp. 24–38.

Bond, N. and Falk, J. (2013). 'Tourism and Identity-Related Motivations: Why Am I Here (and Not There)?' *International Journal of Tourism Research*, 15(5), pp. 430–442.

Bourque, J., Inglis, J.T. and LeBlanc, P. (1993). 'Preface.' In J.T. Inglis (ed.), *Traditional Ecological Knowledge: Concepts and Cases*. Ottawa: International Program on Traditional Ecological Knowledge, pp. vi–vii.

Bowman, M. (2000). 'More of the Same? Christianity, Vernacular Religion and Alternative Spirituality in Glastonbury.' In S. Sutcliffe and M. Bowman (eds.), *Beyond New Age: Exploring Alternative Spirituality*. Edinburgh: Edinburgh University Press, pp. 83–104.

Brady, B. (2022). 'Mountains Talk of Kings and Dragons, the Brecon Beacons.' In D. Gunzburg and B. Brady (eds.), *Space, Place and Religious Landscapes: Living Mountains*. London: Bloomsbury, pp. 173–190.

Bronner, S.J. (2017). *Folklore: The Basics*. Abingdon: Routledge.

Bruchac, M.M. (2014). 'Indigenous Knowledge and Traditional Knowledge.' In C. Smith (ed.), *Encyclopedia of Global Archaeology*. New York: Springer Science and Business Media, pp. 3814–3824.

Bruner, E.M. (2001). 'The Maasai and the Lion King: Authenticity, Nationalism, and Globalization in African Tourism.' *American Ethnologist*, 28 (4), pp. 881–908.

Buchmann, A. (2006). 'From Erewhon to Edoras: Tourism and Myths in New Zealand.' *Tourism Culture and Communication*, 6 (3), pp.181–189.

Burns, T.A. (1977). 'Folkloristics: A Conception of Theory.' *Western Folklore* 36 (2), pp. 109–134.

Ceríaco, L.M.P., Marques, M.P., Madeira, N.C., Vila-Viçosa, C.M. and Mendes, P. (2011). 'Folklore and Traditional Ecological Knowledge of Geckos in Southern Portugal: Implications for Conservation and Science.' *Journal of Ethnobiology and Ethnomedicine*, 7 (26), pp. 1–9.

Correia, A., Kozak, M. and Ferradeira, J. (2013). 'From Tourist Motivations to Tourist Satisfaction.' *International Journal of Culture, Tourism and Hospitality Research*, 7 (4), pp. 411–424.

Csapo, E. (2005). *Theories of Mythology*. Oxford: Blackwell.

Cusack, C.M. and Wilson, D.B. (2016). 'Scotland's Sacred Waters: Holy Wells and Healing Springs.' *Journal of the Sydney Society for Scottish History*, 16, pp. 67–84.

Dancausa, G., Hernández, R.D. and Pérez, L.M. (2020). 'Motivations and Constraints for the Ghost Tourism: A Case Study in Spain.' *Leisure Sciences*, pp. 1–22. doi: 10.1080/01490400.2020.1805655

Digance, J. (2006). 'Religious and secular pilgrimage: Journeys redolent with meaning.' In D.J. Timothy and D.H. Olsen (eds.), *Tourism, Religion and Spiritual Journeys*. Abingdon: Routledge, pp. 36–48.

Dundes, A. (1965). *The Study of Folklore*. Hoboken: Prentice-Hall.

Dundes, A. (1971). 'Folk Ideas as Units of Worldview.' *Journal of American Folklore*, 84 (331), pp. 93–103.

Dundes, A. (1996). *Folklore Matters*. Knoxville: The University of Tennessee Press.

Dundes, A. (2007). 'Folklore as a Mirror of Culture.' In S.J. Bronner (ed.), *The Meaning of Folklore: The Analytic Essays of Alan Dundes*. Logan: Utah State University Press.

Eaton, M.A. (2015). '"Give Us a Sign of Your Presence": Paranormal Investigation as a Spiritual Practice.' *Sociology of Religion*, 76 (4), pp. 389–412.

Ellis, B. (1996). 'Legend-Trips and Satanism: Adolescents' Ostensive Traditions as 'Cult' Activity.' In G. Bennet and P. Smith (eds.), *Contemporary Legend: A Reader*. New York: Routledge, pp. 167–186.

Espirito Santo, D. and Hunter, J. (2021). *Mattering the Invisible: Technologies, Bodies and the Realm of the Spectral*. Oxford: Berghahn.

Everett, S. and John Parakoottathil, D. (2018). 'Transformation, Meaning-Making and Identity Creation Through Folklore Tourism: The Case of the Robin Hood Festival.' *Journal of Heritage Tourism*, 13 (1), pp. 30–45.

Falk, J.H., Ballantyne, R., Packer, J. and Benckendorff, P. (2012). 'Travel and Learning: A Neglected Tourism Research Area.' *Annals of Tourism Research*, 39 (2), pp. 908–927.

Forestry England (2022). 'UFO Trail at Rendlesham Forest.' Available Online: https://www.forestryengland.uk/rendlesham-forest/ufo-trail-rendlesham-forest [Accessed 20 August 2022].

Garcia, B.R. (2012). 'Management Issues in Dark Tourism Attractions: The case of Ghost Tours in Edinburgh and Toledo.' *Journal of Unconventional Parks, Tourism and Recreation Research*, 4(1), pp. 14–19.

Gentry, G.W. (2007). 'Walking with the dead: The place of ghost walk tourism in Savannah, Georgia.' *Southeastern Geographer*, 47 (2), pp. 222–238.

George, E.W. (2010). 'Intangible Cultural Heritage, Ownership, Copyrights, and Tourism.' *International Journal of Culture, Tourism and Hospitality Research*, 4 (4), pp. 376–388.

Goldstein, D., Grider, S. and Thomas, J.B. (2007). *Haunting Experiences: Ghosts in Contemporary Folklore*. Boulder: University Press of Colorado.

Hallam, J. (2019). 'Embedding the Sustainable Development Goals (Sdgs) in the Curriculum.' *Environmental Education*, 120, pp. 12–14.

Hanks, M. (2016). *Haunted Heritage: The Cultural Politics of Ghost Tourism, Populism, and the Past*. Abingdon: Routledge.

Hanks, M.M. (2011). 'Re-imagining the National Past: Negotiating the Roles of Science, Religion, and History in Contemporary British Ghost Tourism.' In H. Silverman (ed.), *Contested Cultural Heritage: Religion, Nationalism, Erasure, and Exclusion in a Global World*. New York: Springer, pp. 125–139.

Harsono, S. (2017). 'Folklore Tourism in Jepara.' *Culturalistics: Journal of Cultural, Literary, and Linguistic Studies*, 1 (1), pp. 1–7.

Harvey, G. (2005). *Animism: Respecting the Living World*. London: Hurst & Company.

Hemme, D. (2005). 'Landscape, Fairies and Identity: Experience on the Backstage of the Fairy Tale Route.' *Journal of Tourism and Cultural Change*, 3 (2), pp. 71–87.

Hill, A. (2010). *Paranormal Media: Audiences, Spirits and Magic in Popular Culture*. Abingdon: Routledge.

Holloway, J. (2010). 'Legend-Tripping in Spooky Spaces: Ghost Tourism and Infrastructures of Enchantment.' *Environment and Planning D: Society and Space*, 28 (4), pp. 618–637.

Holly, D. H. and Cordy, C.E. (2007). 'What's in a Coin? Reading the Material Culture of Legend Tripping and Other Activities.' *Journal of American Folklore*, 120 (477), pp. 335–354.

Holm, P., J. Adamson, H. Huang, L. Kirdan, S. Kitch, I. McCalman, J. Ogude, et al. (2015). 'Humanities for the Environment - A Manifesto for Research and Action.' *Humanities*, 4 (4), pp. 977–992. doi:10.3390/h4040977.

Holmes, G., Smith, T.A. and Ward, C. (2018). 'Fantastic Beasts and Why to Conserve Them: Animals, Magic and Biodiversity Conservation.' *Oryx*, 52 (2), pp. 231–239.

Honko, L. (1964). 'Memorates and the Study of Folk Beliefs.' *Journal of the Folklore Institute*, 1 (1/2), pp. 5–19.

Hopper, N.G., Gosler, A.G., Sadler, A.G. and Reynolds, S.J. (2019). 'Species' Cultural Heritage Inspires a Conservation Ethos: The Evidence in Black and White.' *Conservation Letters*, 12 (3), p. e12636. doi: 10.1111/conl.12636.

Houran, J., Hill, S.A., Haynes, E.D. and Bielski, U.A. (2020). 'Paranormal Tourism: Market Study of a Novel and Interactive Approach to Space Activation and Monetization.' *Cornell Hospitality Quarterly*, 61 (3), pp. 287–311.

Hufford, D.J. (1982). *The Terror That Comes in the Night: An Experience-Centred Study of Supernatural Assault Traditions*. Philadelphia: University of Pennsylvania Press.

Hume, L. (2000). 'The dreaming in contemporary Aboriginal Australia.' In G. Harvey (ed.), *Indigenous Religions: A Companion*. London: Cassell, pp. 125–138.

Hunter, J. (2022). 'The Folklore of the Tanat Valley: Fairies, Giants and Forgotten Ecological Knowledge.' *Newsletter of the Fairy Investigation Society*, Jan 2022, pp. 31–47.

Ironside, R. (2018). The Allure of Dark Tourism: Legend Tripping and Ghost Seeking in Dark Places. In D. Waskul and M. Eaton (eds.), *The Supernatural in Society, Culture and History*. Philadelphia: Temple University Press, pp. 95–115.

Ironside, R. and Massie, S. (2020). 'The Folklore-Centric Gaze: A Relational Approach to Landscape, Folklore and Tourism.' *Time and Mind: Journal of Archaeology, Consciousness and Culture*, 13 (3), pp. 227–244.

Josephson-Storm, J.A. (2017). *The Myth of Disenchantment: Magic, Modernity, and the Birth of the Human Sciences*. Chicago: University of Chicago Press.

Kim, G., Vaswani, R.T., Kang, W., Nam, M. and Lee, D. (2017). 'Enhancing Ecoliteracy through Traditional Ecological Knowledge in Proverbs.' *Sustainability*, 9, pp. 1–16.

Kimmerer, R.W. (2002). 'Weaving Traditional Ecological Knowledge into Biological Education.' *BioScience*, 52 (5), pp. 432–438.

Kimmerer, R.W. (2011). 'Restoration and Reciprocity: The Contributions of Traditional Ecological Knowledge.' In D. Egan, E.E. Hjerpe and J. Abrams (eds), *Human Dimensions of Ecological Restoration: Integrating Science, Nature and Culture*. Washington, DC: Island Press, pp. 257–276.

Kimmerer, R.W. (2013). *Braiding Sweetgrass: Indigenous Wisdom, Scientific Knowledge, and the Teachings of Plants*. Minneapolis: Milkweed.

Kimmerer, R.W. (2018). 'Mishkos Kenomagwen, the Lessons of Grass: Restoring Reciprocity with the Good Green Earth.' In M.K. Nelson and D. Schilling (eds.), *Traditional Ecological Knowledge: Learning from Indigenous Practices for Environmental Sustainability*. Cambridge: Cambridge University Press, pp. 27–56.

Kõivupuu, M. (2020). 'Tradition in Landscape, Landscape in Tradition: Discourse of Natural Sanctuaries in Estonia.' *Time and Mind: Journal of Archaeology, Consciousness and Culture*, 13 (3), pp. 267–281.

Krisjanous, J. and Carruthers, J. (2018). 'Walking on the Light Side: Investigating the World of Ghost Tour Operators and Entrepreneurial Marketing.' *Qualitative Market Research: An International Journal*, 21 (2), pp. 232–252.

Lewis, G. and Scambary, B. (2016). 'Sacred Bodies and Ore Bodies: Conflicting Commodification of Landscape by Indigenous Peoples and Miners in Australia's Northern Territory.' In P.F. McGrath (ed.), *The Right to Protect Sites: Indigenous*

Heritage Management in the Era of Native Title. Canberra: Australian Institute of Aboriginal and Torres Strait Islander Studies, pp. 221–252.

Light, D. (2007). 'Dracula Tourism in Romania Cultural Identity and the State.' *Annals of tourism research*, 34 (3), pp. 746–765.

Lőrincz, A. (2021). 'Intangible Heritage: The Change of Significance of Hungarian Embroidery over Time.' In T. Sádaba, N. Kalbaska, F. Cominelli, L. Cantoni, and M.T. Puig (eds.), *Fashion Communication*. Berlin: Springer, Cham, pp. 265–277.

Malkki, L. (1995). *Purity and Exile: Violence, Memory and National Cosmology among Hutu Refugees in Tanzania*. Chicago: University Chicago Press.

McCue, P. (2012). *Zones of Strangeness: An Examination of Paranormal and UFO Hot Spots*. Bloomington: AuthorHouse.

Meehan, Eileen R. (2008). 'Tourism, Development, and Media.' *Society*, 45 (4), pp. 338–341.

Natale, S. and Pasulka, D.S. (2020). *Believing in Bits: Digital Media and the Supernatural*. Oxford: Oxford University Press.

Nelson, M.K. and Shilling, D. (2018). *Traditional Ecological Knowledge: Learning from Indigenous Practices for Environmental Sustainability*. Cambridge: Cambridge University Press.

Noakes, R. (2020). *Physics and Psychics: The Occult and the Sciences in Modern Britain*. Cambridge: Cambridge University Press.

Nolan, M.L. and Sidney, N. (1989). *Christian Pilgrimage in Modern Western Europe*. Chapel Hill and London: The University of North Carolina Press.

Obradović, S., Pivac, T., Besermenji, S., and Tešin, A. (2021). 'Possibilities for paranormal tourism development in Serbia.' *Eastern European Countryside*, 27 (1), pp. 203–233.

Özel, Ç. H. and Kozak, N. (2012). 'Motive based Segmentation of the Cultural Tourism Market: A Study of Turkish Domestic Tourists.' *Journal of Quality Assurance in Hospitality & Tourism*, 13 (3), pp. 165–186.

Paphitis, T. (2013). '"Have You Come to Take the King Away?': A Survey of Archaeology and Folklore in Context.' *Papers from the Institute of Archaeology*, 23 (1). doi:10.5334/pia.434.

Pharino, C., Peare, P. and Pryce, J. (2018). 'Paranormal Tourism: Assessing Tourists' Onsite Experiences.' *Tourism Management Perspectives*, 28, pp. 20–28.

Pine, B.J. and Gilmore, J.H. (1999). *The Experience Economy: Work Is Theatre & Every Business a Stage*. Boston: Harvard Business Press.

Possamai, A. and Lee, M. (2011). 'Hyper-Real Religions: Fear, anxiety and Late-Modern Religious Innovation.' *Journal of Sociology*, 47 (3), pp. 227–242.

Rappaport, R.A. (1979). *Ecology, Meaning, and Religion*. Berkeley: North Atlantic Books.

Restall, B., and Conrad, E. (2015). 'A literature review of connectedness to nature and its potential for environmental management.' *Journal of Environmental Management*, 159, pp. 1–15.

Richards, G. (1996). 'Production and Consumption of European Cultural Tourism.' *Annals of tourism research*, 23 (2), pp. 261–283.

Richards, M. (1969). 'The Supernatural in Welsh Place-names.' In G. Jenkins (ed.), *Studies in Folk Life: Essays in Honour of Iorweth C. Peate*. London: Routledge & Keagan Paul, pp. 303–314.

Richards, R. (1934). 'Some Giant Stories of the Upper Tanat Valley.' *Montgomeryshire Collections*, 43, pp. 168–172.

Rumsey, A. (1994). 'The Dreaming, Human Agency and Inscriptive Practice.' *Oceania*, 65, pp. 116–130.

Shapland, M. (2021). 'Material Culture and Consciousness: A Thought Experiment.' *Time and Mind: Journal of Archaeology, Consciousness and Culture*, 14 (4), pp. 517–535.

Sherwood, S.J. (2013). 'A Visit to Point-Pleasant: Home of the Mothman.' *Paranthropology: Journal of Anthropological Approaches to the Paranormal*, 4 (1), pp. 25–35.

Spooner, B.C. (1965). 'The Giants of Cornwall.' *Folklore*, 76 (1), pp. 16–32.

Stone, P. (2006). 'A Dark Tourism Spectrum: Towards a Typology of Death and Macabre Related Tourist Sites, Attractions and Exhibitions.' *Turizam: Znanstveno-stručni časopis*, 54 (2), pp. 145–160.

Taylor, B. (2020). 'Plants as Persons: Perceptions of the Natural World in the North European Mesolithic.' *Time and Mind: Journal of Archaeology, Consciousness and Culture*, 13 (3), pp. 307–330.

The Guardian (2013). 'Elf Lobby Blocks Iceland Road Project.' Available Online: https://www.theguardian.com/world/2013/dec/22/elf-lobby-iceland-road-project [Accessed 18 December 2018].

The Guardian (2017). 'New Zealand River Granted Same Legal Rights as Human Being.' Available Online: https://www.theguardian.com/world/2017/mar/16/new-zealand-river-granted-same-legal-rights-as-human-being [Accessed 9 June 2019].

The Irish Times (1999). 'Fairy Bush Survives the Motorway Planners.' Available Online:https://www.irishtimes.com/news/fairy-bush-survives-the-motorway-planners-1.190053 [Accessed 5 June 2019].

The Press and Journal (2018). 'Loch Ness Monster Worth Nearly £41m a Year to Scottish Economy.' Available Online: https://www.pressandjournal.co.uk/fp/news/highlands/1562103/loch-ness-monster-worth-nearly-41m-a-year-to-scottish-economy/ [Accessed 10 August 2022].

The Scotsman (2019). 'Threat to Ancient Scots Yew, UK's Oldest Tree, as Tourists Rip of Branches for Souvenirs.' Available Online: https://www.scotsman.com/news/environment/threat-ancient-scots-yew-uks-oldest-tree-tourists-rip-branches-souvenirs-633219 [Accessed 29 August 2020].

Thompson, R.C. (2010). '"Am I Going to See a Ghost Tonight?": Gettysburg Ghost Tours and the Performance of Belief.' *The Journal of American Culture*, 33 (2), pp. 79–91.

Tilley, C. (1994). *Phenomenology of Landscape*. Oxford: Berg.

Tuhiwai Smith, L. (2012). *Decolonizing Methodologies: Research and Indigenous Peoples*. London: Zed Books.

Tunbridge, J. (1994). 'Whose Heritage? Global Problem, European Nightmare.' In G. Ashworth and P. Larkham (eds.), *Building a New Heritage: Tourism, Culture and Identity in the New Europe*. Abingdon: Routledge, pp. 123–134.

Viken, A. (2022). 'Tourism Appropriation of Sámi Land and Culture.' *Acta Borealia*, 39, pp. 1–20.

Waskul, D. and Waskul, M. (2016). *Ghostly Encounters: The Hauntings of Everyday Life*. Philadelphia: Temple University Press.

Weber, M. (1946). 'Science as a Vocation.' In A.I. Tauber (ed.), *Science and the Quest for Reality*. London: Palgrave Macmillan, pp. 382–394.

Wright, J. (2021). *Subtle Agroecologies: Farming with the Hidden Half of Nature*. Abingdon: CRC Press.

Yunkaporta, T. (2019). *Sand Talk: How Indigenous Thinking Can Save the World*. London: Text Publishing Company.

Yunxia, W. (2019). 'The Symbols of Folklore Tourism Culture of the Waterside Residents in Hainan and Its Dissemination and Development.' *Proceedings of 3rd International Workshop on Arts, Culture, Literature and Language*. Available Online: https://webofproceedings.org/proceedings_series/ART2L/IWACLL%202019/IWACLL19062.pdf [Accessed 28 August 2022].

Part I

Re-making and Re-shaping the Past

1 Rebuilding the Sacred Union with Basque Fountains and Springs

María Martínez Pisón

Introduction

As humankind evolved and developed technology, it experienced a progressive separation from the wilderness and began to modulate its exchanges with the environment on its own terms. However, the primal forces of nature, the seasonal changes, and their cycle of eternal return could not be ignored. Humans re-enacted symbolically the *regressus ad origem*, reviving the cosmogonic myths through seasonal festivals, rituals, and customs as a way to maintain balance (Eliade, 2005, p. 48). Over the years, Basque folk traditions have incorporated diverse influences from the civilisations and communities who became part of the history of the Basque lands: Celts, Iberians, Romans, Suebi, Visigoths, Franks, Muslims, Jews, Gypsies, and Agotes. Some components of Basque folk traditions were substituted and re-shaped over time, but the core of seasonal ceremonies, rites of passage, propitiatory sacrifices, and sympathetic magic prevailed.

Christianised Basque ancestors kept in their memory hundreds of sites known to be the dwellings and sanctuaries of local numens and spirits.[1] Many of them have been noted by famous historians and ethnographers as being traditional pilgrimage places or devotional shrines. But there are also magical landscapes and folk rites performed in holy spaces that have been carefully preserved by locals who profess animist beliefs, hold dual-faith practices, or value their elders' legacy, working for a mindful revitalisation of Basque traditions (Etxepare Euskal Institua, 2022). Some of them are concerned about the intrusion of curious visitors misinterpreting their customs and express reservations about their commodification. Others manifest a preoccupation for the effects of climate change and environmental damages caused by avaricious companies and careless tourists, which deteriorate their homeland, endanger communitarian partnerships, and jeopardise their future wellbeing (Pérez, 2015, pp. 22–26).

The Evolution of Tourism in Euskal Herria

Foreign tourists often visit the seven historical regions which constitute Euskal Herria to explore its prehistoric caves, megalithic monuments,

DOI: 10.4324/9781003374138-3

28   *María Martínez Pisón*

artistic manifestations along the pilgrimage Way of Saint James, and places associated with the witch hunts. The first guests arrived during the blooming of Romanticism, moved by the urge to escape from industrialised areas, to reconnect with untamed nature, and to explore legendary locations (Humboldt, 1801; Thiers, 1823; Flauvert, 1840; Hugo, 1943). During that period the first writings about Basque mythology were published – describing the glorious past of the Navarrese Kingdom, ruled over by the Foral Regime – which emphasised the virtues of embracing a traditional rural lifestyle (Chaho, 1845, 1847; Goizueta, 1851; Cerquand, 1875; Navarro Villoslada, 1879; Arana, 1882). These collections of folklore and myth nurtured Euskarian Reenactment and stimulated the birth of Basque Nationalism.

Considering these precedents, subsequent archaeological research conducted in Basque lands focused its efforts on disclosing the prehistoric origins of its cultural heritage and spirituality, which is deeply chthonic and replete with zoomorphic entities. More than 150 caves with prehistoric paintings have been discovered in Euskal Herria and three of them are recognised as World Heritage Sites. However, the intense tourist exploitation of the most significant caves forced their closure and the creation of reproductions and virtual tours. Several regions also produced a guide of good practices for the preservation of cave art (Lasheras et al., 2012, pp. 614–615).

The lessons learned in the management of palaeolithic remains marked a turning point in the patrimonial administration, accompanied by the implementation of new measures to guard Basque megalithic constructions, such as the Foral Law 14/2005 of Cultural Heritage (Navarra, 2005, BON n° 141). Moreover, an official register designed to prevent the despoilment of archaeological sites is now open to the citizenship to notify of any new findings.

In the last two decades, but particularly around the commemorative events of 400th anniversary of the Zugarramurdi witch trials (2008), a drift towards magical tourism occurred. In the early years of the twenty-first century, writers such as Martínez de Lezea and Bergara revitalised Basque mythology as a remarkable trait of euskaldun cultural heritage, sparking a fresh interest in folk beliefs for younger generations. At the same time, foreign books about modern esotericism, neopaganism, and witchcraft were increasingly translated into Spanish, and online groups of magical practitioners became more popular.

In 2007, the caves of Zugarramurdi and the Witches' Museum were inaugurated, attracting a large number of tourists. In 2009, the Navarrese Government launched a marketing campaign to advertise witchcraft touring itineraries. Over the following years, several exhibitions about Basque witch trials, theatre performances of *"akelarres,"*[2] publications, documentaries, and conferences about the witch and her forbidden arts ignited a passion for learning more about magic and folklore. These initiatives led to the publication of several guides exploring mythical routes as a strategy to incentivise rural tourism. In 2016, the Department of Tourism of Euskadi developed a website presenting seven families of spirits with their correspondent mythical maps, selecting some of their most attractive dwellings to create enchanted paths and interpretative signage around them, and to organise activities for families and groups.

Another important tourist appeal in the region is the practice of hiking and adventure sports. These outdoor activities have grown exponentially in popularity over the course of the pandemic and have provoked a direct impact on the environment and welfare of the community (Lehendakaritza & Turismo, merkataritza eta konsumo saila, 2021, pp. 59–70). In order to reduce the deterioration of ecosystems and cultural heritage, Eusko Jaurlaritza[3] and the Government of Navarre have recently launched advertisement campaigns[4] to involve tourist, and the tourism sector more generally, in a sustainable and ethical model of tourism, offering codes of conduct for responsible hosts and guests (Basque Tour, 2022; Nafarroako Ezagutu Sarea, 2022).

However, there is a missing element to entwine nature, people, and folklore: the hidden symbolism, oral narratives, and traditions attached to those sites, particularly water sources as recipients of the emotional and spiritual memory of the land. Initiatives such Euskal Herriko Ahotsak (Ahotsak, 2022), Ahozko Historiaren Artxiboa (AHOA, 2006), Nafarroako ondare materiagabearen artxiboa (Navarchivo, 2022), or Eleketa (Euskal Kultur Erakundea, 2022), which are focused on the recollection of historical memory and local experiences around folklore, could help to reassess oral wisdom, raise awareness, and grant greater significance to the visitor's perception of these sacred sites.

Water and Aquatic Spirits in Basque Cosmovision

Water represents the source of creation, the primal symbol of rebirth and regeneration for its connection to the alchemical processes of dissolution and coagulation. It is also an element of purification and healing for body and soul, popularly used to cleanse, neutralise evil influences, to bless, and to cure different diseases (Peillen, 2019, p. 255). Nevertheless, an important distinction between celestial waters and inland waters must be established. The water in the vault of heaven is considered masculine because it acts as a fertilising element for the land, while the water present on the surface of the Earth is perceived as feminine due to its nurturing nature. Additionally, sea water is seen as a test of survival, a place of death, and the road to exile (Peillen, 2019, p. 258).

Watercourses symbolise the life path and have a direct connection to destiny, while still waters such as wells or lakes are understood as portals to fairyland and the underworld, where enchanted mansions and sunken villages can be found. Certain fountains and springs are also linked to ghost appearances and witch gatherings (Goicoetxea, 2012, p. 121). Moreover, some lagoons on top of the mountains are known for being sites where numens associated with weather changes and storms reside. For that reason, these aquatic environments have become devotional shrines and liminal communication spaces with fate figures, nature spirits, and phantoms (Barandiarán, 1973, pp. 238–239).

30 *María Martínez Pisón*

Fountains, springs, and ponds are the natural dwelling places of the *Lami(n)ak* – fairy creatures with human form, but with one or both feet like an animal's. If they live near rivers, wells, or springs, they have duck or goose feet. If they wander in high hills or rocky spots, they present goat feet or falcon talons; if they dwell on the coast, they show a fishtail (Barandiarán, 1920, p. 439). In Lapurdi and Nafarroa Beherea, feminine and masculine fairy spirits from the same family are included in the same group. In Zuberoa, the *Lamin/a* is accompanied by a masculine partner, called *Maide* (Caro Baroja, 2009, pp. 39–40). In Ataun (Gipuzkoa), the masculine companion of the *Lamia* is the *Intxixu*, although this term is also employed to designate a male witch in other regions (Satrústegui, 1999, pp. 502–506).

In the Navarre and French Pyrenees, there is an assimilation between the figure of the *Lamina* and the *Sorgin*. Both of them share the powers of shapeshifting and affecting health, love, fertility, and wealth. In Baztan Valley, it is also believed that the *Lamiak* and the *Sorginak* have the power to conjure tempests. In some places, *Lamiak* are described as strange and ancient inhabitants of the underground, living in caves or on the edges of the forest. During the day, they usually hide inside caverns or at the bottom of lakes and wells; during the night, they come out wrapped in pale clothes like wandering souls, yelling and rejoicing. Sometimes, they appear flying like the *Sorginak* (Satrústegui, 1999, p. 500).

Lamiak generally stay away from public settings, religious ceremonies, and Christian sanctuaries and behave in a more passive and benevolent manner, unless you disobey the rules of communal living, fail to fulfil their wishes, miss a promise, or break a pact. They are sensual, seductive, and capricious creatures. There are hundreds of folktales describing infatuation and forbidden love between a *Lamin/a* and a man, often with a tragic ending. They give contradictory or figurative messages to challenge human wit and test people's true intentions with deceiving appearances or tricky ordeals. Their most precious belongings are their golden comb and jewellery, but they also own wonderful treasures and valuable secrets. A noble service must be offered to receive their gifts. Some midwives or healers who assisted them successfully were rewarded with a golden spindle, abundance, or good fortune (Azkue, 1968, pp. 233–234, 393, 425, 442–444). Peasants used to deliver offerings of grain, bread, cakes, dairy products, cider, and bacon to attract the favour of the *Lamiak* and get their help to complete hazardous tasks, as Barandiarán claimed (1982, p. 85).

Laminak are skilled in milling and baking and prepare the most delicious bread, but it is forbidden to bring it to the mortal world. Every Spring, they celebrate by holding a ball in their hidden dwellings and drink from a magical cup which contains the secret of poetry. Some of them are wonderful singers, musicians, and dancers, inspiring artists. However, the art that they truly master is spinning, as their essence is tied to the act of weaving fate. Another traditional craft performed by the *Lamiak* is washing clothes at night. When a *Lamin/a* is seen laundering and wringing, it is interpreted as an omen of death (Azkue, 1942, pp. 146–148). On the other hand, Oihenart (1926, p. 156) reported the belief in a female fairy spirit called *Sorsain* in Zuberoa who presided births. The phonetic similarity between this entity, the midwife (*"sortzain"*), and the witch (*"Sorgin"*) has created a popular association and blurred their idiosyncrasies. Additionally, the guilds of midwives, spinners, laundresses, and water carriers were seen as potential magical practitioners due to the folkloric relationship with these fairy spirits (Azkue, 1949, p. 425; Satrústegui, 1999, p. 509).

Local toponomy is full of fountains, springs, wells, lakes, waterfalls, banks, and sacred stones near the riverside and river mills related to the Lamiak (see Figure 1.1). According to Erkoreka (1978, pp. 466–468; 1979, pp. 119–122), some of the most significant locations are Lamaiturri (Araba), Lamiosin (Gipuzkoa), Lamuxain (Lapurdi), Lamiñerreka (Biscay), Laminatea (Gipuzkoa), Lamisalo (Navarre), Laminosine (Nafarroa Beherea), Laminapozu (Biscay), Lamikila (Araba), Laminenziluak (Zuberoa), Lamiategui (Navarre), Lamindau (Biscay), and Laminen-eskatza (Gipuzkoa).

In Basque lore, water spirits have strong bonds with certain plants, insects, amphibians, fluvial birds, fishes, and equids, all of which may act as messengers or magical allies in divination practices, folk healing procedures, and sorcery rituals. Thorny bushes, but particularly hawthorn and dog rose, are plants related to the fairy faith in the Basque Lands and used as protective and healing elements in folk medicine (Marliave, 2006, p. 57). Basque peasants make hawthorn crosses, which are blessed on 3 May to protect their houses from lightning, and shepherds often carry a branch in their bags to drive away sickness and misfortune. Farmers also put hawthorn bushes under oxen to protect them from being cursed (Aguirre, 2013, p. 143). Christianity adapted the virtues of this plant and associated it with Marian imagery. Local legends affirm that Our Lady of Arantzazu appeared on top of a hawthorn bush, and a piece of it is guarded in her sanctuary (Oñate, Gipuzkoa).

Figure 1.1 Waterfall of Toberia (Araba).
(Photograph by Author).

32 María Martínez Pisón

Thousands of pilgrims go there on 15 August to bless hawthorn branches growing wild (Marliave, 1995, pp. 19, 55–56).

The Goddess Mari, honoured as "*Andra Mari*" (Lady Mari) on the same date, sometimes presents herself as a "*Dame Blanche*," or white mare in her aspect of Queen of the *Lamiak*, although she is also considered the first witch, as some of her nicknames and symbols indicate (Barandiarán, 1973, pp. 157–159). Garmendia (1982) reports that representations of Mari as Queen of Fairies can be seen in Baztan Valley's parodies called "*Erregiña eta saratsak*" (The Queen and the willow maidens) and "*Maiatzeko erregiña*" (May Queen). Many peasants also leave elder crowns or white roses in Andra Mari's shrines during May festivities, asking for health or love (Irigaray, 1933).

Furthermore, the name "*Erregina*" is applied to the Queen Bee, considered a psychopomp animal in Basque folklore, which brings prosperity and harmony to work in the community, but it is also connected to the Otherworld. Bees were adopted as members of the family and the Queen Bee was named "*andere ederra*" (pretty lady). The owners of the household were compelled to inform them in the first instance about significant events and rites of passage, especially funerals (Barandiarán, 1973, p. 81), since they were understood as sacred couriers to communicate with Mari and the *Lamiak*.

The dragonfly is etymologically related to these mythical figures, the *Sorginak* and their master *Etsai*, as it is observed in the terms "*mari-orratz*" (Mari's needle), "*ura-andra*" (lady of the water), "*sorgin-mandatari*" (witch's messenger), or "*infernuko zaldi*" (horse of Hell). A similar association can be found in the butterfly, named "*mari-sorgin*" (Mari the Witch), and the ladybug, known as "*Andra-Mari*," "*marigorringo*" (Mari of the red skirt), or "*maritxu-tellatako*" (Little Mari of the roof tile). The presence of a butterfly is interpreted as the arrival of good or bad news, depending on the colour of the lepidopterous, or the particular time of their appearance (morning or evening). They are often seen in nocturnal flights as icons of the soul separating from the body, or as manifestations of the deceased in purgatory. Meanwhile, the ladybug is seen as a weather forecaster (Bähr, 1928, pp. 94–101), using formulae such as "*Andra Mari gorringo, bihar eguzki ala ebi egingo?*" (Lady Mari of the red skirt, will it be sunny or rainy tomorrow?).

Another species that serves as an atmospheric predictor is the batrachian, taking its croak as a sign of rain. Some dialectical derivations as "*ugarixo*" or "*urin*" also show this association with the water ("*ur/ug*"), an element which is etymologically related to abundance ("*ugari*"). In fact, there is no better image of fullness than the swamps filled by toad's eggs and the meadows populated by frogs in Spring. Moreover, the inflated throat of the batrachian is reminiscent of the womb of a pregnant woman. For that reason, the female specimen of the "*rubeta*" (Bufo bufo) is known as "*andrapoa*" (Lady Toad), maintaining a folkloric connection with Mari in her dual nature as nurturer and provider of prosperity, but also leader of magical creatures (Bähr, 1928, pp. 121–122). Some folk healers poured the urine of a woman over a toad to determine if she was expecting a child, or employed it to avoid bleeding

Rebuilding the Sacred Union with Basque Fountains and Springs   33

during labour, although it was generally used for skin conditions or infectious diseases (Vallejo & González, 2015, pp. 1292, 1306). Folk magicians and sorcerers employed batrachians to secure marriages, make love spells, inflict the evil eye, and to break hexes. Moreover, in the French-Basque territories it was believed that the Devil gave the "*Sorginak*" toads as spirit allies so they could serve them as talismans or ingredient for ointments (Charro, 2000, pp. 21–22).

Several varieties of *Motacilla, Anser domesticus*, and *Bubulcus ibis* are considered manifestations of Basque fairies. *Motacilla alba*, named "*iturri-txori*" (bird of the fountain), is taken as an omen of love and prosperity, while *Motacilla cinerea* or "*buztanikara hori-beltx*" (black washerwoman) is seen as a bringer of bad news and death. *Motacilla flava*, popularly known as "shepherd's trickster," often announces unexpected changes, infidelity, and misfortune (Aranzadi, 1909, pp 162–163). *Anser domesticus* is a representation of Mari as Queen of Fairies, gifting people with good fortune, pregnancy, or abundance. *Bubulcus ibis* is associated with ox drivers and interpreted as a sign of a pleasant journey or new beginnings (Martínez Pisón, 2021, p. 5).

It should be highlighted that the *Lamin/a* is also named "*emasuge*," producer of serpents. In old folktales, this entity was described as having copper skin, referring to the scales of the snake (Caro Baroja, 2009, p. 14). There are almost forgotten versions where the test to receive a *Lamia*'s treasure requires kissing her in a serpentine shape. Actually, Mari may appear as a snake, raven, or vulture in her dreadful forms (Barandiarán, 1973, p. 159). Following the same logic, "*Lamia*" is employed to designate a voracious fish.

Traditions, Rituals, and Customs around Watercourses

Basque lore has preserved belief in the existence of a sacred spring over the vault of heaven ("*ur goiena*") and an interior lake under the Earth's crust, from which groundwater and fountains emerge ("*ur barrena*"). A balanced exchange of celestial and terrestrial water guarantees equilibrium in the universe and the cyclical renewal of creation (Satrústegui, 1988, p. 180). Following this assumption, the neighbours of Urdiain and other towns of the Arakil Valley and Ultzamaldea (Navarre) fetch water from the local fountains at the beginning of the New Year to drink it in community and in order to purify themselves, absorbing the magical properties of the renovated fluids. While they are performing this ritual, they sing verses asking for health, protection, and prosperity.

Ur goiena, ur barrena,	*Superior water, inferior water,*
Urteberri egun ona,	*Good New Year's Day,*
Graziarekin osasuna,	*Health and grace,*
pakearekin ontasuna,	*Fortune and peace.*
Jaungoikoak dizuela egun ona.	*May the Lord of Above grants a nice day.*

(Satrústegui, 1988, pp. 165–167)

34 *María Martínez Pisón*

The ceremonial greeting to the renewed waters retained some divinatory elements in Cinco Villas region, as this folk song from Etxalar shows:

Ela, Ela!	*Hello, hello!*
Nor da, nor da?	*Who is it? Who is it?*
Ni naiz, urteberri.	*I am the New Year.*
Zer dakartzu berri?	*What news do you bring?*
Uraren gaina,	*The cream of the water,*
Bakea ta osasuna.	*Peace and health.*

(Azkue, 1990, p. 1095)

The first 12–13 days of the New Year were considered augural moments to foresee what the newly beginning cycle would bring. Ancient *"aztiak"* developed an annual divination system called *"zotalegun/ak"* or *"sortelegun/ak"* based on the observation of signs in nature. This predictive method has parallels with other forms of divination, such as the Roman *"tempora,"* or the Spanish *"cabañuelas,"* with Sephardic origins (Azkue, 1942, p. 208). The *"zotalegun"* was practiced by shepherds and farmers in different Basque regions, but it remains in Ataun (Gipuzkoa) and Beskoitze (Lapurdi) and has been rekindled by modern magical practitioners (Martínez Pisón, 2017).

In Baztan Valley, the new water is understood as the bearer of blessings in exchange for a Christmas offering, usually money or food delivered to the ones carrying the sacred liquid to each household in the community. The logic behind it is rooted in the etymological relationship between *"Ur"* (water), *"Urte"* (year), and *"Urtats"* (gift). This can be noticed in the following song from Elizondo:

Urteberri berri,	New Year, what news
zer dakarrazu berri?	do you bring?
Uraren gañean	From celestial water,
bakia ta osasuna.	peace and health.
Urtex, Urtex,	Presents, presents,
Urtetxa nahi dugu.	we want gifts.

(Satrústegui, 1988, p. 171)

New Year's Day is the only time when it is permitted to drink water gathered from a sacred fountain at night, since darkness is ruled by *Gaueko* with strict rules. Several mythical creatures like *Laminak*, *Sorginak*, or other phantoms are able to enchant water courses under the light of *Ilargi* (the Moon Goddess). As a ritual act to prevent any harm, peasants used to place a piece of hot coal from the fireplace in the water container.

Summer Solstice (*"Udaburu"* or *"Izkiota"*) is also a suitable date to perform rituals and magic around fountains, springs, and holy wells, counting on the beneficent influence of *Eguzki*, the Sun Goddess. Midsummer is contemplated as a time for purification, renewal, and revitalisation and water is particularly important for healing. In many Basque locations certain rivers,

Rebuilding the Sacred Union with Basque Fountains and Springs 35

springs, and fountains are used to wash oneself, or water is drunk for cleansing purposes. In the event that no spring could be found, this purification could be executed using the morning dew of Saint John's Day.

The Christianisation of pagan water sanctuaries required the construction of hermitages under the advocation of different saints next to the original sites. Saint Claire and Lucy turned into the caregivers of fountains, and were said to cure eye diseases. Saint Gregory was assigned to heal hearing disabilities. Mary Magdalene and Saint Anne were associated with stomach disorders. Saint Quiteria became the guardian against rabies, while Saint Rose and Saint John were in charge of skin conditions. Saint Blas, Roque, and Stephen assumed the protection of children's illnesses. Saint Agatha and Saint Casilda were the custodians of expectant and nursing mothers, infertile women, and females with gynaecological issues. Archangel Michael became the stronghold to overcome severe fevers, migraines, and psychological alterations caused by evil spirits (Goicoetxea, 2012, pp. 33–51).

Some of the most frequently visited places are the banks of the Zadorra (Araba), the saltwater spring next to the Ega River (Navarre), Santa Marina fountain (Gipuzkoa), Sanjuaniturri (Navarre), Andre-Dena-Mariako-Iturri (Zuberoa), Saint John's fountain (Lapurdi), and the sulphurous waters of Urbedeinkatu (Navarre). Sanjuaniturri is a famous pilgrimage site for healing skin problems and tourists visit it due to the legend that tells that the *Basajaun* (Lord of the Forest) once lived there. There is a statue inside a cave that some villagers venerate as the image of Saint John and others worship as the *Basajaun*. Visitors usually light candles, bring flowers, or leave votive offerings as part of a propitiatory rite. Then, they drink three sips from the three springs in the area, dip a cloth in the water, and apply it to the affected areas. Later, the cloth is left over some brambles until it dries and the parish priest then burns the rag.

Several rites of passage marking the entrance to adulthood are also performed during the Summer Solstice, including the selection of sacred fountains as suitable locations for these ceremonies to take place in. A blessing ritual for newly-weds addressed to promote fertility has been preserved in Iturgoyen (Navarre). At dusk, a group of women adorn a cart with branches of beech, boxwood, and roses. Afterwards, two boys dressed in goatskins and wearing cowbells get ready to pull the cart. The couple gets into the carriage and travel around the town. The porters turn and shake the cart, trying to overturn it. If the couple remains unharmed they dance with the boys pulling the cart. Then, the couple is taken to bathe in the fountain. Later, the rest of the community join them in the water for communal cleansing (Rodríguez & Lazcano, 2017, p. 21).

Another popular custom is the practice of hydromancy. It can be done in sacred aquatic sites, or at home, employing water taken from sacred springs. In the Valley of Ayala (Araba), an egg is introduced into a water container on Saint John's Eve and it is left to repose. In the morning, the bubbles and forms in the liquid are read and interpreted (Goicoetxea, 2012, p. 153). In Donibane Garazi (Nafarroa Beherea), marriageable girls take a glass of water and wait until midnight. They write down three names of possible

36 *María Martínez Pisón*

suitors on a piece of paper and place them folded into the water. The most faithful candidate will be visible at sunrise (Azkue, 1942, p. 310).

A specialised form of hydromancy employed to discover if someone has been hexed, called "*begizkune*," is performed in Bermeo and Zeanuri (Biscay). Firstly, it is necessary to bless the house with water from three sacred fountains, sprinkling it in the four directions while the folk magician recites: "*txarradun kanpora, ona etor barrua*" (let evilness go away, bring goodness in). Afterwards, she/he asks the participants to pray, usually the Creed repeated three times. Then, the "*begizkunearena*" puts a frying pan in the fire and introduces a piece of tin or lead. The affected neighbour sits down and is covered with a blanket. The performer removes the pan with the molten metal and makes the sign of the cross three times over the patient: over the shoulder, back, and head. She/he holds the pan and spills the metal in the holy water. The forms are studied to find out the cause and the treatment which should be applied (Erkoreka, 1995, pp. 119–121).

Conclusions

Basque popular beliefs and customs are predominately syncretic, although part of the indigenous animistic background has survived the test of time. Regardless of whether people participate in traditional festivities or folk rites as a means to reconnect with their cultural identity, or perform sacred rites intentionally, there is a large consensus about the need to treasure what remains of these ancestral traditions and learn from them for the future. Reviewing these mythical narratives with an environmental vision permits us to re-examine the past, redirect our interactions, and reconstruct a bond with the natural world. Following Satrústegui's considerations:

> Myth corresponds to a superior category of knowledge which reveals the conception of humanity about the world, the forces of nature and the transcendent origin of the techniques our ancestors were discovering. We are taking the risk of jumping into the void if we break up with an ancestral past which is perfectly compatible in their essential elements with the most reformist currents.
>
> (Satrústegui, 1980, p. 8)

This reconciliation would require the adoption of a reconstructionist and folklore-centric approach to tourism, beginning from an interdisciplinary perspective that integrates scientific knowledge, popular wisdom, and proper contextualisation. Strengthening communitarian networks and obtaining the full support of tourism administrations to change tourist's attitudes and behaviours towards the natural environments that sacred sites occupy are essential. A mixture of different cultural and religious elements coexist in local folk rites, offering numerous possibilities for building bridges with neighbouring regions and foreign countries by revealing those common features and elements of shared history.

Rebuilding the Sacred Union with Basque Fountains and Springs 37

Notes

1 Numens are protective deities of a place. Spirits are entities with feelings, intelligence and communication skills (plants, animals, fairies, the dead, etc.).
2 Term used by the Inquisitors to name the witch gatherings, incorrectly translated as "meadow of the goat." The right word to say assembly is "*batzarre.*"
3 Official name of the Basque Government (Euskadi), which enacted the law 6/2019 of Basque Cultural Patrimony to preserve local heritage. The Department of Tourism of Euskadi created an observatory to supervise the evolution of this sector (Enfokatur) and joined NECSTour.
4 "Turista maitea" and "Navarra, otro turismo" campaigns emerged from the Territorial plan of touristic sustainability in destinations (2021–2023) and Territorial plan of touristic sustainability of Navarre (2022).

References

Aguirre, A. (2013). 'El rayo y el trueno en Euskal Herria.' *Antropología Cultural*, 17, pp. 135–149.
Ahozko Historiaren Artxiboa (2006). *Zer da AHOA?*. Available Online: https://www.ahoaweb.org/ahozko-historia/zer-da-ahoa.php [Accessed 19 March 2022].
Arana, V. (1882). *Los últimos iberos: Leyendas de Euskaria*. Madrid: Librería de Fernando Fé.
Aranzadi, T. (1909). 'Nombres vascos de aves.' *Revista Internacional de los Estudios Vascos*, 3 (2), pp. 160–167.
Azkue, R.M. (1942). *Euskalerriaren Yakintza*. Bilbao: Euskaltzaindia-Escasa Calpe.
Azkue, R.M. (1968). *Ipuñak*. Bilbao: La Gran Enciclopedia Vasca.
Azkue, R.M. (1990). *Cancionero popular vasco*. Bilbao: Euskaltzaindia.
Bähr, G. (1928). 'Los nombres vascos de la abeja, mariposa, rana y otros bichos.' *Revista Internacional de los Estudios Vascos*, 19 (1), pp. 77–122.
Barandiarán, J.M. (1920). 'Fragmentos folklóricos. Paletnografía vasca.' *Euskalerriaren Alde: Revista de Cultura Vasca*, X, pp. 182–190, 224–232, 396–402, 431–443, 452–470.
Barandiarán, J.M. (1973). *Obras completas I: diccionario ilustrado de mitología vasca y algunas de sus fuentes*. Bilbao: Gran Enciclopedia Vasca.
Barandiarán, J.M. (1982). *Mitología vasca*. San Sebastián: Txertoa.
Basque Tour (2022). *Código ético del turismo*. Available Online: https://basquetour.eus/codigo-etico-turismo-euskadi.htm [Accessed 18 March 2022].
Caro Baroja, J. (2009). *Lamiak sorginak eta jainkosak*. Donostia: Gaiak.
Cerquand, J.F. (1875). *Légendes et récits populaires du Pays Basque*. Pau: L. Ribaut.
Chaho, J. A. (1845). *Aïtor: légende cantabre*. Paris: Ariel.
Chaho, J.A. (1847). *Histoire primitive des Euskariens-Basques*. Bayonne: Jaymebon.
Charro, A. (2000). 'Sapos: historia de una maldición.' *Revista de folklore*, 235, pp. 20–32.
Eliade, M. (2005). *Mitos, sueños y misterios*. Barcelona: Kairós.
Erkoreka, A. (1978). 'Laminak: Recopilación de leyendas (I).' *Cuadernos de etnología y etnografía de Navarra*, 30, pp. 451–492.
Erkoreka, A. (1979). 'Laminak: Recopilación de leyendas (II).' *Cuadernos de etnología y etnografía de Navarra*, 31, pp. 65–124.
Erkoreka, A. (1995). *Begizkoa: mal de ojo*. Bilbao: Ekain.
España, Ley 6/2019, de 9 de mayo, de Patrimonio Cultural Vasco. BOE, 29 de mayo, 128, pp. 56452–56492.

Etxepare Euskal Institua (2022). *Tradiciones vascas* Available Online: https://www.etxepare.eus/es/tradiciones-vascas [Accessed 6 March 2022].

Euskal Herriko Ahotsak (2022). *Euskal Herriko hizkerak eta ahozko ondarea.* Available Online: https://ahotsak.eus/english/ [Accessed 6 March 2022].

Euskal Kultur Erakundea (2022). *Programa Eleketa: recopilación del patrimonio oral.* Available Online: https://www.eke.eus/es/cultura-vasca/ondarea/ahozko_ondarea [Accessed 19 March 2022].

Flauvert, G. (1840). *Voyage dans les Pyrénées et en Corse.* Paris: Arlea.

Garmendia, J. (1982). 'El "mayo", los "maios" y las "mayas".' *Anuario de Eusko Folklore*, 1, pp. 117–118.

Goicoetxea, A. (2012). *Las aguas en la medicina popular del País Vasco: ritos y creencias.* Madrid: Opera prima.

Goizueta, J.M. (1851). *Legendas vascongadas.* Madrid: Establecimiento Tipográfico de D.F. García Padrón. Available Online: https://loyola.biblioteca.deusto.es/handle/11656/4879 [Accessed 28 August 2022].

Hugo, V. (1943). *En voyage: Alpes et Pyrenees.* Paris: Jules Rouff.

Humboldt, W. (1801). *Journey to the Land of the Basques.* London: Academic Press.

Irigaray, A. (1933). Folklore baztanés. *Yakintza*, Vol. 1, pp. 130–135.

Lasheras, J. A. et al. (2012). 'La Cueva de Altamira y el arte rupestre paleolítico de la Cornisa Cantábrica. Buenas prácticas para la gestión del arte rupestre paleolítico en España.' *Actas del Primer Congreso Internacional de Buenas Prácticas en Patrimonio Mundial: Arqueología*, Mahon (Spain), 9–13 April 2012. UCM, pp. 613–620.

Lehendakaritza & Turismo, merkataritza eta konsumo saila (2021). *Percepción de la sociedad vasca sobre el turismo.* Available Online: https://www.euskadi.eus/contenidos/documentacion/o_21tef5/es_def/adjuntos/21tef5.pdf [Accessed 4 March 2022].

Marliave, O. (1995). *Pequeño diccionario de mitología vasca y pirenaica.* Editorial José J. de Olañeta.

Marliave, O. (2006). *Dictionaire de magie et sorcellerie dans le Pyrénées.* Bordeaux: Sud Oest.

Martínez Pisón, M. (2017). Zotalegun, sortelegun, sotelegun. *Por encima de todas las zarzas.* Available Online: https://porencimadetodaslaszarzas.com/2017/01/14/zotalegun-sortelegun-sotelegun/ [Accessed: 5 March 2022].

Martínez Pisón, M. (2021). *Traditional Crafts in Basque Folklore.* [PowerPoint presentation]. Online conference, 12 June, Zoom.

Nafarroako Ezagutu Sarea (2022). *Sensibilización.* Available Online: https://redexploranavarra.es/sensibilizacion-2/ [Accessed 19 March 2022].

Nafarroako ondare materiagabearen artxiboa (2022) *Artxiboa.* Available Online: http://www.navarchivo.com/en/archive [Accessed 19 March 2022].

Navarra, Ley Foral 14/2005, de 22 de noviembre, del Patrimonio Cultural de Navarra. BON, 25 de noviembre 2005, n° 141, pp. 6–45.

Navarro Villoslada, F. (1879). *Amaya o los vascos en el siglo VIII.* Pamplona: F. Maroto.

Oihenart, A (1926). 'Noticia de las dos Vasconias, la Ibérica y la Aquitana.' *Revista Internacional de los Estudios Vascos*, 17 (2), pp. 141–174.

Peillen, T. (2019). *El imaginario en las creencias populares y cultas.* Zarautz: Dakit.

Pérez, R. (2015). 'La nueva cultura del agua, el camino hacia una gestión sostenible.' *Cuaderno de Trabajo*, 68, pp. 1–53.

Rodríguez, M.P. and Lazcano, V. (2017). 'San Adrián y el carro de los novios.' *Calle Mayor*, 613, p. 21.

Satrústegui, J.M. (1980). *Mitos y creencias*. San Sebastián: Txertoa.

Satrústegui, J.M. (1988). *Solsticio de invierno: fiestas populares, Olentzero, tradiciones de Navidad*. Estella: Gráficas Lizarra.

Satrústegui, J.M. (1999). 'Lamias y sirenas a través de la simbología.' *Cuadernos de Etnología y Etnografía de Navarra*, 31 (74), pp. 497–520.

Thiers, A. (1823). *Les pyrénées et le midi de la France*. Paris: Chasles Libraire.

Vallejo, J.R. and González, J.A. (2015). 'Los anfibios en la medicina popular española, la farmacopea de Plinio y Dioscórides.' *História, Ciências, Saúde: Manguinhos*, 22 (4), pp. 1283–1319.

2 Bedecked in Ribbons and Bows

Dressed Trees as Markers of Heritage, Hope, and Faith in Southern England

Ethan Doyle White

Introduction

Throughout the nineteenth century, it was not uncommon in parts of England to find people affixing rags to bushes or trees in the hope of securing relief from their ailments. This custom is virtually unheard of today, but in many areas we can still find trees covered in ribbons, bows, and all manner of material culture. These contemporary "dressed trees" do not all serve the same function, instead evidencing a diverse range of human-arboreal engagements. Some mark spaces of both prehistoric ritual activity and modern Pagan religiosity; others stand in churchyards and facilitate prayers to the Christian God. Certain dressed trees commemorate the dead, and in other instances set forth spaces for play. Many represent folk customs, arising from within local communities and serving no commercial purpose whatsoever, but elsewhere institutions and organisations have adopted the practice for their own ends, often to attract visitors and tourists, taking us into the domain of the folkloresque.

Dressed Trees: Defining a Concept

Here, "dressed trees" are defined as trees and bushes onto which humans have deliberately affixed material culture to the trunk, branches, or around the base. The term "dressed trees" is, to my knowledge, my own coining, but derives from older references to "tree dressing." Prior discussions have generally called these "rag trees" or "rag bushes" (Layard, 1879; Hartland, 1893; Grinsell, 1990) or, following a Scots word for rags, "clutie trees" (Box, 2003, p. 24), although these terms fail to reflect the diverse materials used in contemporary dressing customs. As observed since at least the late nineteenth century (Walhouse, 1880), dressed trees and bushes appear internationally, from India (Haberman, 2013) to Israel (Dafni, 2002), and in a few instances we can identify how such customs began, as with the affixing of yellow ribbons to trees in the United States (Santino, 1992b; Pershing and Yocom, 1996; Tuleja, 1997).

Recent centuries of English history saw people affixing material culture to trees located close to wells as part of a custom intended to cure maladies.

DOI: 10.4324/9781003374138-4

Bedecked in Ribbons and Bows   41

John Brand described "shreds or bits of rag" on bushes above "the rag-well" in Benton, now in Tyne and Wear (Brand, 1854, p. 380), while Robert Charles Hope reported bushes "covered with rags and tattered pieces of cloth" around a "rag well" at Newcastle (Hope, 1893, p. 100). In Yorkshire, ribbons were reported on bushes around St Helen's Well in Gargrave (Whitaker, 1812, p. 185) and around its namesake in Thorparch (Hope, 1893, p. 185). Rags were also affixed to thorn trees near Lincolnshire wells at Holy Well Dale near Winterton and at Great Cotes in Ulcery (Hope, 1893, p. 87). In Cornwall, rags were reported on a thorn bush by St Madderne's Well (Hope, 1893, p. 12).

Not all dressed trees accompanied wells. A Cornish custom held that pushing nails into an oak cured toothache (Walhouse, 1880, p. 99), while nailing hair or nail clippings to the Beaumont Tree, an elm at Silsoe, Buckinghamshire, allegedly cured ague (Anonymous, 1945, p. 307). A few tree dressing customs were not linked to healing, perhaps most famously the Arbor Tree, a black polar in Aston-on-Clun, Shropshire, which was dressed in flags each May from at least the 1910s (Box, 2003). There may be other examples left unrecorded; in his late-nineteenth-century cross-cultural discussion of "rag-bushes," the English folklorist Edwin Sidney Hartland only mentioned British examples from Wales and Scotland (Hartland, 1893), perhaps reflecting the tendency of English folklorists to focus on the "Celtic fringe." In some cases, these customs apparently informed fiction; W. H. Hudson's short story "An Old Thorn," first published in 1911, describes a Wiltshire "wishing-tree" to which people attached ribbons or strips of silk or scarlet cloth (Hudson, 2020 [1911], p. 112).

For heuristic reasons, this chapter focuses on contemporary tree dressing in southern England, with a particular emphasis on Greater London, a region where the author has recorded dressed trees since 2010. The study omits Cornwall, not out of any comment on Cornish identity's (complicated) relationship with Englishness, but due to the author's lack of direct experience with Cornish examples and the fact that Cornwall's tree dressing customs appear distinct from those elsewhere. Unlike other parts of southern England, Cornwall contains many wells where material has been deposited both around the water and on adjacent flora (as at St Nectan's Glen and the Madron, Alsia, and Sancreed Wells), in some cases juxtaposing dressed trees with other depositional practices like coin trees (Houlbrook, 2016). These Cornish customs warrant full discussion on their own terms.

Dressed trees typically represent what Jack Santino (1992a, pp. 158–59) called "folk assemblages," thus encompassing "the creation of a single aesthetic entity by grouping together disparate things." They also generally constitute the combined efforts of multiple people, often acting independently, representing examples of what Lynne McNeill termed "serial collaboration" (McNeill, 2007, p. 282). As folk assemblages created through serial collaboration, dressed trees can be seen in tandem with other placemaking customs that have proliferated across early-twenty-first-century Britain, including coin trees (Houlbrook, 2018), love-locks (Houlbrook, 2021), and painted pebbles.

42   *Ethan Doyle White*

Dressed Trees as Markers of Heritage

In southern England, tree dressing has arisen at various prehistoric sites that archaeologists surmise originally served a ritual function. In this they differ from coin trees, which display "little evidence to suggest that they occupy sites of historic ritual significance" (Houlbrook, 2018, pp. 245–46). Perhaps the most famous archaeological site containing a dressed tree is Avebury (Wiltshire), the largest surviving Neolithic/Bronze Age stone circle, where a small number of ribbons, coloured cord, and folded notes have been tied to a large beech tree at the ring's eastern perimeter. Atop a hill to the south of Avebury stands the West Kennet Long Barrow, an Early Neolithic chambered tomb. Although there are no trees atop the hill, several flank the trackway leading to the barrow from the A4 road, on which ribbons can regularly be found.

Knowlton (Dorset) boasts a ruined medieval church inside a Neolithic earthen henge. At the henge's north-eastern end are two adjacent yew trees now adorned with ribbons and other items. By the King's Men, a stone circle forming part of the Rollright Stones complex on the Oxfordshire/Warwickshire border, material has been affixed primarily to an ash on the ring's western side. At the Coldrum Stones (Kent), a beech overhanging the denuded Early Neolithic chambered tomb has been dressed with hundreds of ribbons and other material. Dressed trees at prehistoric sites are also found further north, as in Derbyshire, where examples stand near the Nine Ladies and Doll Tor stone circles.

Archaeologists are not the only individuals visiting these locations. Since at least the 1960s, and especially since the 1980s, modern Pagans have utilised southern England's prehistoric ceremonial sites as ritual spaces, often leaving offerings either to named deities, ancestors, or to the "spirit of the place" (Blain and Wallis, 2007; Doyle White, 2014; Doyle White, 2016). Some of the objects affixed to dressed trees certainly suggest that the person responsible was Pagan. A crevice in a Knowlton yew housed two stones decorated with occult sigils, one combining runic characters (observed in August 2019; see Figure 2.1); similarly, in early 2014 the name of the Norse god Thor was carved into the Coldrum Stones beech in runic script, while a metal runic medallion was later hung from its branches (observed September 2020). Wheat sheafs were also placed at Knowlton Henge and the Coldrum Stones, perhaps during a Pagan harvest celebration. Moreover, Andy Letcher has noted that the Dragon Environmental Group, a Pagan organisation opposing road building projects, carried out "several tree-dressing events" in the 1990s (Letcher, 2004, p. 187), while more recently a respondent to the World Druidry Survey reported establishing a "cloughtie tree" on their property (White, 2021, pp. 88–89).

Fieldwork among Pagans using the Coldrum Stones nevertheless indicates that some never contributed to the site's dressed tree (Doyle White, 2016, p. 359), and most items affixed to dressed trees carry no obvious Pagan symbolism. Instead, at all five aforementioned sites, ribbons of various colours

Figure 2.1 Runes at Knowlton.
(Photograph by Author).

constitute the majority of affixed material. At Knowlton Henge, various knitted items were present, including elaborate triangular shapes (see Figure 2.2) and a purple poppy (August 2019), while at the Coldrum Stones similar knitted items were accompanied by wooden and soft toys, holed stones, a branch of berries, a pink scarf, a red Chinese "good luck" decoration, and a Darth Vader air freshener (September 2020). This is not material a casual passer-by would have; these objects have been deliberately selected by people intent on contributing to the assemblage.

Written material often appears at dressed trees. At Avebury, several folded paper notes, bound in ribbon, were tied to the branches, unreadable unless removed (Oct. 2019; see Figure 2.3). Elsewhere, paper notes are readily legible. At the Coldrum Stones, a hanging note read: "Hope the twins will be good from brother Ralph x" (September 2020). Other notes clearly serve a different function; a letter at the foot of a Knowlton yew was written by two people to their deceased friend. Other material may similarly memorialise a loved one. A decorated piece of fabric on the yew bore the knitted name "Ophelia," possibly that of a departed individual; a nearby dog's leash tied up in a bow probably memorialised a pet, placed at this popular site for dog walkers (August 2019).

Part of a UNESCO World Heritage Site, Avebury is one of Britain's best-known archaeological attractions, and while Knowlton Henge and the Coldrum Stones do not have the same level of fame, they are both among the most famous archaeological sites in their respective counties. There are nevertheless comparable heritage sites where no dressed tree is evident. The

Figure 2.2 Knitted Item at Knowlton.
(Photograph by Author).

Coldrum Stones is part of a group of chambered tombs called the Medway Megaliths, most of which have trees immediately adjacent, but none sustains tree dressing customs. Dorset is home to various stone circles, most notably the Nine Stones, but these again have no dressed trees. Avebury shares its World Heritage Status with Stonehenge, but here there is no dressed tree either. It is possible that, in much of southern England, interest in tree dressing is only sufficient to maintain one example in a given area.

The origins of these dressed trees can be estimated. The tree overhanging the Coldrum Stones shows no signs of being decorated in footage from 1989, nor in a 1994 photograph, but images from 2002 show it bedecked in ribbons. An online comment regarding Knowlton Henge from 2002 refers to a few items placed at the base of the yew trees but makes no mention of objects hanging from the branches, material evident in footage from 2011. Authorities managing the Rollright Stones noted that their earliest records of arboreal deposits come from 2009, with a noticeable assemblage evident by 2011 (George Lambrick, personal communication), while the National Trust team managing Avebury related that the custom became popular there from about 2016 (personal communication). Adam Stout observed that people started

Figure 2.3 Ribbon with Note at Avebury.
(Photograph by Author).

affixing ribbons around the Glastonbury Thorn on Wirral Hill, Somerset, during the late 1990s, a custom that continued until the removal of the trunk and surrounding railings in 2019 (Stout, 2020, pp. 112, 117). It thus appears that tree dressing at southern English heritage sites emerged during the 1990s and 2000s, with different chronologies at different sites.[1]

At Avebury, the National Trust have expressed concerns about tree dressing's impact on grazing livestock, wildlife, and the trees themselves. Hoping to discourage the practice, the Trust removes the affixed material, especially after the summer holidays, although they retain the objects for two months to allow their depositors to collect them if desired (personal communication).[2] The Rollright Trust, a charity managing the Rollright Stones, have similarly removed material on an ad hoc basis when they feel that it is beginning to look messy, but they do not altogether discourage additions (Lambrick, personal communication).

Dressed Trees as Memorial Spaces

Folk assemblages have long been associated with memorialising the dead. These can develop at graves and formal memorials, but also locations of violent death (Monger, 1997; Richardson, 2001, pp. 257, 260), sometimes accruing around trees. Perhaps the best example is in Barnes (London Borough of Richmond upon Thames) at the roadside location where Marc Bolan, the glam rock star who fronted T-Rex, died in a September 1977 car crash. The sycamore tree which Bolan's car struck was soon decorated with written messages and (although now much denuded) has since remained a centre of devotion for Bolan fans. The Performing Rights Society erected a memorial stone by the tree in 1997, with the T-Rex Action Group (TAG) adding a Bolan bust in 2002. The tree itself, along with neighbouring trees and other adjacent features, is regularly decorated with material including ribbons, sparkly fabrics, fake flowers, vinyl records, photographs, and jewellery (September 2018; see Figure 2.4). The quantity of material expands each September, at the time of Bolan's death, before TAG members remove much of it later in the year.

Elsewhere, tree dressing may be a more private process for the bereaved. A young elder tree adjacent to the River Brent near Hanwell (London Borough of Ealing) has a selection of items, including lightbulbs and pink, purple, and red ribbons, affixed to it (May 2021). The memorial's purpose is revealed by two laminated poems dedicated to Alice Gross, a local teenager who was murdered and concealed in the river in 2014. The choice of memorialisation may have emerged from an earlier custom, that of tying yellow ribbons around the locality to raise awareness of Gross' initial disappearance (Horrox, 2014). This echoes the use of ribbons to memorialise the deceased in non-arboreal

Figure 2.4 Marc Bolan Memorial Tree.
(Photograph by Author).

contexts, as on the gates of the Crossbones graveyard in Southwark (London Borough of Southwark), a place where rituals commemorating the "outcast dead" have occurred since 2004 (Hausner, 2016).

Dressed Trees as Spaces for Prayer

While historic trees like the Glastonbury Thorn have long carried Christian symbolism, recent decades have seen various Anglican congregations establish dressed "prayer trees." Encouraged by the Church Support Hub, a website for exchanging ideas among Anglican congregations (Amanda Spence, personal communication),[3] these proved especially popular following the emergence of COVID-19 in 2020, as churches were forced to suspend indoor services and open-air churchyards replaced them as foci for religious activity.

In summer 2021, at least three Anglican churches in southeast London had "prayer trees" in their churchyards: the Church of St Mary the Virgin in Lewisham (London Borough of Lewisham), the Church of St Paulinus in Crayford (London Borough of Bexley), and the Church of St Martin of Tours in Chelsfield (London Borough of Bromley). For its prayer tree, the Lewisham church adopted a mature sycamore, that at Crayford used a young holly, while Chelsfield selected an old yew. In each case, the tree appears to have been selected due to its location adjacent to a path close to the church, thereby emphasising accessibility. At St Paulinus' Church, tree dressing initially began as part of a ritual commemorating the dead at All Souls' Day in November 2020 before the holly was reformulated as a "prayer tree" with a broader function several months later (Spence, personal communication). Here, ribbons were also affixed to the churchyard railings, where a poster invited people to attach a "Ribbon for Remembrance."[4]

Unlike the dressed trees at prehistoric sites, "prayer trees" often propose certain intentions for those contributing to the assemblage, encouraging contributors to pray to the Christian God or memorialise the dead.[5] A sign beside the Lewisham tree invited visitors to affix a ribbon to netting strung around the trunk "as you ask God for help, remember a loved one, or simply place your troubles in God's loving hands." At Crayford, a notice on the trunk suggested that those attaching ribbons pray for hope "as we come out of lockdown," an explicit reference to COVID-19's impact. Some of the contributions to these assemblages suggest more precise concerns motivating certain individuals. At Lewisham, some heart-shaped fabric bearing the words "Windrush Day" testified to the concerns of the Afro-Caribbean community, who represent a significant proportion of the local population (Anim-Addo, 1995).

Dressed Trees as Spaces for Play

Dressed trees can also serve as a locus for play. In Bexley Wood (London Borough of Bexley), material including model fairies, garden gnomes, and children's toys were placed on and around a dead oak and surrounding beech trees. Local lore holds that the tree was established in memory of a deceased child; one online comment reports having observed the assemblage since 2003. Anecdotal observation suggests that most visitors are families with young children, which would be congruent with the choice of material deposited. The quantity of material grew substantially in Spring 2020, during the COVID-19 pandemic, and included a "Covid Snake" comprising decorated pebbles – a tradition that appeared throughout Britain during that period, although not usually in spatial conjunction with a dressed tree. The Bexley Wood custom likely informed the emergence of another dressed tree at the nearby Churchfield Wood (London Borough of Bexley), where a "fairy home" had been created around the base of an oak (Figure 2.5), similar to those found elsewhere in England (Fortean Times, 2015). Here, the greater thematic unity and aesthetic cohesiveness of the assemblage suggested that only one individual, or a small number of individuals, had established and continued the tradition.

Arboreal associations with fairies carry a longer pedigree, reflected, for instance, in the dead tree, now at London's Kensington Gardens, onto which

Figure 2.5 Churchfield Wood Fairy Tree.
(Photograph by Author).

Ivor Innis carved fairies in 1922 (Wilks, 1972, p. 128). From the material culture itself, it is unclear if those contributing to the Bexley assemblages regard fairies as romanticist whimsy or as beings that literally exist. A young child's letter at the base of the Bexley Woods oak (May 2020) explained that they were giving their old toys to the fairies; this child, at least, was apparently a believer. Considering the ongoing belief in fairies among certain esoteric subcultures (Magliocco, 2018), it is possible that some adults contributing to the assemblages also regard these trees as the actual abode of fairy folk.

This ambiguity between literal belief and "make-believe" play can also be seen at those dressed trees termed "wishing trees." Here, different individuals can perform the same act – adding material culture while making a wish – while holding different views on its efficacy. One such "wishing tree" was created outside Goldsmiths' College in New Cross (London Borough of Lewisham) in 2014; its creator, student Martin Hasani, expressed a desire to introduce "rural folklore into urban settings," with the assemblage featuring bright ribbons and Buddhist prayer flags (JoeJourneys n.d.).[6] The popularity of the "wishing tree" designation may owe something to the "Wish Tree" project launched by Japanese artist Yoko Ono in 1996, during which people wrote down wishes on paper notes before affixing them to trees at many international locations.

In March 2020, at the start of the COVID-19 lockdown, the artist Lou Baker created four "wishing trees" around Bristol. Two utilised the mesh railings around young trees, outside Baker's home and on Horfield Common; the other two involved hawthorn bushes at Purdown and on Clifton Downs. Baker encouraged others to contribute, with the trees soon attracting ribbons, poems, and hearts, often decorated with supportive messages. Many contributors communicated with Baker via social media, some inspired to create additional "wishing trees" elsewhere (Baker, 2020; King, 2020; Baker, personal communication). Although designed as an art project, Baker notes that many contributors probably understood the assemblages as a "feel-good community project" amid the anxieties of the pandemic (personal communication). The Purdown tree was disassembled by persons unknown, while Baker cleared up the other three in late 2020 or 2021, although she observed further additions made after this point.

Institutional Promotion

While representatives of institutions like the National Trust have generally discouraged tree dressing, it is probable that institutional support for the custom has contributed significantly to its spread. A key player here has been the environmental charity Common Ground, which in 1990 initiated an annual Tree Dressing Day on the first weekend of December (Price, 2018).

Various institutions have adopted Common Ground's initiative, among them the Woodcraft Folk, an educational movement for young people (Woodcraft Folk, 2012). Other youth groups have also embraced it; in 2003, Tree Dressing Day was celebrated in Stanton Park near Swindon (Wiltshire)

50 *Ethan Doyle White*

(Gazette and Herald, 2003), and in 2017 at Knyveton Gardens in Bournemouth (Dorset), with the council providing red ribbons marking World AIDS Day (Grassby, 2017). Museums and heritage attractions have held events to observe Tree Dressing Day, including Fulham Palace (London Borough of Hammersmith and Fulham) in 2015 (TimeOut, 2015), the Richard Jefferies Museum (Wiltshire) from 2016 (Suzie Simmons, personal communication), and the Weald and Downland Museum (West Sussex) from at least 2017. In 2020 the Rural Life Living Museum (Surrey) held a tree dressing event during which children made hanging bird feeders (Katie Hill, personal communication). An alternative approach was taken by the Horniman Museum (London Borough of Lewisham), which erected an indoor "cloutie tree" in 2018. Visitors are invited to affix coloured notes to the tree on which they have written "a wish for well-being" or a comment "to say thank you for something good that has happened" (Horniman Museum, n.d.; personal observation).

During the pandemic, local government also utilised tree dressing. In September 2020, London's Royal Borough of Greenwich established eight "wishing trees" around the area. Part of its "Residents' Rainbow" project – which brought criticism for costing £95,000 – each tree contained ribbons onto which residents' messages had been printed, many offering thanks to individuals or institutions for their work throughout the pandemic. Each tree had ribbons of a specific colour, but after several weeks the ribbons were redistributed, giving each tree a multi-coloured selection, before being removed the following month (Greenwich, 2020; Chamberlain, 2020). In June 2021, the London Tourism Co-Operative established eight "wishing trees" around the city (Beale, 2021), each in an area reliant on tourism, hoping these attractions might help reverse the massive downturn in visitor numbers caused by COVID-19.

Employing folk assemblages to attract tourists has been identified elsewhere, as at St Nectan's Glen, Cornwall (Houlbrook, 2016, p. 353). There, much as in the Horniman Museum, the visitors' ability to contribute to an assemblage is probably part of the attraction – especially for visitors with children. Conversely, in several of the London cases, institutions have commissioned ready-made installations that superficially resemble folk assemblages but which require no additional contributions from visitors; rather than folklore, they are examples of "the folkloresque" (Foster, 2016).

Conclusions

This has only been a preliminary analysis of tree dressing customs in contemporary southern England, based on anecdotal encounters with these assemblages over the preceding decade. In those cases where the trees have been in the care of specific organisations, contact has been made with their representatives, although the study has not involved in-depth fieldwork or interviews with those contributing to these assemblages.

Bedecked in Ribbons and Bows 51

Provisional observations can nevertheless be made. That there are multiple reasons for the creation and maintenance of dressed trees in southern England should come as little surprise given that similar conclusions have been reached by studies elsewhere (for instance Dafni, 2002). However, of note is that the purpose of English tree dressing as it appeared in the nineteenth century (i.e. for curing ailments) is no longer prevalent, if practiced at all. Shifts in the availability of mainstream medicine have meant that folk remedies involving trees have declined. Changes in the use of material are also observable. In contrast to earlier British tree dressing traditions, where torn pieces of cloth were favoured, now the most common material is ribbon. This reflects changing economic factors, with a much broader range of material being available and affordable. Comparisons could be drawn with how coins have replaced pins as the preferred material to throw into wells around Britain.

This study has also highlighted how COVID-19 and the lockdowns it prompted contributed considerably to the growth of this custom. Dressed trees provided accessible and safe foci at which people could express their frustrations, fears, and grief through physical actions; as spaces of serial collaboration they also offered those feeling lonely and isolated the sensation of being part of a broader community. For parents, they sometimes offered places to try and entertain children, and for some Christians they were spaces at which worship could continue. The end of lockdowns generally saw a decline in tree dressing activities – by the close of 2021, many of the dressed trees that were flourishing during 2020 looked decidedly barren – and there may be no future resurgence. COVID-19 also provided an opportunity for local government and related institutions to use tree dressing as a means of encouraging tourism, at least in Greater London, an act that probably promoted knowledge of the custom to a wider audience and may contribute to new developments in coming years.

Notes

1 This broadly accords with Houlbrook's findings regarding deposition at St Nectan's Glen, Cornwall (Houlbrook 2016, p. 354).
2 Love-locks from a Leeds bridge are also temporarily retained after removal (Houlbrook 2021, p. 75, 157).
3 The Church Support Hub's "National Day of Reflection" webpage suggests that churches "Invite people to tie yellow ribbons to a prayer tree or railings as sign of their prayer and support for all who are bereaved." The suggestion that yellow be used probably draws on the established US tradition, although in practice English congregations have used ribbons of many colours.
4 Placing ribbons on railings could be seen elsewhere, as at Trinity Church, a Methodist and United Reformed church in Enfield (London Borough of Enfield).
5 Paralleling the custom, common in Anglican churches, of lighting a candle for a deceased loved one.
6 The tree was no longer dressed by October 2021.

52   *Ethan Doyle White*

References

Anim-Addo, J. (1995). *Longest Journey: A History of Black Lewisham.* Deptford: Deptford Forum Publishing.

Anonymous. (1945). 'Beaumont's Tree.' *Folklore*, 56 (3), p. 307.

Baker, L. (2020). 'Lou Baker, Wishing Trees, Participation in Isolation, 24.3.20 and Ongoing.' Available Online: https://issuu.com/loubakerartist/docs/lou_baker wishing_trees__participation_in_isolati [Accessed 28 August 2022].

Beale, H. (2021). 'Wishing Trees Planted Across London to Inspire Families to Look Towards a Better Future.' Available Online: https://www.swlondoner.co.uk/news/18062021-wishing-trees-london-better-future/ [Accessed 27 August 2022].

Blain, J. and Wallis, R. (2007). *Sacred Sites, Contested Rites/Rights: Pagan Engagements with Archaeological Monuments.* Brighton and Portland: Sussex Academic Press.

Box, J. (2003). 'Dressing the Arbor Tree.' *Folklore*, 114, pp. 13–28.

Brand, J. (1854). *Observations on the Popular Antiquities of Great Britain, Volume II.* New edition. London: Henry G. Bohn.

Chamberlain, D. (2020). 'Greenwich Council's 'Residents' Rainbow' Cost Over £200 Per Message.' Available Online: https://853.london/2020/11/12/greenwich-councils-residents-rainbow-cost-over-200-per-message/ [Accessed 27 August 2022].

Dafni, A. (2002). 'Why are Rags tied to the Sacred Trees of the Holy Land?' *Economic Botany*, 56 (4), pp. 315–327.

Doyle White, E. (2014). 'Devil's Stones and Midnight Rites: Megaliths, Folklore, and Contemporary Pagan Witchcraft.' *Folklore*, 125 (1), pp. 60–79.

Doyle White, E. (2016). 'Old Stones, New Rites: Contemporary Pagan Interactions with the Medway Megaliths.' *Material Religion: The Journal of Objects, Art and Belief*, 12 (3), pp. 346–372.

Fortean Times. (2015) 'Too Many Fairy Doors.' *Fortean Times*, 327, pp. 24–25.

Foster, M.D. (2016). 'Introduction: The Challenge of the Folkloresque.' In M.D. Foster and J.A. Tolbert (eds.) *The Folkloresque: Reframing Folklore in a Popular Culture World.* Logan: Utah State University Press, pp. 3–33.

Gazette and Herald. (2003). 'Youngsters Reckon It's the Best Dressed Tree Around.' Available Online: https://www.gazetteandherald.co.uk/news/7293575.youngsters-reckon-its-the-best-dressed-tree-around/ [Accessed 27 August 2022].

Grassby, J. (2017). 'Trees Decorated with Red Ribbons to Mark World Aids Day.' *Daily Echo.* Available Online: https://www.bournemouthecho.co.uk/news/15701795.trees-decorated-with-red-ribbons-to-mark-world-aids-day/ [Accessed 27 August 2022].

Grinsell, L.V. (1990). 'Some Sacred Trees and Rag-Bushes in Cyprus.' *Folklore*, 101, pp. 227–228.

Haberman, D.L. (2013). *People Trees: Worship of Trees in Northern India.* Oxford and New York: Oxford University Press.

Hartland, S.E. (1893). 'Pin-Wells and Rag-Bushes.' *Folklore*, 4 (4), pp. 451–470.

Hausner, S.L. (2016). *The Spirits of Crossbones Graveyard: Time, Ritual, and Sexual Commerce in London.* Bloomington and Indianapolis: Indiana University Press.

Hope, R.C. (1893). *The Legendary Lore of the Holy Wells of England.* London: Elliot Stock.

Horniman Museum. (n.d.) 'Cloutie Tree (World Gallery - Gallery text).' Available Online: https://www.horniman.ac.uk/object/authority/subject-1007/ [Accessed 27 August 2022].

Horrox, Camilla. 2014 (10 October). 'Alice Gross Yellow Ribbons of Hope to be Removed,' *My London.* Available Online: https://www.mylondon.news/news/local-news/alice-gross-yellow-ribbons-hope-7914799 [Accessed 27 August 2022].

Houlbrook, C. (2016). 'Saints, Poets, and Rubber Ducks: Crafting the Sacred at St Nectan's Glen.' *Folklore*, 127 (3), pp. 344–361.

Houlbrook, C. (2018). *The Magic of Coin-Trees from Religion to Recreation: The Roots of a Ritual*. Cham: Palgrave Macmillan.

Houlbrook, C. (2021). *Unlocking the Love-Lock: The History and Heritage of a Contemporary Custom*. New York and Oxford: Berghahn.

Hudson, W.H. (2020 [1911]). 'An Old Thorn.' In J. Miller (ed.) *Weird Woods: Tales from the Haunted Forests of Britain*. London: British Library, pp. 93–116.

JoeJourneys. n.d. 'New Cross Wish Tree.' Available Online: https://www.joejourneys.com/new-cross-wish-tree [Accessed 27 August 2022].

King, J. (2020) 'Tree with 'Ribbons of Hope' on Clifton Downs.' *Bristol Post*. Available Online: https://www.bristolpost.co.uk/news/bristol-news/tree-ribbons-hope-clifton-downs-4135529 [Accessed 27 August 2022].

Layard, E. (1879). 'Rag-Bushes.' *Nature*, 20, p. 457.

Letcher, A. (2004). 'Raising the Dragon: Folklore and the Development of Contemporary British Eco-Paganism.' *The Pomegranate: The International Journal of Pagan Studies*, 6 (2), pp. 175–198.

Magliocco, S. (2018). '"Reconnecting to Everything: " Fairies in Contemporary Paganism.' In M. Ostling (ed.) *Fairies, Demons, and Nature Spirits: 'Small Gods' at the Margins of Christendom*. London: Palgrave Macmillan, pp. 325–347.

McNeill, L. (2007). 'Portable Places: Serial Collaboration and the Creation of a New Sense of Place.' *Western Folklore*, 66 (3–4), pp. 281–299.

Monger, G. (1997). 'Modern Wayside Shrines.' *Folklore*, 108, pp. 113–114.

'National Day of Reflection 2021.' *Church Support Hub*. Available Online: https://churchsupporthub.org/national-day-of-reflection-2021/ [Accessed 27 August 2022].

Pershing, L. and Yocom, M.R. (1996). 'The Yellow Ribboning of the USA: Contested Meanings in the Construction of a Political Symbol.' *Western Folklore*, 55 (1), pp. 41–85.

Price, A. (2018). 'Tracing the 'roots' of Tree Dressing Day in the Common Ground archive.' *Exeter University Special Collections*. Available Online: http://specialcollections.exeter.ac.uk/2018/11/30/tracing-the-roots-of-tree-dressing-day-in-the-common-ground-archive/ [Accessed 27 August 2022].

Richardson, M. (2001). 'The Gift of Presence: The Act of Leaving Artifacts at Shrines, Memorials, and Other Tragedies.' In P.C. Adams, S. Hoelscher and K.E. Till (eds.), *Textures of Place: Exploring Human Geographies*. Minneapolis: University of Minnesota Press, pp. 257–272.

Royal Borough of Greenwich. (2020) 'A Spectrum of Gratitude from Royal Greenwich Residents.' Available Online: https://www.royalgreenwich.gov.uk/news/article/1695/a_spectrum_of_gratitude_from_royal_greenwich_residents [Accessed 27 August 2022].

Santino, J. (1992a [1986]). 'The Folk Assemblage of Autumn: Tradition and Creativity in Halloween Folk Art.' In J.M. Vlach and S. Bronner (eds.), *Folk Art and Art Worlds*. Logan: Utah State University Press, pp. 151–169.

Santino, J. (1992b). 'Yellow Ribbons and Seasonal Flags: The Folk Assemblage of War.' *Journal of American Folklore*, 105, pp. 19–33.

Stout, A. (2020). *Glastonbury Holy Thorn: Story of a Legend*. Glastonbury: Green & Pleasant.

TimeOut. (2015). 'National Tree Dressing Day.' Available Online: https://www.timeout.com/london/things-to-do/national-tree-dressing-day [Accessed 27 August 2022].

54 *Ethan Doyle White*

Tuleja, T. (1997). 'Closing the Circle: Yellow Ribbons and the Redemption of the Past.' In T. Tuleja (ed.), *Usable Pasts: Traditions and Group Expressions in North America*. Logan: Utah State University Press, pp. 311–331.

Walhouse, M.J. (1880). 'Rag-Bushes and Kindred Observances.' *The Journal of the Anthropological Institute of Great Britain and Ireland*, 9, pp. 97–106.

Whitaker, T.D. (1812). *The History and Antiquities of the Deanery of Craven in the County of York* (second edition). London: J. Nichols and Son.

White, L.A. (2021). *World Druidry: A Globalizing Path of Nature Spirituality*. Belmont, CA: Privately published.

Wilks, J.H. (1972). *Trees of the British Isles in History and Legend*. London: Frederick Muller.

Woodcraft Folk. (2012). 'Tree Dressing Day.' https://woodcraft.org.uk/activities/tree-dressing-day [Accessed 27 August 2022].

3 "Unite and Unite, and Let Us All Unite"

The Social Role of the Calendar Custom in English Communities

Sophie Parkes-Nield

Introduction

England is home to a diverse calendar of vernacular traditions taking place in communities which continue to be performed today even though their original purpose may be unknown, or has fallen out of use. Yet historian Ronald Hutton tells us that contemporary society typically favours the "celebration of private relationships and the individual lifecycle" (1996, pp. 426–427), rather than collective, society-wide holidays that our ancestors might have enjoyed. What, then, is the social role of the calendar custom in contemporary English communities, and what do customs contribute to the lives of the people living there and visiting? Do calendar customs have the power to unite our communities and strengthen their tourism appeal? If so, how?

Though there is some discrepancy about what constitutes a calendar custom (Shuel, 1985, p. 6), folklorist Steve Roud's approach, as outlined in his book *The English Year*, is adhered to here: the "'traditional' customs and festivals that take place within communities and are organised by members of that community, and have been around long enough to have been passed on to successive generations" (2006, p. xiii). This intangible cultural heritage is significant, UNESCO maintains, because it enables and promotes "cultural diversity in the face of growing globalisation [encouraging] mutual respect for other ways of life" (2021a). Intangible cultural heritage can also appeal to tourist bodies that wish to promote their places as culturally significant, though it is worth observing that the United Kingdom is not one of the 180 states to have ratified the Convention for the Safeguarding of the Intangible Cultural Heritage 2003 (*The States Parties to the Convention for the Safeguarding of the Intangible Cultural Heritage (2003)*, 2021b).

An excellent introduction to the nature, content, and proliferation of England's calendar customs and, more widely, Britain's, can be found at CalendarCustoms.com, an online directory in which users can document their experiences of such events. This contributes to the website's aim to "celebrate the diversity of British culture and tradition and to encourage others to support events so that they can continue in perpetuity for future generations to enjoy." CalendarCustoms.com also seeks to crowdsource information

DOI: 10.4324/9781003374138-5

56 *Sophie Parkes-Nield*

to enable visitors to "get to the right place at the right time on the right day and to know what to expect when they arrive" (Shepherd, 2019).

In 1985, photographer Brian Shuel, in the introduction to his collection of photographs of British calendar customs, noted that one of his motivations for photographing these events was to make them visible to readers, because these "hotbeds of tradition and ritual [...] like to keep it to themselves" (Shuel, 1985, p. 6). But with online interventions, such as CalendarCustoms.com, and groups such as "Traditional Calendar customs and Ceremonies" hosted by Facebook, where users can also ask questions and disseminate related information to a like-minded community of users (Facebook, 2021), twenty-first century communities may have little opportunity to "keep it to themselves."

In making this shared information publicly available, and inviting contributions, CalendarCustoms.com actively encourages calendar custom tourism: for interested individuals from outside the host communities to spectate. Given Roud's observation that calendar customs are organised locally, the internet, and in particular social media, has become a vital tool in discovering calendar customs.

The title of this chapter is derived from the traditional "Cornish May Carol," (n.d.) sung every year at the Padstow May Day celebrations where, according to the local tourist board, 30,000 people gather to welcome the onset of summer, including many former Padstonians who return home for the purpose (Visit Cornwall, 2020). In 2020, immediately after the cancellation of the town's celebrations due to the national outbreak of COVID-19, an interview was conducted with a Padstonian heavily involved in the orchestration of May Day despite his permanent residency in Maine, the United States. He felt the absence of the custom deeply and described his and his peers' attempts to observe the day and generate the kind of camaraderie usually experienced during the festivities:

> Everybody either sat around and played music and watched old May Day videos or tried to get themselves out of the doldrums, so to speak, by doing something similar to what we would have done normally. I had a lot of video calls with friends and a virtual pint over the video.
>
> (personal communication, 5 May 2020)

Though only the viewpoint of one organiser, volunteered for the interview by his community, this insight goes some way to demonstrate the social role a calendar custom can have for its host community. It is thanks to May Day that he, a man living over three thousand miles away, maintains close connections with friends and neighbours and has the occasion to return to his hometown each year. "I'd skip Christmas and New Year; there's nothing else in the calendar but May Day" (personal communication, 5 May 2020), he says. The social role of May Day from his perspective, then, is to bring together those with a connection to the town to renew relationships. May Day becomes a "communal pace-maker [that] recharges the community and the good fellowship of the people of Padstow" (Rowe, 2006, p. 40).

"Unite and Unite, and Let Us All Unite"   57

Outsiders are not unwelcome; the archivist, collector, and documentarian of calendar customs, Doc Rowe, has famously been visiting Padstow's May Day since the 1960s (Rowe, 2006), and as Padstow is known for its tourism, local people understand that tourists will be present. The organiser told me that local people feel "the contrast of it being such a local custom and a local tradition, and also having so many visitors come to the place," but the significance of the event for the townspeople is such that it "wouldn't matter if nobody showed up. I mean, if we could block the entire town off for the day and have it as our day we would" (personal communication, 5 May 2020). And, as already outlined above, Visit Cornwall makes available May Day information to tourists, recognising the value of the event to the visitor economy: a "huge and remarkable" (Rowe, 2006, p. 6) custom that is integral to the town's calendric cycle, and a curious, colourful draw.

With qualitative data gleaned from organisers only – not from other residents or spectators, or those that abstain from participation – and from only three customs amid many more, there is much work to be done in ascertaining a representative perception of the calendar custom's social role in England. However, by assessing the organisers' intentions in planning and performing their custom, we can begin to understand the perceptions of their communities, synthesise the reported reception of their activities, and understand the reasons behind their compulsion to undertake responsibility, accountability, and significant amounts of unpaid work to organise these customs, or as John Widdowson acknowledges, "the individual who participates in a given custom for such praiseworthy reasons as his realisation that somebody must carry on the tradition, and who therefore unselfishly volunteers to do so" (Widdowson, 1993, p. 25). The diversity of the case studies – one with a long performance history, one a revival, and one created more recently – also goes a little towards ameliorating the representation question.

It is also worth noting that although there is not sufficient scope here to interrogate the impact of the COVID-19 pandemic on the three case studies, interviews informing this chapter came at a time when all three customs were unable to take place in their usual format, if at all. Absence gave the organisers additional time and space to consider the social role of their customs, but at the time of writing it is unclear how the pandemic will affect their future.

The Castleton Garland Ceremony

Each year on 29 May – Royal Oak Day – the streets of Castleton in Derbyshire are crowded with people observing a King and Consort parading on horseback, the King's body obscured by a "garland' – a heavy cage decorated with flowers. Royal Oak Day typically commemorates 1660's restoration of Charles II, but, like the history of many English customs, the origins of the Castleton Garland Ceremony are unclear: whether it is a direct celebration of Royal Oak Day, or an amalgam of May garland, or even rushbearing traditions, continues to be a point of speculation (Roud, 2006, p. 279).

58   *Sophie Parkes-Nield*

Historically, village bell ringers were responsible for the coordination of the event, but later a Garland Committee was formed for this purpose (Hole, 1976, p. 115). An interview with a key organiser about his lifelong involvement in the custom found him keen to stress his village roots. For example, his wife was:

> [...] born on her mother's front room carpet in Castleton [...] When people say "well, what do you know about Castleton?," I can say [we], together, have lived here 129 years between us.
>
> (personal communication, 2 June 2021)

The organiser believes that the Castleton Garland Ceremony is most important to "the old village families" – those who have been resident for many generations. When Garland Day could not take place in its usual guise in 2020 and 2021, he organised a COVID-compliant observation of the event for these old village families, as he felt the absence of the custom would be experienced more significantly for them, "really deep down." He struggled to articulate why this might be, saying "it's something inside, you know, and people get incredibly emotional about it [...] I can't describe why it's emotional. It just is" (personal communication, 2 June 2021). Dorothy Noyes, in her study of the La Patum festival in Berga, Catalonia, was told much the same thing by her informants during her fieldwork: "The Patum was ineffable: there was no one who did not say this [...] the important thing was the way it made them feel" (Noyes, 2003, p. 31). This is typical of intangible cultural heritage, where the "untouchable, such as knowledge, memories and feelings" comes into play, meaning that "since human activity of the past exists only as tangible evidence, intangible cultural heritage must be tied, in whatever form it takes, to the present" (Stefano et al., 2012, p. 1).

From the organiser's comments, it is clear that he, too, believes that the significance of the Garland Ceremony is the way it makes him, and other long-resident families, feel. By opening up this small ceremony to these families only, he equates the resonance of the custom with the longevity of village residence: that continuity and repetition of performance across generations results in a deeper significance than for those families that may have moved to the village more recently. This is unsurprising given the organiser's own personal connection with the custom, but his description of the changing nature of the village also influences this perception and has affected the performance of the custom itself. Recently, he explained, the constitution was amended so that Castleton boys as well as girls could participate; it has since changed again to enable children from neighbouring villages to take part. These changes have been made to accommodate the fact that the village is home to far fewer young families due to a lack of affordable family housing, and the proliferation of holiday lets and "party houses." For the organiser, then, the custom provides the opportunity for the old village families, and for those with direct, familial connection to the village but living elsewhere, the occasion to reunite (personal communication, 2 June 2021), much like the social role that Padstow's May Day festivities fulfil.

There is also the apparent popularity of the custom with tourists to consider. Castleton itself has long been a tourist destination, with Georgina Boyes noting the growth of the railway in the late nineteenth century resulting in development of local amenities to better accommodate greater numbers of visitors (1993, p. 112), a trend which has continued today, illustrated by the organiser's observations of the abundant holiday homes, and at least one pub dubbed "the tourist pub" – the one frequented not by residents but only by visitors (personal communication, 2 June 2021).

Though May customs involving garlands have been widespread across England (Rowe, 2006, p. 36), the ceremony's status as "deservedly well known, and very photogenic" (Roud, 2006, p. 278) makes Garland Day an attractive tourist proposition: the opportunity to see something unusual and with a long, documented but not concrete heritage, allowing for speculation and (re)interpretation, in a festive landscape: "The end of the day often sees visitors and villagers alike dancing a spirited impromptu dance through the streets" (Rowe, 2006, p. 64).

Much like Visit Cornwall disseminating May Day information to prospective visitors, a wealth of promotional material about the Castleton Garland Ceremony is found on Peak District tourism websites (a selection include: DerbyshireUK, 2017; Peak District National Park, 2018; Peak District Online, 2020; The Peak Hotel, 2021), while Marketing Peak District and Derbyshire include events "as part of our tourism strategy to increase visitor spend in the area" (personal communication, 2 November 2021). Castleton Visitor Centre, at the epicentre of the village, hosts two exhibition cabinets about the ceremony. Placed towards the back of the Visitor Centre among other exhibits depicting local agricultural and educational history, the Stuart-style costumes used in the custom are the focus of the displays, while an interpretation panel proffers theories regarding its origins.

In making exhibition material available, the Visitor Centre curators show that the Castleton Garland Ceremony, as performed today and in the past (the interpretation panel is titled "The Ancient Castleton Garland Ceremony"), is part of village life: that to live in Castleton is to recognise the custom. Boyes states that the cultural shift in appreciation for calendar customs in the latter part of the nineteenth and twentieth centuries – largely courtesy of the rise in folkloristics – has helped to cement the reputation of the Castleton Garland Ceremony as an authentic, and therefore important, survival of old village life. This "re-styling," Boyes confirms, "satisfied both local critics and visitors" (Boyes, 1993, p. 118), and, as a result, the Castleton Garland Ceremony gives credence to the notion that Castleton is a special place, a place which is lived in by generations of dedicated village families with their own expression of village identity *and* one which has tourist worth. However, the organiser understands that not all local people welcome the event, saying:

> There are people who are against it, don't like it. About ten days in advance, we put the [road closure orders] up around the village [...] and people will still come to the barriers and argue.
>
> (personal communication, 2 June 2021)

60 *Sophie Parkes-Nield*

He does not indicate whether these people are the old village families, or whether they are more likely to be holidaymakers and newer residents, and there are further questions to be asked here: does the organiser believe that residents without a deep familial connection to the village are unable to make a link between their own contemporary life in the village and the cultural heritage that preceded it? Do newer residents feel excluded from village life because of this apparent focus on longevity? Further research would be required to understand the reasons behind this apparent lack of enthusiasm from some quarters, and whether there are established patterns of engagement that correlate with the demographics of the subjects.

The Saddleworth Rushcart

Greater Manchester's Saddleworth Rushcart also has its roots in documented history. Rushbearing is not unique to Saddleworth; numerous other festivals occur across England today, and historically it was commonplace (Hole, 1976, p. 172), although how it was conducted differed from region to region. Saddleworth hamlets saw multiple carts built during wake celebrations, until the tradition was outlawed by police in the early twentieth century due to a fatal accident (Ashworth, 1999; personal communication, 11 January 2021).

Today's event was revived in 1974–1975 by Saddleworth Morris Men in the image of its historical predecessor (Ashworth, 1999). That this is a tradition with a documented history in Saddleworth is of utmost importance to the organisers. One of the organisers elaborates:

> When we bring out that cart on Saturday morning, all those guys in those sepia photographs are watching us [...] It crackles as we bring it out because we're doing the same thing at the same time of year at the same place that's been done for two hundred years.
>
> (personal communication, 11 January 2021)

All aspects of the event – cutting the rushes, building the rushcart, riding the cart as the "jockey," its route around the Saddleworth villages, the dancing – are presided over by the Saddleworth Morris Men, while morris dance sides from across the country are invited to process the cart on the day. It is also often an official event of the Morris Ring (2021), illustrating its significance to the morris dance world. To be involved in the event in a role other than spectator, then, the individual must be part of the morris community. As such, the Saddleworth Rushcart could be considered exclusive, its social role designed to satisfy the singular group that governs it, performing an enactment of Saddleworth identity that Saddleworth people can only observe. Put plainly: the custom is performed *for* and *by* the morris dance community, only some of whom will be Saddleworth people.

It is undeniable to the organisers, however, that the audience contributes greatly to the perceived success of the event: "The warmth you get from the locals, that's what does it for me" (personal communication, 11 January

2021). This support from local people, though, the organisers believe, has taken time to establish:

> I seem to remember a spell, maybe early nineties, mid-nineties, where I don't think we felt that appreciation. I think to some people we were a bit of a thorn in their side – stopping the traffic in Uppermill, how dare we do that? – but I think there's been a change in recent years.
> (personal communication, 11 January 2021)

Organisers cite recent, local social media activity to demonstrate the strength of support for the event in light of its absence due to COVID-19, but they are also aware that there is a contingent of local people who do not necessarily feel at home at such an event and leave the area when it takes place (personal communication, 11 January 2021). The current Rushcart Secretary feels that the Saddleworth Rushcart is not as well attended as other local events, believing morris dance to have less of a "broad appeal" and local people not knowing, understanding or valuing the event's history and its significance to the area (personal communication, 5 June 2021).

The organisers indicate that for an individual outside of the morris community to feel part of this custom is to recognise and place value on Saddleworth's history and intangible cultural heritage, stating, "It's in their history. It's part of the fabric of Saddleworth" (personal communication, 11 January 2021). The social role of the Saddleworth Rushcart, therefore, is to bring the morris community together through the act of reminding Saddleworth people of that heritage. Like the organiser of the Castleton Garland Ceremony, the organisers of the Saddleworth Rushcart find significance in their own connection to the custom, either through familial relationship and living in the area, or simply from participating every year, in their own unbroken tradition (personal communication, 11 January and 5 June 2021).

Comparable to Castleton's Visitor Centre, information about the Saddleworth Rushcart is housed at Saddleworth Museum, but with greater prominence: a replica rushcart, complete with a manikin in full Saddleworth Morris Men kit, occupies the main window of the Museum's ground level on Uppermill High Street. This display is kept up to date with the most recent rushcart banner (at the time of writing, in late 2021, the banner commemorates the life of the Duke of Edinburgh), while inside, interpretation panels offer greater detail about the tradition's history and revival. This exhibition was curated independently of the Saddleworth Morris Men, although the side were informed of its development (personal communication, 8 October 2021).

Organisers acknowledge that it is the cart itself that audiences like to engage with best, saying, "They want to see it and they want to touch it. They want to ask about it and they want to nick a rush out of it" (personal communication, 11 January 2021), and Museum curators have appealed to this curiosity by placing the cart at the centre of Saddleworth's most bustling village. Both the historic tradition and the contemporary event, Museum curators seem to say, is at the very heart of the community.

62   Sophie Parkes-Nield

The Marsden Imbolc Fire Festival

In contrast to both the Castleton Garland Ceremony and the Saddleworth Rushcart, there is no historical precedent for the Marsden Imbolc Fire Festival, which occurs every two years on the first Saturday in February. Created in the 1990s, the festival's organisers had a social role in mind for its inception: to bring together the community during the winter months, to counteract "the most depressing time of year," and to appreciate the local landscape (personal communication, 25 February 2021). Like calendar customs with a lengthier record of performance, the main event follows a programme established over the years: a noisy, torch-led procession through the village culminates in a nearby arena where a giant Jack Frost puppet, representing the hardship of winter, goes to battle with the Green Man, the bountiful spring, in a display of "iconography that was more accessible to people," the organisers felt, than real, documented folklore (personal communication, 25 February 2021).

The organisers have not tried to hide their invention, but the custom has still been ascribed folkloric and even religious meaning by its audience, and it could be the very lack of historical evidence – unlike the documentation that underpins the Castleton Garland Ceremony and the Saddleworth Rushcart – that enables these personal interpretations to flourish. The organisers explained how they have been told of babies born to women who had touched the Green Man the preceding year, or subsequent weather patterns influenced by the event (personal communication, 25 February 2021). Pagans have observed the festival from a religious perspective and although the organisers are not pagan themselves, they have been invited to reciprocal pagan events (personal communication, 25 February 2021). This desire to "bring a supernatural element to our festival," the organisers believe, is the need for local people to make a connection to the place in which they live, and to celebrate its uniqueness as the event helps people "get a sense of being rooted in a place" (personal communication, 25 February 2021). Certainly, with the event held in darkness at the mercy of early February weather, it fosters an atmosphere of reverence to nature.

In its early days, the organisers sought to involve residents more closely:

> I didn't like the idea of [the custom] being totally imposed upon the community, so we wanted to get more community involvement. I then organised to do workshops in schools and public workshops, which we've done ever since.
>
> (personal communication, 25 February 2021)

Over the subsequent years, the festival has been adapted in an attempt to nurture an environment in which all residents, regardless of background, skills, or interest, can contribute and participate. This might be as simple as a family attending a lantern making workshop, or more integral to the organisation of the event itself, with performers, stewards, fundraisers, and workshop facilitators sourced directly from the community. Organisers have also set out to welcome individuals that might ordinarily be excluded from taking on responsibility, such as people with learning difficulties or ex-offenders, and are also open to ideas brought forward by the community: when the festival was besieged by heavy snow, for instance, the organisers were delighted when one family created small snow sculptures along the procession route. As such, the organisers believe their inclusive intentions give the festival its essence, stating, "The festival can embody the people that manage it" (personal communication, 25 February 2021).

The intended social role of the Marsden Imbolc Fire Festival, then, appears further reaching and more active than the Castleton Garland Ceremony or the Saddleworth Rushcart: it has a social agenda in mind, and finds ways to include local people through different opportunities. Though there is a practical side to this – the size of the organising team is small, at just three people, so it is necessary to bulk up with volunteers – there is also the hope, on the organisers' part, that community involvement will result in community ownership, and resilience, of the event.

The festival has also attracted visitors, people "that are interested in folklore that will travel" (personal communication, 25 February 2021), and audience numbers have swollen from several hundred to over five thousand during the lifetime of the custom. Much like the Castleton Garland Ceremony and the Saddleworth Rushcart, the custom is seen by the organisers to be integral to life in the village, citing two high profile pieces of evidence: the amount of festival memories shared on Marsden social media pages – including by those that no longer live in the village – and the people that have "come to live in Marsden virtually on the strength of [the festival]," including the incumbent Jack Frost puppeteer (personal communication, 25 February 2021).

Conclusion: "The fun, the freedom, the families, the fame" (Shuel, 1985, p. 11)

Though the fieldwork sample here is small, these three case studies are different in nature: the village-wide custom with a long performance history; the morris dance community reviving a previously moribund tradition; and a new custom consciously created by residents. As such, the intended social role of the customs differ too.

For all three customs, promoted public performance encourages local people to have a meaningful, collective experience by witnessing something on their doorstep which does not take place in the same way anywhere else. Organisers of all three customs are keen to stress the uniqueness of their custom, and how this might contribute to place identity: providing an impetus to stay resident in a village, to move there in the first place, or to appreciate what it means to live there. In the case of the Castleton Garland Ceremony and the Saddleworth Rushcart, this performance has occurred over generations, and the organisers therefore place value on both continuity and a direct connection to the past – that to live in this place is to engage with this custom,

64   *Sophie Parkes-Nield*

as people have done through time. Scott McCabe observed the same in his research into Ashbourne's Shrovetide football game, stating:

> [...] a sense of place is made not through legend or recreation of events, but in a determined effort to continue the event as a means to provide a symbolic system of continuity to the past [...] The game is played in the full knowledge that people have for centuries visited the event and the town and will continue to do so for centuries to come.
>
> (McCabe, 2006, p. 116)

The significance of the past to the contemporary practice is reiterated by the appearance of both customs in local exhibits at Visitor Centres and Museums, demonstrating to visitors the strength of the cultural heritage of the area. Similarly, those that have a direct connection to the custom, but no longer live in its host community, may use the custom as an anchor in the calendar to return and reunite with old friends, neighbours and relatives. This is another method of valuing the past, albeit a relatively recent past belonging to an individual or a family unit, and this is certainly not unique to the customs featured here. McCabe, for instance, observed the same in Ashbourne, with "'ex-pat' Ashburnians" returning not to participate or follow the game explicitly, but to catch up with former acquaintances (McCabe, 2006, p. 108), while the Kirkwall Ba' custom "helps to reaffirm social networks" in the same way, drawing people into the environment and "physically displaying the local community" (Fournier, 2009, p. 194).

Though the Marsden Imbolc Fire Festival is in its infancy in comparison, organiser insights demonstrate that the festival may go on to enjoy similar status and that this process is already underway as people who have left the area share their memories of the festival online, and children that attended the first workshops in the 1990s are now returning with their own children (personal communication, 25 February 2021).

Further research is required to understand whether those that do not know or value the heritage of their home community, or do not equate the activities of forebears as having any relevance to their own contemporary existence, are less likely to find the custom significant.

The Marsden Imbolc Fire Festival's lack of historical emphasis offers local people freedom to explore what the custom means to them: through folklore, and by contributing their own ideas and skills. This has the potential to broaden the appeal of the custom and its social role while widening active participation, meaning that diverse experiences of living in a place may be considered and valued; inclusivity acknowledged by UNESCO that "contributes to social cohesion, encouraging a sense of identity and responsibility which helps individuals to feel part of one or different communities and to feel part of society at large" (UNESCO, 2021a). For a custom to last beyond an ageing committee or singular group, and to remain a genuine reflection of the contemporary experience of a place, organisers should consider their custom's social role – or risk a custom becoming customary for a select few before relinquishing it to the history books.

References

Ashworth, P. (1999). *Rushcarts in Saddleworth*. n.p.

Boyes, G. (1993). 'Dressing the Part: The Role of Costume as an Indicator of Social Dynamics in the Castleton Garland Ceremony.' In J. Buckland and J. Wood (eds.), *Aspects of British Calendar Customs*. Sheffield: Sheffield Academic Press, pp. 105–118.

Cornish May Carol (n.d.). 'Caedmon TC 1224 / Topic 12T 197 ('Songs of Christmas' / 'Songs of ceremony').' Available Online: https://www.vwml.org/record/RoudFS/S302972 [Accessed 7 September 2021].

DerbyshireUK (2017). 'Castleton in Derbyshire.' Available Online: http://www.derbyshireuk.net/castleton.html [Accessed 6 October 2021].

Facebook. (2021). 'Traditional Customs and Ceremonies.' Available Online: https://www.facebook.com/groups/Traditionalcustomsandceremonies [Accessed 27 September 2021].

Fournier, L.S. (2009). 'The Embodiment of Social Life: Bodylore and the Kirkwall Ba' Game (Orkney, Scotland).' *Folklore*, 120 (2), pp. 194–212. Available Online: https://www.tandfonline.com/doi/abs/10.1080/00155870902969376?journalCode=rfol20 [Accessed 22 September 2021].

Hole, C. (1976). *British Folk Customs*. London: Book Club Associates.

Hutton, R. (1996). *The Stations of the Sun: A History of the Ritual Year in Britain*. Oxford: Oxford University Press.

McCabe, S. (2006). 'The Making of Community Identity through Historic Festive Practice: The Case of Ashbourne Royal Shrovetide Football.' In D. Picard and M. Robinson (eds.), *Festivals, Tourism and Social Change: Remaking Worlds*. Bristol: Multilingual Matters. Available Online: https://www.degruyter.com/document/doi/10.21832/9781845410490-008/html [Accessed 22 September 2021].

Morris Ring. (2021). 'Index of Morris Ring Meetings.' Available Online: https://themorrisring.org/about-mr/history/previous-meetings [Accessed 29 September 2021].

Noyes, D. (2003). *Fire in the Plaça: Catalan Festival Politics after Franco*. Philadelphia: University of Pennsylvania Press.

Peak District National Park. (2018). 'Visitor Centres – Castleton.' Available Online: https://www.peakdistrict.gov.uk/visiting/visitor-centres/castleton [Accessed 29 September 2021].

Peak District Online. (2020). 'Castleton Garland Day.' Available Online: https://www.peakdistrictonline.co.uk/castleton-garland-day/ [Accessed: 29 September 2021].

Roud, S. (2006). *The English Year: A Month-by-Month Guide to the Nation's Customs and Festivals, from May Day to Mischief Night*. London: Penguin.

Rowe, D. (2006). *May Day: The Coming of Spring*. Swindon: English Heritage.

Shepherd, H. (2019). 'About This Site.' Available Online: https://calendarcustoms.com/about/ [Accessed 4 June 2021].

Shuel, B. (1985). *Guide to Traditional Customs of Britain*. Exeter: Webb and Bower.

Stefano, M.L., Davis, P. and Corsane, G. (2012). *Safeguarding Intangible Cultural Heritage*. Woodbridge: Boydell Press.

The Peak Hotel. (2021). 'Castleton Ancient Garland Ceremony.' Available Online: https://www.thepeakhotel.co.uk/post/castleton-ancient-garland-ceremony [Accessed 29 September 2021].

UNESCO. (2021a). 'What is Intangible Cultural Heritage?' Available Online: https://ich.unesco.org/en/what-is-intangible-heritage-00003 [Accessed 28 October 2021].

UNESCO. (2021b). 'The States Parties to the Convention for the Safeguarding of the Intangible Cultural Heritage (2003).' Available Online: https://ich.unesco.org/en/states-parties-00024 [Accessed: 28 October 2021].

Visit Cornwall. (2020). 'Padstow May Day.' Available Online: https://www.visitcornwall.com/whats-on/traditional-cultural/north-coast/padstow/padstow-may-day [Accessed: 4 June 2021].

Widdowson, J. (1993). 'Trends in the Commercialization of English Calendar Customs: a Preliminary Survey.' In J. Buckland and J. Wood (eds.), *Aspects of British Calendar Customs*. Sheffield: Sheffield Academic Press, pp. 23–35.

4 "The Spik O the Place"[1]

Dialect and Its Place in the Folkloric Cultures and Traditions of North-East Scotland

Peter H. Reid

Dialect as Folklore

In 1946, FitzRoy Somerset, 4th Baron Raglan, President of the Folklore Society, observed: "it seems to me, high time that we broke new ground." He was giving his presidential address to the society and was attempting to set out what he saw as the scope of folklore. In his observations, he also noted that "dialect [in folklore terms] has received very little scientific study" (Raglan, 1946, p. 102). His theme was timely, for the previous year Louise Pound had also set out to explore the interconnections between dialect and folklore. She highlighted that dialect and folklore had been less closely associated than they should be and that the two subjects had, hitherto, largely been treated independently:

> Dialect, in the sense in which we now ordinarily use the word, is *lore*, linguistic lore, and linguistic lore exists in tradition alongside the folk beliefs and folkways, the folk legacies that we usually term lore.
>
> (Pound, 1945, p. 146)

It is true that many of the antiquarian scholars of the nineteenth century had often combined dialect and folklore in their studies. Sternberg (1851) in his *Dialect and Folklore of Northamptonshire*, Worth (1886) in his *History of Devonshire*, Brown (1891) in his *History of Nottinghamshire*, and others, cover similar ground in making connections between folkloric traditions and dialect. However, as is common of local historical writers of this period, their work essentially created little more than (eminently valuable) glossaries which, in the words of Sternberg (1851, p. iii), "embrace a collection of the lingual localisms; popular superstitions, fairy-lore, and other traces of Teutonic heathenism." Few references are given beyond their own well-meaning but amateur ethnography and, certainly, modern-day notions of language and dialect as central parts of cultural heritage and identity are rarely explored. Raglan and Pound were not, therefore, simply highlighting a truism; both were justified in their appeals for connections to be made more strongly and more explicitly between dialect as folklore, a theme which had already emerged strongly in some other countries such as Sweden, where systematic research into folklore and dialect was well-established (Hedblom, 1961, p. 1). Writing

DOI: 10.4324/9781003374138-6

68   *Peter H. Reid*

40 years later, Widdowson still considered the connections between dialect and folklore traditions to be "a neglected heritage." He commented:

> By searching into the traditions practised today, and recognising their firm anchorage in history, folklorists can provide reassurance by identifying the structures and patterns which impart a sense of stability and permanence to our culture.
>
> (Widdowson, 1987, p. 41)

Those ideas of the reassurance given by traditions and the sense of stability and permanence are important because they help inform the ties that bind people, places, and communities together. Widdowson's sense of a "neglected heritage" recalls the concerns articulated by WJ Thoms in 1846 when he first coined the word *folklore*. Writing in the *Athenæum*, Thoms had two main concerns – loss and survival:

> No one who has made the manners, customs, observances, superstitions, ballads, proverbs, &c., of the olden time his study, but must have arrived at two conclusions: – the first, how much that is curious and interesting in these matters is now entirely lost – the second, how much may yet be rescued by timely exertion.
>
> (Merton [pseud. Thoms], 1846, p. 862)

Thoms also recognised how cultural traditions and folklore shaped our understanding; all of those elements – manners, customs, observances, superstitions, ballads, proverbs – were areas of study where facts "which trifling in themselves, become of importance, when they form links in a great chain" (Merton [Thoms], 1846, p. 863). And that chain thus created is our collective cultural and folkloric inheritance.

Just as there were pleas to make connections between folklore and dialect, so too have there been appeals to understand better the links between language (encompassing dialect) and tourism. Whitney-Squires noted that "relatively few studies focus on the nexus between tourism, language, and indigenous community-based initiatives" (2016, p. 1160). In a Scottish context, Butler (1978) examined the precarious state of Gaelic on Skye and the implications of increasing visitor numbers, but there has been little work in this area since. Whitney-Gould also notes that tourism literature "lumps" language together with "traditions and practices" and that such a superficial approach results in underestimating the importance of language to cultural identity and heritage (2018, p. 1910). The consequence is that the use of local languages and dialects is often undervalued and considered superficial (Jaworski and Thurlow, 2013).

Doric and Its Place in the Tradition of North-East Scotland

The issues just discussed – from that initial conceptualisation of the word folklore by Thoms, to the superficiality of literature addressing language (or dialect) and tourism – collide fortuitously in an examination of Doric in North-East Scotland. The definition of folklore in the Oxford England Dictionary is "the traditional beliefs and customs of a community passed on by word of mouth" (OED, 2001). That "word of mouth" is mentioned here is significant for this chapter because it implies that spoken language is an important aspect of folklore, and the Doric dialect itself is principally a spoken one without standardised orthography (although much important literature does exist). Doric is, first and foremost, a spoken tongue.

Doric[2] is the name given to the dialect spoken in the North-East of Scotland (see Figure 4.1). It is a dialect of the Scots language, similar to, yet distinctively different from, that which is spoken elsewhere in Scotland. It is a living language (Millar, 2018). The 2011 Census showed that the highest concentrations of Scots speakers live in the North-East and in Shetland. It is widely used, possesses a distinctively rich vocabulary, and is marked by certain "shibboleths" which set it apart from General Scots (McClure, 2002, pp. 21–22). The most important of these is the replacing of *wh* in words like *whit* (what) *whan* (when), *whaur* (where) with the letter *f* so that in Doric it is *fit, fan, far* (see Figure 4.2).

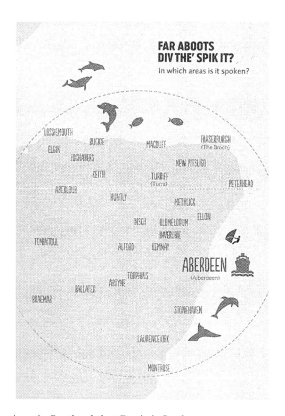

Figure 4.1 The Area in Scotland that Doric is Spoken.
(Image: Robert Gordon University).

70 Peter H. Reid

Figure 4.2 The Doric "F" Words.
(Image: Robert Gordon University).

"The Spik O the Place" 71

Doric is one of the principal ways in which the people and communities of North-East Scotland are bound together. McClure noted: "Doric defiantly persists as an integral part of the region's identity and self-image" (McClure, 2002, p.15). It is fundamental to the identity of the region, whether in its *Toonsers* form (associated with the City of Aberdeen itself) or in its richer and more mellifluous *Teuchter* form (spoken in the countryside and rural hinterlands). It has been described, perhaps uncharitably, as "a significant part of an insignificant identity" (Loester, 2017, p. 344). Yet, this is decidedly not an *insignificant* identity.

The landscape of the region – particularly the affinity with the land and the mountains, sea and coasts – provides strong cultural and folkloric markers in North-East Scotland. Much of the intangible cultural heritage of the region is evoked from an almost spiritual connection with, and sense of belonging to, the very tangible landscape. An obsessive concern for, and relationship with, the land has been at the heart of the narratives of folk traditions in the region for generations (and prevails even long after most people have ceased to have a direct connection with farming). Cuthbert Graham, a leading topographical historian of the area, explained that the North-East "has been dominated by a single theme – a single myth in the deep psychological sense – a passion for the land" (Graham, 1981). Much of the folklore, myth, legend, and dialect is derived directly from this spiritual sense of, and connection to, the land. Flora Garry, one of the greatest Doric poets, said:

> It [land] was a sort of religion. It was the thing they lived for and thought about. It was every day that they were practising this religion. Religion, using the word in a different sense, meaning the Kirk on a Sunday, was in a way a much more superficial thing than this feeling they had about the parks and crops and the beasts.
>
> (Garry, 1991)

A similar obsession can be observed in the relationship with the sea, a bond that has spawned a bewildering array of folklore traditions that, like those connected to the land, help define the culture, mentality, and outlook of the people. Peter Anson, the leading ethnographer of North-East Scotland's fisher communities, profoundly understood the region, its folkloric traditions, and culture:

> Folklore is still a force. While retaining ancient characteristics it is adapting itself to changes in ways of living and environment. Some customs have withered away and their memory has become romantic to us. Others have prospered to such an extent that they are ordinary, even tawdry and occasionally commercialised.
>
> (Anson, 1965, p. 7)

Landscape and sea come together as principal markers (even perhaps generators) of folklore and cultural heritage. In Doric-Land they are tied to the

72 Peter H. Reid

rhythm of the seasons, the rituals of agricultural life, the majesty of the landscape, the perils of the sea, the hardiness of the people, the simplicity of life, and expressed through the mither tongue.[3] For centuries, fishing and farming have been central to the economic, social, and cultural identity of the North-East of Scotland (Hood, 2009; Knox, 2001), and relationships with both sea and land have shaped the culture and identity of these communities, as well as underpinning its folkloric inheritance. Knox argues that the sense of "north-easterness is related to ways in which the dialect and culture have been mobilised" (Knox, 2001, p. 315). Nicolaisen, a great scholar of the North-East, described folklore and dialect as the coming together of the *spatial* and the *cultural* with the "old-fashioned notions of tradition" (Nicolaisen, 1980, p. 137).

These "old-fashioned notions of tradition" are supported by a sense that Doric, the native voice of individuals and communities, is one of the most "uncorrupted" and "pure" varieties of dialects, linked to the continuation of traditional industries, the rural character of the area and its relative geographical isolation (Loester, 2017, p. 342). In addition to this obsessive concern for the landscape, which shaped both dialect and folklore, two other critical factors are very evident. As mentioned previously, Thoms emphasised two prevailing characteristics in his letter discussing folklore in 1846, and today, these remain two of the obsessive drivers for those concerned with the folklore, traditions, culture, and heritage of North-East Scotland: the notions of *things lost* and *things to be preserved*. These are the fundamental preoccupations of Doric culture.

McClure has mentioned its "defiant" survival in an increasingly fragmented and globalised world. Doric is a remarkably durable element in the cultural landscape, and there has been a long, valiant fight to keep it alive:

> It would be a pity indeed to sacrifice the beauty of our Doric on the altar of a fetish called gentility. There were people who were always telling us the Doric was dowie and dying, and that it was well on the way to being a 'bonnie corpse.' But, if it was a corpse it was a mighty lively one. Surely we are not to allow all this gracious and precious inheritance of ours to pass away from us. We were told it was vulgarian and more likely to prove a handicap than an asset to youth. That is utterly and completely wrong. We were bilingual. We used the English language as finely and as freely as the English did. All English literature was ours, but our literature was not theirs.
>
> (Symon, 1932, p. 4)

Symon was also an important Doric author, a Great War poet whose work has had a similar impact on Scots as that of Brooke or Sassoon has on the English. She emphasises the cultural place of the dialect, as well as a cultural exclusivity of which she was proud. Her belief, nearly a century ago, that reports of Doric's demise were exaggerated, still resonates today as the obsession with *things lost* and *things to be preserved* continues to be played out.

Doric and the Visitor

What place, therefore, does Doric occupy for visitors and tourists coming to North-East Scotland? How does this cultural inheritance manifest itself in the twenty-first century? The region sometimes has an erroneous reputation for being insular. Historically and culturally, it was outwards facing (principally across the North Sea to the Low Countries and the Baltic), although separated by geographical barriers from the rest of Scotland. In the last 60 years, the region's more cosmopolitan feel has been due, in no small part, to the energy industry drawing people from across the world. Although globalised in this sense, it does not have the same tourist appeal as highly-visited places like Edinburgh or the Highlands and Skye, and a significant proportion of tourism has hitherto been business-related. That said, tourism is important, and has become increasingly so over the last decade. Although not a "hidden jewel" in the traditional sense – National Geographic (2010) rated the Moray Firth coastline number eleven in the top 99 stretches of coast on the planet – it does have capacity for further growth and diversification in tourism terms.

Anson, mentioned earlier, noted that folklore is sometimes exploited and given over to "tawdry commercialism." This is (still) something largely absent in North-East Scotland where the cultural experience remains authentic. In part this is due to the fact that the region has not being subject to the numbers of visitors found in other Scottish tourist hot-spots, and partly because of the zealousness with which the indigenous population guard their heritage and traditions, with Doric being possibly the most significant of these cultural and folkloric markers.

Chris Foy, Chief Executive of Visit Aberdeenshire, makes no bones about the importance of the dialect, believing that the region embraces the visitor "with a warm and authentic Doric welcome" (Foy, 2019) noting:

> [it is] tricky to understand but woven with complexities, glorious variances and brimming with the most wonderful, colourful expressions.
>
> (Foy, quoted in BBC, 2021)

Foy's comment highlights the extent to which both VisitAberdeenshire and its parent body, VisitScotland, see the dialect as a central element in the region's culturally distinctive and authentic offer to visitors:

> Doric [...] is full of fascinating words and phrases such as *loon* (lad), *quine* (girl/woman) and *fit like*? (how are you?), that you won't find elsewhere in Scotland. Taking some time to appreciate this unique language and, more importantly, the deeper cultural heritage of the North-East, will enrich any visit to this less discovered part of Scotland.
>
> (VisitScotland, 2021)

VisitAberdeenshire also, helpfully, gives guidance on one important facet, the tendency for lavatories in many places to be indicated by signs saying "loons" or "quines":

74   *Peter H. Reid*

Loons and quines are boys and girls. You might hear these words being added on to the sayings above: "fit like, loon?" or "far hiv ye bin, quine?" These words are also useful to know as they may just be the only way for you to differentiate between the ladies and gentlemen bathrooms.

(VisitScotland, 2022)

VisitScotland also makes much of the rich supernatural folklore that characterises the region, and this folklore is frequently rooted in, or transmitted through, Doric. The fact that Bram Stoker, author of Dracula, holidayed on the Buchan coast at Cruden Bay features heavily. Nearby Slains Castle[4] – the "inspiration for Dracula" according to VisitScotland – is a major component in the promotion of the supernatural element to visitors. A number of Stoker's other works are set along this part of the coast, including the *Watter's Mou* (a Doric title), and *The Mystery of the Sea*. In his work *Crooken Sands*, Stoker himself uses Doric liberally, and draws on the life of Jamie Fleeman (1713–1778) the Laird of Udny's Fule (the last family jester or fool in Scotland):

"Na! Na!" came the answer, 'there is nae sic another fule in these parts. Nor has there been since the time o' Jamie Fleeman – him that was fule to the Laird o' Udny'.

(Stoker, 1894, p. 16)[5]

Just as Stoker and Dracula are important for attracting visitors to the Buchan coast, they have also been channelled back into the cultural life of the region. In 2019, the story was reinvented as *Doricula*, a Doric retelling, mixing street theatre and highly physical circus performance, which played in locations across the North-East to locals and visitors alike, as well as at touring festivals in France and Italy.

Spikkin Aboot oor Heirskip[6]

Over the last decade (and particularly since the formation of the Doric Board to promote the dialect in 2016), there has been a move to something more meaningful; rather than speaking *about* the dialect third-hand, it is now something that has visibility and audibility as part of visitors' everyday experiences in the region. Certainly, in the past, visitors encountered it as, perhaps, background noise in shops or restaurants, but recently it has come to the fore in a more deliberate and explicit way. The example above around lavatory signs is one manifestation of this but there are many others.

A particularly important facet of this has been the engagement of visitor attractions and heritage sites. For some this is nothing new. The Grassic Gibbon Centre in Kincardineshire (towards the south of the Doric-speaking lands) has had the dialect at its heart since inception. This is hardly surprising given the run-away popularity of Lewis Grassic Gibbon's novel *Sunset Song* (habitually voted Scotland's favourite book). Dialect is very much at the heart of Grassic Gibbon's narrative and therefore the story that the Centre tells. For other small heritage attractions in the region (like Fraserburgh Heritage Centre or Buckie Fishing Heritage Centre), Doric is a natural element of the experience where *couthy* (friendly or comfortable) front-of-house staff greet visitors in their mither tongue. Macduff Aquarium, a popular attraction, tells stories of some of the most characterful fish in Doric with Cedric, a Flapper Skate, featuring in a range of Doric stories and storytelling events.

Perhaps more significant, however, is the embracing of Doric by Scotland's two principal heritage conservation bodies, the National Trust for Scotland (NTS) and Historic Environment Scotland (HES), which own between them 40 properties or sites across the region. NTS's rejuvenation of House of Dun, completed in 2021, is an interesting example. House of Dun is a grand baroque mansion house overlooking the Montrose Basin. The Doric dialect here is often called "Mearns" after the name of the district, and a few miles further south the vernacular shifts to that of Angus Scots (with the loss of the "f" shibboleth that marks out Doric at its purest).

House of Dun, an impressive property, was home to the aristocratic Kennedy-Erskine family. A member of that family, Violet Jacob (née Kennedy-Erskine), was one of the most noteworthy Scots poets of the twentieth century. Her father was Laird of Dun, her grandmother was a natural daughter of King William IV. She belonged to an elite social class and yet, as a child, she had a carefree upbringing, mixing with all of the children on the estate:

> […] she lairned the leid o the grieves, the orramen, the ploomen and the cottars fa aa warket the fairm.
>
> (Gweed Wirds, 2022)

She was not unique in this respect but, unlike the majority of her upper-class contemporaries, Jacob retained Mearns Doric all her whole life and saw it as part of her very soul. She wrote extensively, including novels, prose, reviews, and most particularly poetry. Her work was deeply informed by the folklore, legends, and traditions around House of Dun, but it owes its unique, distinctive dignity to her use of her mither tongue. John Buchan, author of *The Thirty Nine Steps*, wrote the foreword for her work *Songs of Angus* and noted: "she writes in Scots because what she has to say could not be written otherwise."

Jacob now features as a costumed guide at House of Dun. Her poetry has been recorded by Alistair Heather, a leading Scots language writer and presenter, as part of the audio interpretation. Jacob's poem *The Wild Geese*, narrated by Heather, conveys a strong sense of the place and dialect, as well as of Jacob herself. The outbuildings at Dun have become a folk museum, giving a permanent home to the outstanding collection of objects gathered by Lady Maitland of Burnside. The National Trust for Scotland has described this as "reimagining" the property, and it does so with the indigenous heritage and folklore traditions – dialect included – at its heart.

76   *Peter H. Reid*

In 2019, Historic Environment Scotland in partnership with the Elphinstone Institute at the University of Aberdeen, which researches the culture of the North-East of Scotland, launched a series of children's quizzes for some of its visitor attractions, including Huntly Castle and Spynie Palace. These quizzes were produced in both English and Doric. Digital assets have been created, such as "Stories of Aberdeenshire" (a collaboration between VisitScotland and the Elphinstone Institute at Aberdeen University), which tell folklore tales from across the region including many sound recordings in Doric by storytellers.

The Bonnie Lass o Fyvie

The ports of Aberdeenshire and Banffshire have witnessed trade across the North Sea for centuries and many ballads (and indeed stories and legends) have come from continental Europe. This, coupled with the fact that their "long legacy of farming [and] fishing [creates] an enviable tradition of story-telling which often takes the form of song and verse" (VisitScotland, 2022), enables tourism authorities to describe the region as "the Ballad Capital of World." It is a bold claim, but one that is not without foundation:

> North-East balladry constitutes the richest regional tradition in Britain. The warrant for this assertion lies in both the quantity and the quality of the area's ballads; the tradition has more recorded ballads than any other and it includes what good authority has judged the "best ballads."
>
> (Buchan, 1972, p. 4)

There is compelling, widely accepted evidence that the traditional ballads of the North-East have influenced musical genres such as Bluegrass, Country, and Rock 'n' Roll. It is well-documented that the *Bonnie Lass of Fyvie*, perhaps the most-celebrated and well-loved of North-Eastern Ballads, found its way to the United States where the title was corrupted to *Fennario*. Bob Dylan's *Pretty Peggy-o*, from his 1962 debut album, has its roots in *Fennario* and is a "skilful embroidery on the Bonnie Lass of Fyvie" (Bold, 2021, p. 37). Joan Baez recorded a version of it the following year, and Simon and Garfunkel the year after. Dolly Parton, Richard Thompson, and even the Grateful Dead share their roots with traditional ballads from the region. The musical legacy is strong, and virtually all indigenous songs from the region are in Doric.

The "Stories of Aberdeenshire" project builds on this tradition, showcasing extensively the musical and ballad heritage of the region alongside the other staples of the area, the folklore, and supernatural customs. The Bothy Ballad tradition (songs sung by itinerant farm labourers, often infused with political or economic meaning, and occasionally lewd) remains extraordinarily strong, with events and festivals featuring them attracting audiences from far and wide. The sung and spoken word are cornerstones of the Across the Grain festival (successor to the Doric Festival), which runs in October each year under the auspices of Aberdeenshire Council, and is a big attraction for locals and visitors alike.

A Fly Cup and a Fine Piece

One of the most emblematic encounters that tourists have with Doric culture is in terms of food and drink. The concept of the Fly Cup is one of the most omnipresent, and few visitors the North-East can escape this phenomenon. Various cafés around the region are called "The Fly Cup," including in Portknockie and in Inverurie. A "fly cup" (or more accurately, a fly cuppie) is technically a quick cup of tea or coffee, but is imbued with much more cultural significance and is rarely a swift event. A fly cup is a lingering event, where coffee or tea is partaken, and a *newsie* is had (the exchange of news and gossip). In a private home, a fly cup can take on all the ceremony (and spread) of formal afternoon tea. A "fine piece" is the essential accompaniment to a fly cup, being any type of rich, calorific cake or baking. In Aberdeen itself, this is sometimes named a "funcy piece" (a term regarded with snobbish scorn as déclassé by Teuchters in the hinterland).

Another part of culinary heritage that visitors encounter is the buttery (as it is described by Teuchters), or rowie (as it is called by Toonsers). This heavily salted and fatted flaky bread roll – described, not inaptly, by *The Guardian* as "roadkill croissants' – has its origins in the fishing industry, being created as a long-lasting alternative to ordinary bread for crews at sea. It is, perhaps, the one delicacy central to North-Eastern identity:

> […] it's the characteristic staple of north-east Scotland, as much a part of the local identity as the lush green landscape and the Doric dialect […] Loons and quines knew that taste, and what it meant: home.
>
> (Ross, 2018)

Over the years, the buttery ingredients have changed little. Moves to replace the butter and lard with palm oil have been resisted and, with events such as the World Buttery Championships, there has been a return to traditional methods and ingredients. "If you visit Aberdeenshire and do not eat butteries, you haven't visited Aberdeenshire" (Ross, 2018).

The only other food that can rival (and it does) the buttery as being at the heart of the culinary heritage of the North-East is Cullen Skink, a thick soup made of smoked haddock, potatoes, onions, and milk. It owes its name to the village of Cullen on the Moray Firth coast, with *skink* being a Scots word for a knuckle, or hough, of beef (from Middle Dutch *schenke*). Cullen Skink meant that instead of a beef broth, the fisher folk of Cullen had one of haddock. Cullen Skink has gone from a regional delicacy to an international one, from one made in the kitchens of fisherfolk to one made in Michelin-starred restaurants. Today, it is omnipresent on the menus of virtually every establishment a visitor to the region might eat in.

Conclusion

> So, *mak yer wye tae Aiberdeenshire*, connect with some of the region's *couthy craiturs* to learn more […] "F*it like?*" is sure to spark a warm conversation!
>
> (VisitScotland, 2022)

Thirty years ago, what the region had to offer in the way of tourism was very different. It focused primarily on the "Castle Trail" and the "Whisky Trail" and, although both remain important elements, there was little that showed the indigenous intangible heritage, and almost nothing that included Doric. That this has changed is undoubtedly down to a greater understanding of the value of intangible forms of heritage, such as dialect, and also perhaps due to a greater sophistication in visitors wanting to experience an authentic culture. But it is also due to the dogged persistence of the people of the North-East who value the dialect so highly. This speaks to the point addressed earlier about the preoccupation with *things lost* and *things to be preserved*, points made by Thoms in 1846. Those for whom Doric means something visceral have striven to promote and protect it and, through the establishment of the Doric Board in 2016, to ensure that it is strongly visible in the everyday life of the region for locals and visitors alike. In 2022, stickers proclaiming "We spik Doric here" are being offered to businesses across the region as part of the Board's activities (see Figure 4.3).

That Doric is at the very heart of the cultural identity and heritage of the region is not in doubt. Neither is the fact that the region makes much of its warm unspoilt authenticity, and is largely unaffected by the tawdry commercialisation that Anson warned about. This is not language tourism in the sense of students coming to learn it as a foreign language. Rather, this is the language of everyday encounters in shops and restaurants. But it is also increasingly visible and valued in heritage and cultural attractions across the region. It can be found in castles, galleries, museums, heritage centres, too; it is in the food and drink experiences, the craft experiences, the music, and festivals. Whitney-Gould points out that language is often lumped with

Figure 4.3 "We Spik Doric Here" Shop Stickers.
(Image: The Doric Board).

"The Spik O the Place" 79

"traditions and practices." Some visitors to North-East Scotland might see it like this, but they are also likely to encounter a thriving vernacular that encapsulates the culture of the region. Reports of Doric's death have been greatly exaggerated; when it was suggested to Mary Symon that it was a "bonnie corpse" she replied, nearly a century ago, that if it was so then it was "a mighty lively one." Time has not altered that. Exposure to tourism is not a threat for Doric; it is another example of its enduring vibrancy.

Notes

1 Literally the "speak of the place"; a pun, as it usually refers to someone who is the subject of unwanted gossip.
2 The word "Doric" implying rustic or unsophisticated was used to describe dialects in Scotland more generally. It has come to be used specifically to refer to the version of Scots spoken in the North-East of Scotland. The name is not without its critics; many in the region still refer to it as the Buchan tongue.
3 Mother tongue. Doric words and phrases in this chapter are not given in quotation marks, and nor are "apologetic apostrophes" added where words are contracted.
4 The truth is somewhat different. The spectacular ruin of "new" Slains Castle figures strongly in regional promotion of Stoker, Dracula, and the supernatural generally. However, when Stoker visited it was an intact, and then relatively modern, country house. The roof was removed in 1925 simply to avoid taxes.
5 By coincidence, the legend of the Laird of Udny's Fule was well-known to Lord Raglan mentioned at the start of this chapter. Raglan's wife was an Udny, a descendant of the Laird to whom Fleeman served as Fool.
6 Heritage.

References

Anson, P.F. (1965). *Fisher Folklore*. London: The Faith Press.
Bold, V. (2021). 'It's Braw to Ride Round and Follow the Camp: The Linguistic Journey of a Scots Song with Irish Soldier, Through Space and Time.' *Traditiones*, 50 (2), pp. 35–53
Brown, C. (1891). 'Dialect and Folklore.' In *A History of Nottinghamshire*. London: Elliot Stock, pp. 281–290.
Buchan, D. (1972). *The Ballad and the Folk*. London: Routledge, Kegan Paul.
Butler, R.W. (1978). 'The Impact of Recreation on Life Styles of Rural Communities. A Case Study of Sleat, Isle of Skye.' *Wiener Geographische Schriften*, 51/52, pp. 187–201.
Dylan, B. (1962). *Pretty Peggy-O*. New York: Columbia. CS 8579. Available Online: www.bobdylan.com/songs/pretty-peggy-o [Accessed 6 March 2022].
Foy, C. (2019). Quoted by Buchan, R. 'Putting the North-East on the Map.' *Press and Journal*, 17 June, Available Online: https://www.pressandjournal.co.uk/fp/business/1773960/putting-the-north-east-on-the-world-map/ [Accessed 6 March 2022].
Foy, C. (2021). Quoted by MacEacheran, M. *Doric, a Little-Known Form of North-East Scots, Is Undergoing a Pandemic-Inspired Renaissance.* Available Online: https://www.bbc.com/travel/article/20210321-scotlands-little-known-fourth-language. [Accessed 6 March 2022].
Garry, F. (1991). 'Interview with Frieda Morrison.' *Scots Radio*, episode 3, 27 February 2014. Available Online: https://www.scotsradio.com/podcast/february-edition-episode-3/ [Accessed 6 March 2022].

80   *Peter H. Reid*

Graham, C. (1981). *Grampian Hairst: An Anthology of Northeast*. Aberdeen: Aberdeen University Press.

Gweed Wirds: Doric Scrievin Ingang. [Doric Literature Portal]. Available Online: www.thedoric.scot/violet-jacob.html [Accessed 6 March 2022].

Hedblom, F. (1961). 'The Institute for Dialect and Folklore Research at Uppsala, Sweden.' *The Folklore and Folk Music Archivist*, 3 (4), pp. 1–2.

Hood, D.W. (2009). 'Customs and Beliefs: Folk Culture in North East Scotland: Essay for the North-East Folk Archive.' Available Online: http://www.nefa.net/archive/peopleandlife/customs/folk.htm [Accessed 6 March 2022].

Jaworski, A. and Thurlow, C. (2013). 'Language and the Globalizing Habitus of Tourism: Towards a Sociolinguistics of Fleeting Relationships.' In N. Coupland (ed.) *Handbook of Language and Globalization*. Oxford: Wiley Blackwell, pp. 264–286.

Knox, D. (2001). 'Doing the Doric: The Institutionalization of Regional Language and Culture in the North-East of Scotland.' *Social and Cultural Geography*, 2 (3), pp. 315–331.

Loester, B. (2017). 'A Significant Part of an Insignificant Identity: The Rearticulation of North East Scots between Tradition and Globalization.' *Russian Journal of Linguistics*, 21 (1), pp. 335–347.

McClure, J.D. (2002). *Doric: the dialect of North East Scotland*. Amsterdam: Benjamins.

Merton, A. [pseud. William J. Thoms]. (1846). 'Folk-Lore.' *Athenæum*, 982, pp. 862c–863a.

Millar, R.M. (2018). *Modern Scots: An Analytical Survey*. Edinburgh: Edinburgh University Press.

National Geographic. (2010). 'World's Great Islands, Coastlines, and Beaches.' Available Online: https://www.nationalgeographic.com/travel/article/list [Accessed 6 March 2022).

Nicolaisen, W.F.H. (1980). 'Variant, Dialect and Region: An Exploration in the Geography of Tradition.' *New York Folklore*, 6 (3), pp. 137–149.

Oxford English Dictionary. (2001). Oxford: Oxford University Press.

Pound, L. (1945). 'Folklore and Dialect.' *California Folklore Quarterly*, 4 (2), pp. 146–153.

Raglan, Baron. (1946). 'The Scope of Folklore.' *Folklore*, 57, pp. 98–105.

Ross, P. (2018). 'Utterly Butterly: The Scottish Pastries that Look Like 'Roadkill Croissants.' *The Guardian*, 5 July. Available Online: https://www.theguardian.com/travel/2018/jul/05/buttery-rowies-traditional-scottish-pastry-scotland-aberdeen-aberdeenshire [Accessed 6 March 2022].

Sternberg, T. (1851). *The Dialect and Folklore of Northamptonshire*. London: John Russell Smith.

Stoker, B. (1894). *Crooken Sands*. New York: TL De Vinne.

Symon, M. (1932). 'Beauty of Doric.' *Press and Journal*, 16 February, p. 4, col. 4.

VisitScotland (2021). *Stories of Aberdeenshire*. Available Online: https://www.visitscotland.com/blog/aberdeen-city-shire/heritage-culture-aberdeenshire/ [Accessed 6 March 2022].

Whitney-Gould, K. et al. (2018). 'Community Assessment of Indigenous Language-based Tourism Projects in Haida Gwaii (British Columbia, Canada).' *Journal of Sustainable Tourism*, 26 (11), pp. 909–1927.

Whitney-Squire, K. (2016). 'Sustaining Local Language Relationships Through Indigenous Community-based Tourism Initiatives.' *Journal of Sustainable Tourism*, 24 (8–9), pp. 1156–1176.

Widdowson, J.D.A. (1987). 'English Dialects and Folklore: A Neglected Heritage.' *Folklore*, 98 (1), pp. 41–52.

Worth, R.N. (1886). 'Dialect and Folklore.' In *A History of Devonshire*. London: Elliot Stock, pp. 335–340.

5 Folklore, Story, and Place

An Irish Tradition with Vast Touristic Value

Shane Broderick

Introduction

> It is a well-nigh trueism that Irishness and a sense of place go together. So
> closely do we connect identity with location that when we tell others who we
> are, we tell them where we come from.
>
> Patrick Sheeran (1988, p. 191)

Ireland, once lauded as "the land of saints and scholars," has without question one of the richest, most vibrant folkloric traditions in Europe. Over the last 2000 years an unassailable sense of place and connection to the land has been propagated through the oral and written traditions. This chapter will focus on the propagation and dissemination of this sense of place, the people involved, and how this can be implemented and drawn upon in terms of tourism.

A Sense of Place, Written in Stone

The first demonstrable evidence of placemaking in Ireland, and the age-old connection between the people and their sense of place within their surroundings, can be seen in the demarcation of tribal boundaries with monuments known as Ogham stones. These date to several centuries before the introduction and use of the traditional ink and quill manuscripts that Ireland is famous for. These monolithic monuments number roughly 400 examples and are not only found in Ireland but also in areas of Irish settlement in Britain, such as Wales, Scotland, and the Isle of Man (Moore, 2010, p. 7). The highest concentration, however, can be found in a south/south-west distribution in Ireland (Westropp, 1873, p. 201). The eponymous "Ogham," found on these stones constitutes the earliest recorded version of the Irish language, with most of script on these monuments being in Irish, excepting the Scottish examples, which are almost entirely in Pictish (MacNeill, 1909, p. 329).

The "letters" of this alphabet were inscribed in the form of straight or diagonal lines along a stem line on the Ogham stone itself. The stem line could be natural or carved onto the stones, and are traditionally read from bottom left, up, and around (Downey and O Sullivan, 2014, p. 26). It has

DOI: 10.4324/9781003374138-7

Folklore, Story, and Place 83

been postulated that it was originally a secret language or cypher (Granville, 1901, p. 133) and that it may have originally been used on wood (none of which survives in the archaeological record) before being used on stone. It has also been suggested that it may have been used as a type of sign language using the fingers to represent the letters (ibid, p. 135). The alphabet has mythical origins with tales reporting that it was invented by Ogma, a god of the *Tuatha dé Dannan* associated with eloquence (Windele, 1853, p. 44), while other tales give a biblical origin to the alphabet (this co-occurrence of a "native" pagan origin and a biblical origin is part and parcel of the syncretised nature of Irish cosmology). This alternative "biblical" tradition can be found in the *Auraicept na nÉces* (The Poets Primer), a book focusing on the training of the native *Filidh* (modern Irish: *Filí*, poets). It recounts how a mythical figure by the name of *Fénius Farsaid* was responsible for inventing not only the Irish language but also the three sacred languages of Latin, Greek, and Hebrew by selecting the best parts of the world's languages from the tower of Babel (McLaughlin, 2009, p. 1; Downey and O Sullivan, 2014, p. 27). This of course appears to be a calculated effort by the recorders of the tale to put Irish cosmology on a global (and biblical) scale. So how does this relate to a sense of place?

Early Medieval Irish texts expound that Ogham stones had "official recognition as documents confirming title to land" (McManus, 2004 in Downey and O Sullivan, 2014, p. 28), and as such were literal witnesses to a person's right to rule. Further evidence of this connection to land and place can be found by translating the writing from the stones themselves, which point to their possible function being tied to land ownership and the demarcation of tribal boundaries. Almost all examples read the same and follow a similar formula of:

[Name of] A [son of] B [son of] C
[Name of] A [of the kindred of] B
[Name of] A [Descendant of] B.

(MacNeill, 1909, p. 344)

Or:

X *Maqi* Y àX Son of Y
X *Avi* Y à X grandson of Y
X *Maqui Mucoi* Y à X descendant of Y.

(Downey and O Sullivan, 2014, p. 27)

Especially important to note here in relation to the current topic is the use of *Mucoi*. This shows tribal affiliation and was usually followed by the name of a legendary ancestor who gave their name to the *tuatha* (petty kingdom, tribe) that the person being commemorated on the stone belonged to. The term *Mucoi* itself did not survive the change into subsequent forms of the Irish language (*Gaeilge*) but was replaced by the prefixes *Dál*, *Síol*, and *Corcu*,

84 *Shane Broderick*

or the suffixes of –rige, -ne or –acht, to form the name of the *Tuatha* (MacNeill, 1909; White, 2021, p. 14). Some of these tribal names for territories have stood the test of time and can be still found today, for example, *Corca Dhuibhne* on the Dingle peninsula in County Kerry.

As the monumental use of Ogham went out of fashion and the traditional form of writing on vellum became more widespread, largely due to the expansion and influence of Christianity (White, 2021, p. 17), the development and propagation of a strong sense of place shifted firmly in the hands (or mouths) of the many-talented members of the class of native poets, the *Filidh*.

The *Senchaidh Sírcuimneach*, the "Long Memoried Custodian of Tradition"

In the hierarchical society of medieval Ireland, only one person came close to the status of the King (*Rí*), and that was the poet (*fili*, plural: *Filidh*). In fact, the highest ranking of them, the *ollamh* (the word still used in modern Irish for "Professor"), essentially had an equal status to that of the average petty king (Kelly, 2016, p. 46). Their name translates to "seer" and it is believed by some that the *Filidh* took on some of the functions of the Druids (Brezina, 2007, p. 10) and were the custodians of *Senchas* (traditional lore). As repositories of this lore, they acted as a *Senchaid*, an "authority on all things ancient" (Mallory, 2016, pp. 63–64). The many functions of the *filidh* depended on which of the seven grades they obtained through formal training. This grade determined the status, level of training, honour price, privileges, and the size of the retinue they could keep with them (Ireland, 2016, p. 36). Metrical and linguistic pursuits were a cornerstone of their profession and composing poems, such as extolling the virtues of a king through praise poetry, was the main source of their income. However, they were just as renowned for shaming and condemning them through satire *(Áer)*. On top of praise and satire they also had to have an encyclopaedic knowledge of the illustrious genealogies of the kings they visited, battles they fought in, and any other notable achievements (Mac Cana, 1974, p. 126). This not only helped to legitimise the rule of the king in question (whose ancestors might have ruled the *túath* for centuries) but also acted as the anchor for any of his kin who would follow him, cementing their deeds, and the deeds of those that came before them, firmly into the "place" they ruled. These deeds and notable events were often carried by the *Filidh* to other territories, acting as publicity agents or envoys for their kings (Breathneach, 1983, p. 55). It should be noted that the freedom of movement afforded to the *Filidh* was not usually granted to the average person, who would not be allowed to leave the *Túath* they resided in (with the exception of going on pilgrimage, or to attend an assembly). It stands to reason that this would have compounded the sense of place among these people, with the stories focused squarely on the land they lived on.

While on the subject of stories, the telling of tales was another arrow in the overflowing quiver of the *Filidh*. These tales were passed on orally from *fili to*

Folklore, Story, and Place 85

fili. One medieval text tells us that *"Níba fílí gan scéla"*: He is not a poet who does not have stories (Kelly, 2016, p. 47). The number of stories that the *Fili* had to memorise was entirely dependent on their level of training, and as such, the status and title he had obtained. The highest grade (*Ollamh*) was required to know 350 primary stories (*Príomhscéala*), while the lowest grade *(Focloc)* was only required to know 30 (ibid, p. 46). If we take into account that the family of *filidh* could hold a hereditary, landed position for centuries (Mac Cana, 1974, p. 137), it should stand to reason that they would be intimately connected to the natural environment around them. They would no doubt have stories for every single lake, hill, or stone in the landscape. Looking from the point of view of the king, the stories would be important to show where their ancestors came from and how they were connected to the land around them and the territory they ruled over (Brady, 2021). One genre of tales they were required to know was place name lore, with the eighth year of their training committed to learning how to recite these tales orally (Mulligan, 2019, p. 18).

As the influence of Christianity continued to spread and take a foothold, these stories were gradually committed to velum. But the oral and written traditions survived side by side, with each informing the other for centuries to come. The bardic schools also managed to survive alongside the Christian schools and monastic scriptoria (Fyke, 2008).

A Land Imbued with Story and the Formalisation of *Dindshenchas*

The exact mode of transmission of the stories from oral tradition to written is unknown but there are a few theories:

1) *Filidh* reciting to the monks dictating,
2) Monks listening to the stories and writing them in their own words
3) The *Filidh* learning to write and then composing the tales.

(Mallory, 2016)

Even though contact between the oral tradition of the *filidh* and the manu-script tradition of the monastic scriptoria is evident, due in part to the pres-ence of signs of orality in the writing, such as the descriptive passages/ Mnemonic runs known as *lann* (Mallory, 2016, p. 65), early sources and Annals make a clear distinction between the monastic scholar and the native *filidh* (Mac Cana, 1974, p. 126). However, we do have several cases where clerics are listed as having the title of *fili* (ibid., p. 26; Mallory, 2016, p. 24), showing us that an intersection between the two traditions was not an alien concept. Nevertheless, it is also possible that there may have been some small degree of friction from either side. The church may have had an issue with the *Filidh*'s fondness for panegyric poetry, and likely felt that praise should have been directed exclusively towards God (O Riordan, 1998, p. 73), while the *Filidh* refused to take up the new monastic rhyming meters (until finally giv-ing in in the ninth century), referring to them as *nua-chrutha* or "new forms" (Murphy, 1931, p. 96). Their insistence on remaining part of the oral tradition

86 *Shane Broderick*

for many centuries after the introduction of writing may also be evidence of this, though this could simply be down to the preservation of tradition (Breathnach, 2006). Whatever the case, both were responsible for the propagation and transmission of stories and poems that related to the people and places surrounding them. Even though the oral tradition relating to this subject is unfortunately lost to us, we are privileged to have a wealth of information preserved in the manuscripts.

During the eleventh and twelfth centuries we start to see a formalisation and codification of what is referred to as *Dindshenchas* ("The lore of notable places") which involved "the mapping of narrative and lore onto specific and named sites" (Mulligan, 2019, p. 108). This corpus of material, referred to collectively as *Dinshenchas Éireann* (The lore of the notable places of Ireland), is comprised of 200 pieces of prose and 200 pieces of poetry that survive in 20 manuscripts. Interestingly, some of these texts try to integrate local history and topography into a global framework (Ní Mhaonaigh, 2021), similar to the tales of *Fénius Farsaid* mentioned above that attempt to put the Irish language, and by proxy the vernacular Irish literature, on a world stage. While other countries in medieval Europe focused on cartography and the creation of *mappa mundi* (most of which placed Ireland on the periphery), the Irish used "innovative geospacial literature" to map the landscape with words and developed a genre of literature that gave the landscape they occupied a central space in European imagination (Mulligan, 2019, p. 3). This uniquely Irish genre of rich topographical literature brought the landscape that had been imbued with centuries of story to life through words, transforming it into narratives focusing on how notable places got their names. The prose and poetry of the *Dindshenchas Éireann* emphasised places over characters and events (ibid, p. 108), but place lore itself permeates the pages of the annals and hagiographies and form an integral part of our epic literature and sagas. It illustrates how the land and its features were conceptualised through the ages and how the people of the past engaged with their surroundings (Ní Mhaonaigh, 2020).

A thousand years or so later, geospacial etiological tales remained part of the traditional storyteller's repertoire, and it was these traditional storytellers who were the spiritual successors to the *filidh*. Myths, legends, and multi-episodic folktales, similar to the *príomhscéala* of the *filidh* formed part of the repertoire of traditional storytellers. For a full understanding of these more modern tradition bearers, Delargy's lecture *"The Gaelic Storyteller"* gives a concise overview. Or, for a more in depth look, Zimmerman's tome *The Irish Storyteller* will give these repositories of traditional lore far more justice than the current author can in the present chapter.

An Intangible Heritage Encoded in the Language of the Landscape

Through millennia these stories have left an imprint on the land. There is an inherent knowledge contained within the landscape, and the best way to access that is through the Irish language itself (Magan, 2020, p. 7). This is especially evident when looking at place names, for they are "the most direct and visceral way the Irish language is connected to the landscape" (ibid., p. 138). Anyone who has travelled in Ireland will have noticed the bi-lingual road signs. The English transliterations (through which the original meaning of the place name is essentially lost through anglicisation) are a direct result of the Ordnance Survey mapping of the country carried out between 1825 and 1841 (O'Giollán, 2000, p. 42). Fortunately, the original meanings of many of the place names were recorded by a team of Irish Scholars (O Donovan, O Curry and Petrie) who were among the only non-military (and Irish) people hired by the OS to "ascertain the proper nomenclature of the Gaelic toponomy" (Leerson, 1996, pp. 101–102). They were also in charge of documenting many aspects of folk life including *dinshenchas*, habits, superstitions, songs, stories, and so on (O'Giollán, 2000, p. 42), much of which would have been lost following the tragedy of the Great Hunger that was to devastate the country within the space of a couple of decades (Leerson, 1996, p. 103).

Returning to place names, they helped the local people orient themselves within their environment and preserved stories of the mythic past and the monuments contained within the landscape they inhabited (Ní Cheallaigh, 2006, p. 107). Information that is still there for people to access or to pass on to any tourists looking to connect to the land themselves. Sheeran said it best when he stated that to "recollect these place names was to remember the ancient tribes and their memorable deeds" (1988, p. 202). He also states that for any outsiders, or those not fluent in the language of the landscape, "all that Gaelic background of myth, literature and history had no existence" and the "landscape they looked upon was indeed but rocks, stones and trees." Whereas, to those well-versed in the Irish language and the language of the landscape, every field had its own name, depending on its function or characteristics (Magan, 2020, p. 3) and every "place" had its own story to tell. An interesting example of a field name can be found in *Muing na Fola*. A *Muing* is an overgrown piece of boggy ground, while *na fola*, means "of the blood," the reason being it was a soft piece of land where cattle could be "bogged down," i.e. stuck in the mud, so folk cures using bloodletting could be carried out (Robinson, 2003, p. 43). This level of local micro-geography would be unknown to anyone not versed in the *Dindshenchas* of the area, but connecting to the land through the native tongue allows this history to be preserved and the past to be brought to life, especially for any tourists or people from outside the culture. It will also uncover the "encoded reflections of our culture and past practices" (Magan, 2020, p. 138), revealing the "layers of memory contained within each Place name" (ibid., p. 149).

Another interesting example can be found in Cork City. In a picturesque area on the outskirts of the city lies "lovers walk." However, like many other place names, the anglicisation of the original "Siúl Na Lobhar" removes the context and history associated with the area. The correct translation would be "Lepers Walk," pointing to the presence of a Leper hospital in the past – a far less romantic alternative, but a prime example of the encoded history that lies

88 Shane Broderick

hidden in plain sight within the native language of the country. Before moving on to discuss how this can be applied to tourism, it would serve to discuss several ways that folklore is reflected in the landscape and how it has affected the attitudes of the people who have inhabited the land for millennia.

The Imprint of Folklore on the People Who Inhabit the Landscape

The effect that thousands of years of story, myth, and folklore, passed down through both oral and manuscript traditions, had on the people of Ireland and their natural surroundings is clearly evidenced and reflected in how they interact with the world around them. One of the finest examples can be found when looking at a type of monument that litters the Irish landscape in the tens of thousands, referred to as ringforts (*Rath, Lios*). This umbrella term covers a number of earthen and stone enclosures "defined by a penannular bank of earth with a ditch outside" (Lynn, 1975, p. 29). Stout, in his monograph *The Irish Ringfort*, claimed that these are so numerous and so familiar to Irish field workers that they hardly even need a definition (1997 in Ní Cheallaigh, 2006, p. 106). The monuments, which came into use in the early Christian era, usually encompassed a single family dwelling/farm settlement. Looking critically at the flimsy level of defence offered by the enclosures, it is just as likely that they were used as much for the protection of animals as they were for people (Lynn, 1975, pp. 30–32). When this type of habitation went out of use (approximately in the seventeenth century), myth and legend started to build up around them, which has inadvertently led to the preservation of many of these monuments.

These forts resisted the encroachment of modernity and maintained a prominent place in the consciousness of the communities in which they were found, due mostly to their association with "the other crowd," the enigmatic creatures known as fairies (Ní cheallaigh, 2006, p. 107). Even today, it is not unusual to encounter a ploughed field containing a fort that has been left unmolested due to fear of retribution from the "other crowd." Over the centuries, many accounts have built up of death or maiming due to ploughing through these abodes of the fairies, or through the removal or cutting of branches from the trees contained within (Roe, 1939, p. 21). Sudden death, no matter how many years after this offence was committed, was invariably blamed on revenge from the fairies. Generally, people would even avoid getting too close to the forts for fear of being "carried away" or "led astray" by these denizens of the otherworld (Ibid., p. 25). A famous case involving the belief that someone was carried away and replaced by a changeling after coming too close to a fort occurred near Clonmel in 1895. Over several days after falling ill, a young woman by the name of Briget Cleary was effectively tortured by her husband, members of her family, and a few members of the community in the belief that she was a fairy changeling (Burke, 1999). Unfortunately, these events tragically culminated in the death of Briget, but her story illustrates well the position such beliefs held in the minds of the people. The connection of the forts with fairy activity is also evident in

Folklore, Story, and Place 89

certain place names, such as Lisfarbegnagommaun in County Clare. This awkward and clunky anglicisation of "*Lios Fear Beag na gComáin*," meaning "Fort of the little men with Hurleys," owing to the belief that Fairies played the ancient Irish sport of Hurling there. Another example can be found in Lisnagunnel ("*lios na coinnle*"), or "Fort of the Candles," due to otherworldly lights being seen in the fort (Joyce, 1875, p. 191). These associations with otherworldly forces made sure that people kept a wide berth of the forts, ensuring their survival.

Forts were not the only features of the landscape that were treated with fear and suspicion. The enigmatic "fairy tree" (usually a hawthorn, or *Sceach*) was treated with equal fear and avoidance. These hawthorns, often referred to as a "lone bush," are frequently found unmolested in cultivated fields, comparable to the forts due to the innate fear of fairy retribution. Similar to the forts, tampering with the bushes or taking timber from them could result in maiming or death. One story tells of a carpenter who was hired to cut a bough off a lone bush, only for the leg he used to kneel on the branch later to wither away, requiring amputation (Roe, 1939, p. 26). Was this a case of a limb for a limb? Whatever the case, the belief in retribution was so strong that people would often give the trees a wide berth just in case. A famous case in 1999 involving the so-called "Latoon Bush" culminated in a new road being altered to avoid having to remove the bush, which according to folklore was the meeting place for battles between the Munster and Connaught fairies. The renowned *Seanachaí* (traditional storyteller) Eddie Lenihan was responsible for this result, having gained international interest from the media (Lenihan and Green, 2003, p. 13). It was also believed that the forts and trees were all connected through a series of invisible "fairy paths." Such was the belief in these paths that great care had to be taken when building a house. Traditionally, hazel rods were placed in the ground to form the outline of the house and if any were moved come daybreak, the house was deemed to be "in the way" (ibid., p. 148). Building on these paths could result in damage or destruction of the house or, at the very least, night-time disturbances.

The Touristic Potential of Irish Folklore and Myth for Visiting Communities

Now that the sense of place and the effect of folklore on the landscape have been established, it is time to look at how this can be translated into potential touristic value, infused with the oral and manuscript traditions of Ireland. First and foremost, even though the Irish credit themselves with a very strong sense of place, the places themselves – the monuments – are quite often left to wrack and ruin, which according to Sheeran creates a paradox between a "professed and sincere allegiance to places, together with an actual, almost total inability to care and cope with them" (1988, p. 194). The centuries of fear and caution that saved many of these monuments has started to slip, leading to increased destruction of these sites over the past few decades (for examples of this worrying trend, see Magan, 2021). Lack of knowledge of

90 Shane Broderick

the myths, legends, and folklore of the places in question has led to wanton destruction and neglect. So, as a result of this, sustainability and conservation need to be taken into consideration when considering the touristic potential.

Many Ogham stones are situated on private land, making them difficult to visit, although numerous examples can be found in museums. The largest public collection can be visited at the "Stone Corridor" at University College Cork. For the rest of the stones that can be visited *in situ*, the effect of mass tourism has to be taken into account, from people touching the stones to the effect that increased footfall might have on the immediate environment. For a case study specific to Scotland, but dealing with the negative impacts that over-tourism and the invention of folk practice can have on the environment, see Ironside and Massie (2020).

A similar problem arises when looking at ringforts and "fairy trees." Many of these lie on private land or working farms. Reconstructions of ringforts aimed at tourists might remedy this and allow them to see how they would have looked historically. Conservation issues also exist when looking at fairy trees. Many of them have been damaged in recent years due to well-meaning, but often inept, visitors attaching all manner of non-organic detritus to the trees as "offerings" in imitation of an actual folk practice usually associated with holy wells (Walsh, 2019; see also Ethan Doyle White's chapter in this volume).

The oral tradition of the *filidh* may mostly be lost, and as such is very much intangible, but the physical remains of the Bardic schools can be found, such as the O'Daly School near Kilcrohane village, or the Kilclooney Bardic School. These remains would no doubt offer a physical anchor to the stories of *Filidh*. Perhaps on the monastic side of things, a reconstructed *scriptorium* would serve as a fantastic attraction to show how the monks prepared the quills, vellum, ink, and so on (Marry, 1953, p. 208), and how they created the manuscripts containing centuries worth of accumulated knowledge and lore. In terms of *Dindshenchas* tales, the fact is that the location of a number of the sites is unknown, and others are etymological inventions (Mulligan, 2019, p. 78). However, many approximate locations are known and offer excellent tales for anyone touring the country. All it requires on the part of the guide is "fluency in the vernacular of Irish topography" (ibid, p. 76), enabling them to bring the sites to life for visitors to the area. The tales of the known sites would add layers of lore relating to their mythical origins, resulting in an experience that could not be found in the guidebooks or on standard "vanilla" tours.

A similar case can be made for place names. The contextual and encoded information found in native language place names would allow the guide to reveal centuries of folk tradition to visitors, who without this information would simply see fields and stones. Familiarisation and utilisation of the almost two thousand years of oral and manuscript tradition would allow the guide to "bridge the gap of centuries and hear the voice of the nameless storytellers and creators of the heroic literature of medieval Ireland" (Delargy,

Folklore, Story, and Place 91

1945, p. 9), enabling the interpretation and dissemination of this valuable cultural information to tourists. The manuscript collections are without a doubt "the embodiment of the past of a forgotten people" (O'Giollán, 2000, p. 133) and deserve to provide a voice to the nameless and voiceless storytellers of Ireland's rich past.

A huge potential for bringing this material to the fore is a rejuvenation and revival of traditional storytelling. Very few traditional *Seanachaí* remain, so incentives towards taking up the craft would be very beneficial. The fireside setting of traditional storytelling might not be applicable in most cases, but folk parks such as Bunratty, County Clare, and its historic vernacular buildings offer incredible opportunities for storytelling events by the turf fire, similar to how it would have happened at the *Tigh Áirneán* (houses associated with "night visiting" and storytelling) in the past. Utilisation of the tangible heritage in the archaeological record, augmented by the rich and storied manuscript tradition, as well as the invaluable National Folklore Collection, can offer a vast array of options when it comes to designing customised tours of Ireland. The combination of built heritage, myth, and oral history would allow the guide to reach back thousands of years to present this history to the visitor. The locations of myths and sagas can be shown alongside the monastic centres and bardic schools where these tales were constructed. This could help to bring the tangible and intangible together and hopefully preserve the myth, history and sense of place that was cultivated over millennia for many future generations to come.

References

Brady, L. (2021). 'Origin Myths in Early Insular Pseudo-histories: Medieval or Modern.' *Personal notes from online conference, "Pseudo-history Among the Celtic speaking Peoples: Medieval Propaganda,"* 12 June 2021.

Breathnach, L. (2006). 'Satire, Praise and the Early Irish Poet.' *Ériu*, 56, pp. 63–84.

Breathneach, P.A. (1983). 'The Chief's Poet.' *Proceedings of the Royal Irish Academy: Archaeology, Culture, History, Literature*, 83C, pp. 37–79.

Brezina, C. (2007). *Celtic Mythology.* New York: Rosen Central.

Burke, A. (1999). *The Burning of Briget Cleary.* New York: Vintage Publishing.

Delargy, J.H. (1945). 'The Gaelic Story-Teller: With Some Notes on Gaelic Folk-Tales, Sir John Rhŷs Memorial Lecture.' *Proceedings of the British Academy*, 31, pp. 1–48.

Downey, L. and O'Sullivan, M. (2014). 'Ogham Stones.' *Archaeology Ireland*, 28 (2), pp. 26–29.

Fyke, G.K. (2008). *An Bhfuil Gaeilge Agat? Perspectives on the Irish Language in Ireland.* Undergraduate Thesis, University of Mississippi. Available Online: https://egrove.olemiss.edu/hon_thesis/2006/ [Accessed 6 March 2022].

Granville, C.R. (1901). 'On Oghams.' *The Scottish Antiquary or, Northern Notes and Queries*, 15 (59), pp. 132–140.

Hicks, R. (2011). 'The Sacred Landscape of Ancient Ireland.' *Archaeology*, 64 (3), pp. 40–45.

Ireland, C.A. (2016). 'Vernacular Poets in Bede and Muirchú': A Comparative Study of Early Cultural Histories.' *Traditio*, 71, pp. 33–61.

92 Shane Broderick

Ironside, R. and Massie, S. (2020). 'The Folklore-Centric Gaze: A Relational Approach to Landscape, Folklore and Tourism.' *Time and Mind*, 13 (3), pp. 227–244.

Joyce, P.W. (1875). *The Irish Names of Places*. Dublin: McGlashan & Gill.

Kelly, F. (2016). *A Guide to Early Irish Law*. Dublin: Dublin Institute for Advanced Studies.

Leerson, J (1996). *Remembrance and Imagination: Patterns in the Historical and Literary Representation of Ireland in the 19th Century*. Cork: Cork University Press.

Lenihan, E. and Green, C. (2003). *Meeting the Other Crowd*. Dublin: Gill & Macmillan.

Lynn, C.J. (1975). 'The Medieval Ringfort: An Archaeological Chimera.' *Irish Archaeological Forum*, 2 (1), pp. 29–36.

Mac Cana, P. (1974). 'The Rise of the Later Schools of Filidheacht.' *Éiru*, 25, pp. 126–146.

MacGugan, J.H. (2012). 'Landscape and Lamentation: Constructing Commemorated Space in Three Middle Irish Texts.' *Proceedings of the Royal Irish Academy: Archaeology, Culture, History, Literature*, 11C, pp. 189–217.

MacNeill, J. (1909). 'Notes on the Distribution, History, Grammar and the Import of Irish Ogham Inscriptions.' *Proceedings of the Royal Irish Academy: Culture, History, Literature*, 27, pp. 329–370.

Magan, M. (2020). *Thirty-Two Words for Field*. Dublin: Gill Books.

Magan, M. (2021). 'From Ringfort to Road: Destruction of Ireland's Fairy Forts.' *Irish Times Online*, March 13. Available Online: https://www.irishtimes.com/culture/heritage/from-ringfort-to-ring-road-the-destruction-of-ireland-s-fairy-forts-1.4496069 [Accessed 6 March 2022].

Mallory, J.P. (2016). *In Search of the Irish Dreamtime*. London: Thames and Hudson Ltd.

Marry, W. (1953). 'The Medieval Scribe.' *The Classical Journal*, 8 (6), pp. 207–214.

McLaughlin, R. (2009). 'Fénius Farsaid and the Alphabets.' *Éiru*, 59, pp. 1–24.

Moore, F (2010) The Ogham stones of county Kerry. In: Murray G (ed.) *Medieval Treasures of County Kerry*. Tralee: Kerry County Museum, pp. 6–18.

McManus, D. (2004). *The Ogam Stones at University College Cork*. England: Cork University Press. pp. 1–29.

Mulligan, A.C. (2019). *A Landscape of Words: Ireland, Britain and the Poetics of Space, 700–1250*. Manchester: Manchester University Press.

Murphy, G. (1931). 'The Origin of Irish Nature Poetry.' *Irish Quarterly Review*, 20 (77), pp. 87–102.

Ní Cheallaigh, M. (2006). 'Going Astray in the Fort Field: Traditional Attitudes towards Ringforts in 19th Century Ireland.' *The Journal of Irish Archaeology*, 15, pp. 105–115.

Ní Mhaonaigh, M. (2020). 'Mapping a Literary Landscape: Medieval Irish Dindshenchas, Narratives of Place.' DIAS Samhain and Science Series of Talks, Online Lecture, Dublin Institute of Advanced Studies. Available Online: https://www.youtube.com/watch?v=t1_iuPXHIQ0&ab_channel=DublinInstituteforAdvancedStudiesDIAS [Accessed 11 March 2022].

Ní Mhaonaigh, M. (2021). 'The Place of Propaganda and the Propaganda of Place in Medieval Irish Narratives.' personal notes from online conference "*Pseudo-history Among the Celtic speaking Peoples: Medieval Propaganda*," 12 June 2021.

O Crualaoich, G. (n.d.) *Irish Storytelling*. Dublin: Heritage of Ireland.

O Riordan, M. (1998). 'Professors and Performers and Others of Their Kind: Contextualising the Irish Bardic Poet.' *The Irish Quarterly Review*, 23, pp. 73–88.

Folklore, Story, and Place 93

O'Giollán, D. (2000). *Locating Irish Folklore: Tradition, Modernity, Identity.* Cork: Cork University Press.

Robinson, T. (2003). 'The Seanchaí and the Database', *Irish Pages*, 2 (1), pp. 43–53.

Roe, H.M. (1939). 'Tales, Customs and Beliefs from Laoighis.' *Béaloideas*, 9 (1), pp. 21–35.

Sheeran, P. (1988). 'Genius Fabulae: The Irish Sense of Place.' *Irish University Review*, 18 (2), pp. 191–206.

Walsh, L. (2019). 'Wishing Tree Falls under the Weight of Visitors Relics.' *Irish Independent*. Available Online: https://www.independent.ie/irish-news/wishing-tree-falls-under-the-weight-of-visitors-relics-38312824.html [Accessed 27 March 2022].

Westropp, H.M. (1873). 'On Ogham Pillar Stones in Ireland.' *The Journal of Anthropological Institute of Great Britain and Ireland*, 2, pp. 201–205.

White, N. (2021). *'Ogham Stones.' An Chomairle Oidhreachta/ The Heritage Council*. Available Online: https://www.heritagecouncil.ie/content/files/Ogham-Stones.pdf [Accessed 27 March 2022].

Windele, J. (1853). 'Ancient Irish Ogham Inscriptions.' *Ulster Journal of Archaeology*, 1, pp. 43–52.

Part II

Folklore and Indigenous Landscapes

6 Sacred Anishinaabeg Folklore

Okikendawt Mnisiing, the Island of the Sacred Kettles

Renée E. Mazinegiizhigoo-kwe Bédard

Introduction

Weweni ganawendamog 'i minisi ebiitamong.

(Take good care of the island we inhabit.)

In Anishinaabeg[1] sacred folklore, bebaamaadiziwin (touring the landscape, visiting and travelling) is the traditional way tourism is practised at sacred rock locations such as Okikendawt Mnisiing (the Island of the Kettles). Bebaamaadiziwin protocols and morals are embedded in the sacred stories that guide Anishinaabeg on how to attend sacred locations. For Anishinaabeg, the island of Okikendawt Mnisiing is a sacred ecology that encompasses interconnections between nature, people, and manidoowag (Spirit Beings) of various nations. The name of the island originates from izhitwaa-asiniig (sacred rocks) called Okikoog (kettles) found on the island. Anishinaabeg have been visiting, travelling through, performing ceremonies, and living on, or near, the Okikoog for generations. Bebaamaadiziwin traditions echo the traditional movement and practice of Anishinaabeg bebaamaadizijig (visitors, travellers, tourists).

Firstly, in this chapter, the story of Giizhigookwe is offered to outline the nature and context of bebaamaadiziwin protocols. The story is embedded with the original teachings of Anishinaabeg-centred tourism. Secondly, the chapter provides an exploration of the historical and contemporary cultural contexts of Okikendawt Mnisiing as a sacred rock location that is visited and toured by both Anishinaabeg and non-Indigenous peoples alike. Next, the chapter will present an Anishinaabeg-centred paradigm for tourism rooted in the folkloric teachings of Giizhigookwe, which offer an alternative worldview to that embodied in colonial tourism.[2] The chapter also offers Anishinaabeg cultural teachings, instructions, and protocols of bebaamaadiziwin to decolonise tourism by prioritising Indigenous strategies of bebaamaadiziwin. Finally, the chapter will offer some concluding thoughts, goals, and needs related to future research on this topic.

DOI: 10.4324/9781003374138-9

98 Renée E. Mazinegiizhigoo-kwe Bédard

The Origin of Anishinaabe Bebaamaadiziwin (Tourism, Visiting, Travelling): The Story of Giizhigookwe Dancing across the Turtle's Back

The origins of bebaamaadiziwin originate in the sacred folklore of the Spirit Being Giizhigookwe. Her story offers a set of instructions, laws, and an ethics embedded in the collective manidoo-minjimendamowin (spirit memory; blood memory) of all Anishinaabeg. As the first bebaamaadizid (visitor, traveller, tourist) to Aki (Earth), Giizhigookwe's origin story, is one of the oldest sets of remembered folklore connecting human beings to our motion across, and presence within, the land, its gifts, and humanity's collective moral responsibilities to care for it. Her story is shared to situate all readers within Anishinaabeg epistemology, cosmology, ontology, and axiology, which lie outside the dominant colonial worldview. The following is just one version of her story.[3] Bindakwe!

> Hey oh way
> I tell a story,
> A story from the Ancient Ones
> Hey oh way
> I place asemaa for their
> Spirits
> Hey oh way
> I tell a story
> Listen! And Learn!
>
> (Geniusz, Mary Siisip, 2015, p. 7)

One day, long ago, a pregnant woman fell through a hole in the sky. Her name was Giizhigookwe. Down, down, down, she fell, until she was caught by a flock of nikag (geese). They carried her gently to the Earth, which was flooded. There was no land upon which to place her. The waterfowl, animals, insects, and reptiles counselled together to devise a plan to search deep below the water to find dirt. The great snapping turtle agreed to have the dirt placed on its back to provide a home for the Sky woman. After many attempts and failures, one small creature named Wazhashk (muskrat) finally brought up some mud; however, the journey down had caused poor Wazhashk to drown. Giizhigookwe took the mud out of Wazhashk's tiny paw and placed it across the rim and back of the Great Turtle. As she placed the mud down, she also sowed the (miinikaanan) seeds she had brought with her from the Sky World. The seeds were food and plant medicines. First, she held them in her left hand closest to her heart. Then, Giizhigookwe introduced herself and thanked those seeds for the food and medicine they would produce. She spoke softly and kindly to those little seeds. Next, she promised to tend and protect the plants, as well as their grandchildren. She promised to offer them gifts for their sacrifices and never to take too much. As she planted those seeds, she walked around the rim of the turtle's back, praying as she went. When she

Sacred Anishinaabeg Folklore   99

was done sowing the seeds, Giizhigookwe began to dance the seeds gently into the surface of the soil with her feet. Slowly, the plants grew, died, and grew again. The soil also grew and grew. Land animals, insects, and other creatures were gifted back to the land by Gizhew-Manidoo (Great Spirit, Great Mystery, the Creator). The land got so big that the Great Turtle was no longer needed to hold it up. So, the Giant Turtle departed and left Giizhigookwe on the new land to give birth. Her children were known as the Anishinaabeg. The new land was called Mikinaakominisiing (Turtle Island) in remembrance of the Giant Turtle.

Many plant medicines grew on these new lands, among them is asemaa (tobacco). Asemaa is known for their[4] rich and deep sweet scent and grows through Anishinaabe-akiing and beyond. It has been harvested, traded, and shared for thousands of years. Giizhigookwe taught her children and grandchildren how to perform manashkikiwewin, the act of gathering asemaa – or any plant – in a good way. She also taught them how to save seeds, plant them, and tend the asemaa near their lodges, as well as how to dry the asemaa for use in their pipes, to offer prayers to all-of-Creation. Further, she gave her children bebaamaadiziwin – teachings of how to be and move on the land, to be a good and gentle visitor to the land. Giizhigookwe taught them the ethos of niigaanii asemaa, meaning tobacco comes first and tobacco leads before all else. She showed them how to hold the asemaa in their left hands, the arm close to their hearts, and tell asemaa their prayers or intentions. Giizhigoo instructed her children in the protocols and ceremony of offering asemaa, in prayer to Gizhew-Manidoo (ceremony), in gratitude for the bountiful gifts of the land, before entering the forest's sacred spaces, to ask permission to hunt or harvest food, and to plant or pick medicines. In these ways she showed Anishinaabeg how to perform mino-babanametwaawag (leaving a good presence) on the land to maintain the natural balance and harmony of the Earth. The belief encoded in babanametwaawag is that if something is taken, something is to be given, such as asemaa. A gift for a gift is the exchange and ceremony of mutuality

That sweet scent of asemaa is to remind all human beings of the importance of the Earth to human beings. Asemaa represents a reminder of the original teachings from Giizhigookwe, the first bebaamaadizid to Turtle Island. Anishinaabeg continue to pick, dry, and carry the asemaa so that we remember Giizhigookwe's gifts and offerings to the land. Asemaa is also a reminder of how Giizhigookwe, as the first tourist, treated the land with manaadendamowin (respect) and gizhewaadiziwin (kindness). She asked permission before taking anything from the land or entering sacred spaces. She was giving, spoke kindly, walked gently, did no damage, and remained an ally to the land. Today, Anishinaabeg of Okikendawt Mnisiing harvest asemaa from the land to carry in their asemaawazhensan, or asemaa-mashki-modensan (medicine pouches), and mashkiki-gashkibijigan (medicine bundles), so that they may carry the memory of Giizhigookwe and use the sacred tobacco to send their prayers of gratitude for the land's bounty.

Today, Anishinaabeg continue to use Giizhigookwe's teachings, and every child learns their responsibilities to the land through her stories. Her teachings

100   Renée E. Mazinegiizhigoo-kwe Bédard

are also warnings not to abuse the land, but to follow the gchi-inaakonige-winan (Sacred laws; Great Laws) that instruct how to maintain the natural balance of all things in Waawiyekamig (the universe; cosmos). Human beings have waawiindamaagewinan (treaties) with all beings in Creation – organic, inorganic, and Spirit – to mutually uphold the gchi-inaakonigewinan and each other's roles within Creation. Therefore, when Anishinaabeg visit with the Okikoog they honour niigaanii asemaa and provide offerings of tobacco in reciprocation for the gifts the Okikoog and land provide, including spiritual nourishment, wisdom, knowledge, and teachings.

The folklore and sacred sites are encoded with knowledge about the sacred ecology of Anishinaabe-akiing (Anishinaabeg lands; territory) and serve to instruct Anishinaabeg on the protocols of bebaamaadiziwin, ensuring they are still upheld. These teachings inform how Anishinaabeg dance across the Turtle's back as bebaamaadizijig (visitors, travellers, tourists) of this Earth. Niigaanii asemaa!

Okikendawt Mnisiing: The Island of the Sacred Kettles

For generations, Okikendawt Mnisiing was a place visited by Anishinaabeg (nations of the Ojibweg and Nibisiing), as a place of ceremony, to gather or harvest plant foods and medicines, to fish, hunt, and for trapping. Okikendawt Mnisiing is recognised by Anishinaabeg as a location of izhitwaa-asiniig (sacred rocks) and home of the Okikoog. These sacred rocks are also the dwelling place of both the Memegwesiwag – who are the little Spirit Beings of the forest, commonly known as the Little People – and the Animikiig (thunderbirds), along with a host of other manidoowag (Spirit Beings) of both land and water. Anishinaabeg practised bebaamaadiziwin (travelling, visiting or tourism) at Okikendawt Mnisiing through seasonal migration, on or by the Okikoog-territory, for the purposes of bebaamaadiziwin, but also for upholding treaty obligations, which required offerings of asemaa, as well as the moral custodial responsibility to care for the land.

The Okikendawt Mnisiing is an ancient and sacred site of both bebaamaadiz-iwin and Anishinaabe abiwin (Anishinaabeg habitation on the land). The island is situated on the ziibi (river) whose name is Waabnoong bemjiwang ziibi (Place where the waters flow from the East), commonly known by its colonial name – the French River watershed. Additionally, it is also known as Anibesin-akiing ziibi, meaning "the land of the tilting river" (Campbell, 1993, pp. 2–3). Anishinaabeg have been travelling, visiting, and touring around Nibisiing zaaga'igan ("little water" lake, Goulais, 2022), commonly known as Lake Nipissing, and Waabnoong bemjiwang ziibi for thousands of years, stopping at Okikendawt Mnisiing to perform custodial duties for the Okikoog rocks. In Anishinaabemowin (Anishinaabeg language), mnisiing translates to island and okik, akik, or kik, is a kettle, pot, pan, pail, cauldron, or a bucket ("Akik," *The Ojibwe People's Dictionary*). Clayton Dokis, a community member of Okikendawt Mnisiing and cultural guide for the Okikoog explains:

Sacred Anishinaabeg Folklore   101

"Okikendawt Island" (meaning island of the buckets/pails). The name is derived from several bucket formations in the rock due to centuries of water flows to these areas. The buckets were often utilized for tobacco offerings for safe passage through the territory.

(Back Roads Bill, n.d.)

Anishinaabeg acknowledge the Okikoog as sentient and animate beings. The folklore and oral narratives of Anishinaabeg movements across the French River and Lake Nipissing watershed is a living record of a deep relationship with the land and water. Each visit was an act – a ritual – to renew the mani-doo-minjimendamowinan (spirit-memories) of ancestors long past, to maintain mutuality with the okikoog, which has been fostered over generations, and to serve as a renewal of treaty with those sacred locations – a treaty that is always being recalibrated, recalled, reconstructed, and revitalised. For the Anishinaabeg of the French River and Lake Nipissing, it is truly evidence of "ezhianishinaabe-bimaadiziyaang," meaning "the way in which we live" (Noodin, 2014, p. 183). The generations of spirit-memories accumulated over the course of movements across the land are evidence of connections to Anishinaabe-akiing, the territorial land that deeply connected the identity of the people. These spirit-memories offer the ability to visit, to move out of time, and to look in all directions for connections to the land – in the past, present and future. This is the legacy that continues today, the need to remember-to-remember, and to connect in ways that honour the trail of the Anishinaabeg over time.

While Anishinaabeg continue to live and travel upon the watershed, the French River and Lake Nipissing region only became a colonial tourist route in Canada in the early 1600s. Colonial tourism ideologies – of seeking land, knowledge, exploration, and exploitation of the land's resources for human gain – would lead to the formation of the country of Canada. The first colonial tourist was a young 17-year-old French explorer named Etienne Brûlé, sent by French explorer and navigator Samuel de Champlain to chart routes towards the Nayaano-nibiimaang Gichigamiin (Great Lakes) for the purposes of trade, securing resources, and establishing political alliances with the First Nations (Campbell, 1993, pp. 6, 10). Early tourism by explorers, fur traders, and voyageurs led to the establishment of forts, which later transformed into settlements. Increased settlement and competition for resources led to the need for treaties to sort out territorial rights. In 1850, the Robinson-Huron waawiindamaagewin was signed by 17 First Nations signatories, including Michel Migisi (Eagle) L'Aigle Dokis[5] (1818–1906). Migisi Dokis was put in charge of Dokis Indian reserve (later Dokis First Nation). The Dokis First Nation territory included "three miles square at Wanabeyakokaun, near Lake Nipissing and the island near the Fall of Okickandawt" ("Robinson Huron waawiindamaagewin," n.d.). Thereafter, Migisi Dokis' descendants came to be referred to as the "eagles on the river" (Pollard, as cited by Blackaws, 2014, p. 7), and protectors of the river. After the signing of the Robinson-Huron waawiindamaagewin, colonial tourism exploded on the French River and Lake Nipissing watersheds, including development by

102   *Renée E. Mazinegiizhigoo-kwe Bédard*

cottagers, the construction of lodges and resorts, visiting naturalists, vacationists, as well as creation of fishing and hunting clubs (Noël, 2015, p. 96). By the mid-1940s, colonial tourists were pouring in from across Canada, the United States of America and Europe ("The evolution of Canadian tourism, 1946 to 2015." *Statistics Canada*, n.d.). Members of Okikendawt Mnisiing and the territory itself became active participants in the tourist trade of the French River and Lake Nipissing watersheds.

Through time and the rigours of colonial tourism, Anishinaabeg carried forward the teachings, practices, and ethos of bebaamaadiziwin for the survival of the Okikoog, as well as the people, culture, and land. A paradigm of bebaamaadiziwin became encoded into all aspects of the sacred folklore, including the stories, songs, and prayers of the people. When shared, the instructions, guidance and wisdom come alive.

Honouring Giizhigookwe's Paradigm of Bebaamaadiziwin

The late Anishinaabeg scholar Basil Johnston-ban[6] shared in his book *Ojibway Ceremonies*, a story of two young men who unwisely travelled into the domain of the Spirit Beings of a mountain, and the territory of the Okikoog. Upon entering the domain, the young men fail to uphold the asemaa teachings of Giizhigookwe and their responsibilities as bebaamaadizijig (Johnston, 1982, pp. 34–35). The Spirits call out to the land in a prophetic song – stream of folklore – a living story on traditional tourism that teaches Anishinaabeg to follow the protocols of bebaamaadiziwin. They did not offer sacred tobacco to gain permission to enter the domain. They hear voices asking, "Who dares without tobacco? Who dares without offering? [...] Tobacco will allay our anger. Tobacco will clear the cloud [...] Our pipes are cold and empty. Our pipes are cold and empty" (Johnston, 1982, p. 34). The young men ignore the song's warning. Again, without seeking permission, one of the young men steals a glimpse of the animikiig (thunderbirds), and as punishment, ends up falling over the side of the mountain.

The second young man, left alone to find his way, stumbles upon a lake on the side of the mountain, which is likely an izhitwaa-Okik-zaaga'igan (sacred kettle lake). Again, the second young man hears voices that are now singing out for tobacco to fill their pipes. Paddling by the young man was jiimaanensag (tiny canoes) carrying the memegwesiwag (little spirit folk of the forest), who are described in the story as being "no taller than wildflowers" (Johnston, 1982, p. 35). Each carries a small opwaagan (pipe) and sings out to the young man in warning:

> We will stir the waters
> Until one remembers [...]
> Tobacco cleanses my heart.
> Tobacco cleanses my mind.
> Tobacco brings calm.
>   (Johnston, 1982, p. 35)

Sacred Anishinaabeg Folklore   103

Finally, finding meaning in their song, the young man placed asemaa on the surface of the lake as an offering to appease the offences that had been committed. In return, the memegwesiwag offer a response of gratitude and acknowledgment of the bagijigan, singing out that "Tobacco is my friend. Tobacco is our friend. Tobacco makes us friends" (Johnston, 1982, pp. 35–36). The memegwesiwag allow the young man to live and return home unharmed. Through his bagijigan, the second young man finally upholds the gete-waawiindamaagewin (ancient treaty; compact) between the land and human beings. With his offering of niigaanii asemaa, he demonstrates that he has remembered how to be a good bebaamaadizid.

The mountain as a sacred location is the territory of the okik-zaaga'igan (kettle lake), animikiig, and the memegwesiwag as guardians and uphold their side of the Gete-waawiindamaagewin to the Okikoog. In Anishinaabeg sacred folklore, Okikoog zaaga'igan are considered the nesting grounds of the animikiig. Western science explains that the Okikoog zaaga'igan are

> formed when large blocks of ice calve from the main glacier onto an outwashplain. As the glacier retreats the block of ice is left stranded. The ice then gets surrounded and possibly buried by subsequent meltwater deposits and outwash. Eventually, when the temperature increases and the ice block melts it leaves a large depression in the ground that the ice occupied. These are known as kettle holes. Where the depressions subsequently fill with rainwater, they are known as kettle lakes.
>
> ("Kettle holes." *Geography, Tutor2U*, n.d.)

Kettle lakes may range in size from 5 m (15 feet) to 13 km (8 miles) in diameter and up to 45 m in depth ("Kettle." *Encyclopedia Britannica*, n.d.). For Anishinaabeg, the kettle lakes are honoured as the nests of the animikiig.

The Okikoog zaaga'igan also have the Okikoog-waawiyeminagad (kettle spheres), also known as animikiig-waawanoonan (Thunderbird eggs). Across Anishinaabe-akiing there are two kinds of kettle spheres. The first kind of kettle spheres are called boiler rocks; these were rocks that got caught up in the churning glacial waters and gradually carved out the bedrock, sometimes ending up metres down into the bedrock. These can be found inside, or around, the Okikoog-waanikaanan (kettle holes), which are smaller versions around the kettle lakes. Kettle holes can be the size of a bowl, or as big as several metres across and deep ("Kettle." *Encyclopedia Britannica*, n.d.). At Okikendawt Mnisiing, they are found near the rapids and throughout the forest.

The second kind of kettle spheres are called concretion kettle rocks. Round sphere kettles were first recorded in southern Ontario in 1826, along Naadowewi-Gichigami (Lake Huron), on the traditional territory of the Kettle and Stony Point First Nation (Leclair, 2015, n.d.). Concretions "range in size from 0.3–1.5m across" and are some of the oldest Okikoog at "about 370 million years" ("The Kettles of Kettle and Stony Point." *Lambton County Museum*, n.d.) old. However, the ages of both types of kettles might vary due

104   *Renée E. Mazinegiizhigoo-kwe Bédard*

to the manner of their formation. Both kinds of round shaped kettles are known as thunderbird eggs and the Anishinaabeg believe that places they are found are sacred places as a nesting ground ("The Kettles of Kettle and Stony Point." *Lambton County Museum*, n.d.). For Anishinaabeg, all children are seen as the foundation of a nation, so great care was given to the locations known as nesting grounds.

Further, the kettle pots were also recognised as spiritual pots or pipe bowls of the land. According to Norm Dokis, an Anishinaabeg knowledge holder from Okikendawt Mnisiing, the kettle lakes were treated as sacred and seen as the opwaaganag (pipes) (Schwabe, 2021, n.d.), or pipe bowls (opwaaganag-boozikinaagan) of the land (Schwabe, 2022, n.d.). Pipe bowls are fed[7] asemaa when prayers are given, as offerings to the Spirits, and as medicines to heal the wiiyaw (body), inendamowin (mind), ode' (heart) and spirit (ojichaag). These places on Earth are recognised as the pipe bowls of Mother the Earth, created by Gizhew-Manidoo so that human beings will remember on their travels to leave asemaa in gratitude for the Earth and the Spirits who aid in the continued survival of human beings. Anishinaabeg observe bebaamaadiziwin to maintain ancient Anishinaabeg connections to the land (Johnston, 1982, pp. 33–36; Conway, 2016, pp. 17–18).

In Anishinaabeg sacred folklore, the Okikoog and manidoowag are together also "gimiinigoowizimin gaaganawendang" – the "keepers of the gifts" (Davidson-Hunt et al., 2005, p. 196), along with the human beings – and uphold their side of the gete-waawiindamaagewin. Feeding the Okikoog, as the pipe bowls of the land, not only renews the treaty but also demonstrates to the Spirits that human beings remember the ways of Giizhigookwe. The Okikoog understand this sense of sustained relationality and mutuality between nations as "gdoo-naaganinaa" (Simpson, 2008, p. 29), which translates to "the dish with one spoon teachings." In these teachings, the "dish" represents the land that is to be shared peacefully and the "spoon" represents the individuals living on and using the resources of the land in a spirit of mutual co-operation. Often, a bowl or kettle was referred to rather than a dish (Glover, 2020, n.d.). Michi Saagiig Nishnaabeg scholar Leanne Betasamosake Simpson suggests that gdoo-naaganinaa is a "symbol of shared ecology" (Simpson, 2008, p. 39). The act of going and performing renewal ceremonies is an important life principle of Anishinaabe-mino-bimaadiziwin, and "is a way of ensuring human beings live in balance with the natural world, their family, their clan, and their nation" (Simpson, 2008, p. 29). At an individual level, giving gifts as bimaadiziwin is principally about maintaining moral relationships with all-our-relations in the cosmos. It begins with the self-in-relation to the collective, and acting responsibly for the good of all. Human beings do not survive unless they first see themselves as connected to the Earth upon which they stand. Okikoog are some of the original teachers of how to live on the land with all the other beings (organic and inorganic), on the shared territory, which is called inaadiziwin: a philosophy of living and being in accordance with the order of Creation.

Gift-giving is a reciprocal act in Anishinaabe-inaadiziwin. First, always first, comes niigaanii miigiwewinan, first comes gifts! First, niigaanii asemaa, offer semaa. Anishinaabeg historian Cary Miller describes semaa bagijiganan (tobacco offerings) as "gift-giving," and writes that this process is "the cornerstone" of Anishinaabeg kinship and community, functioning as a glue that creates relationships between people and other beings. Gift-giving forges agreements, and forms individual identities (Miller, 2010, p. 32). Similarly, Anishinaabeg scholar Niigonwedom James Sinclair says that "receiving a bagijigan is giving one as well" (Sinclair, 2013, p. 18). For instance, Elder Hartley White suggests that bagijiganan (offerings) demand continual and qualitative relationality between human beings and the Spirit realm in a cyclical of reciprocal exchange (Miller, 2010, p. 32). Moreover, a bagijigan is a gift with accompanying responsibilities and expectations. As Sinclair explains it, every bagijiganan of asemaa is "a gift with strings" (Sinclair, 2013, p. 18).

Failure to offer bagijiganan, particularly semaa, results in the chance that the Okikoog will not be found or appear to the human beings that have given offense (Conway, 2016, p. 18). These places are always watched over by the Memegwesiwag, or other Spirit Beings. Gifts for the guardians of the Okikoog are placed at these sites. The Memegwesiwag can shapeshift and transcend time, space, and dimensions as sentient beings, to appear as a frog, a rabbit, snake, or different small woodland creatures (Conway, 2016, pp. 18–19). These manidoowag, as guardians and teachers of human beings, are always there to ensure that treaty responsibilities are satisfied. To uphold a respectful treaty relationship, human beings offer gifts to the manidoowag guardians for allowing them to enter their territory, to learn from them, and seek their guidance. Gifts can include a pinch of semaa, zenibaanyag (ribbons), waabiziiwanwiin (buck shot), and Makade miigiwewin (gun powder) (Conway, 2016, pp. 18–19).

Gifts, whether to people or manidoowag, were part of a governance structure dependent on an understanding of respect, mutual benefit, and aid. Sinclair offers that: "when accepted, bagijiganan imply responsibilities between parties, a shared relationship, and are used most often to welcome newcomers into communities as relations" (Sinclair, 2013, p. 18). Miller points out that

> deeply ingrained social expectations for respect and obligation framed these exchanges [...] There was as much a right and obligation to receive as to give, an idea embedded in the ascription of familial relationships to all parties in the exchange.
>
> (Miller, 2010, pp. 32–33)

Between human beings and the manidoowag, gift-giving obligations are a spiritual commitment that spans time, space, and other dimensions.

How old are these treaties? Anishinaabeg Elder Dan Pine would describe them as "beads on a string [...] a necklace" (Conway, 2016, p. 88). In this way he suggests that all time – past, present, and the future – are inseparable,

106   Renée E. Mazinegiizhigoo-kwe Bédard

interconnected, overlapping, and cyclical (Conway, 2016, p. 88). Elder Pine teaches that making offerings to sacred rocks will "reestablish our bonds to the earth," and "today, these [ways] are coming back. This was a prophecy" (Conway, 2016, p. 5).

Concluding Thoughts

The knowledge presented here about the sacred kettles of Okikendawt Mnisiing offers just a glimpse into the teachings, stories, ethics, cosmology, and philosophy of the Anishinaabeg of Okikendawt Mnisiing. No single voice among the Anishinaabeg would ever seek to be or act as an authority on the subject and call themselves Anishinaabeg. These sacred places are not meant to be fully seen or known to the outside world, but for the purposes of education and awareness of Anishinaabeg worldviews and Anishinaabeg culture, some of the knowledge is shared here; however, it is done so rather reluctantly. If Anishinaabeg do not speak for themselves and define their ways for themselves there are always going to be outsiders that will readily, and often incorrectly, do it for them. Images of the kettle pots were not shown because it goes against protocol to photograph the sacred locations of the memegwesiwag, any dwelling place of Spirit Beings, or the izhitwaa-Okikoog. The internet is full of photographs for the curious, but it is not part of Anishinaabeg ethical teachings to record, document or reveal the homes of manidoowag. Further, any future research into the kettles of Okikendawt Mnisiing must include the voices of community members, Elders, knowledge keepers, and language speakers from Dokis First Nations and Anishinaabe-akiing should be a requirement. In conclusion, this chapter is to honour the Okikoog, memegwesiwag, the people of Okikendawt Mnisiing, and Giizhigookwe, as well as sacred folklore as an unfolding prophecy teaching us how to dance ethically across the Turtle's Back. Bindakwe!

Notes

1 Anishinaabeg are Indigenous peoples from the lands around Nayaano-wiishkbiwii-nibiimaang Gichigamiin (The Five Freshwater Seas: Great Lakes). Anishinaabeg traditional territory crosses the borders of Canada and the United States of America. Anishinaabeg have lived on the lands of Turtle Island (North American Continent) since time immemorial.
2 Colonial tourism is rooted in the Eurocentric ideology that all land, knowledge, and cultures are open to colonial or imperialist consumption and appropriation.
3 The origins of the knowledge related to the teachings of Giizhigookwe come from Anishinaabeg Elders Edna Manitowabi and Shirley Ida Williams as cultural mentors to the author. Additionally, the author draws on the teachings of those stories recorded and written down by Anishinaabeg Elder Edward Benton-Banai-ban and Anishinaabeg scholar Basil Johnston-ban. See, Benton-Banai, Edward. 1988. *The Mishomis Book: The Voice of the Ojibway*. Minneapolis, University of Minnesota Press; Johnston, Basil. 1976. *Ojibway Heritage*. Toronto: McClelland & Steward.
4 Plant medicines are not described as an "it" and are honoured in the language as a relative in Creation.

Sacred Anishinaabeg Folklore   107

5 Migisi Dokis was known by many names or variations of his name, including Michel Dokis, Michael Dokis, Michel L'Eagle, Migisi, Michel L'Aigle, Ducas, and Dukis. See, LeBelle, Wayne F. *Dokis: Since Time Immemorial*. Field, ON: WFL Communications, 2006. p. 2.
6 In Anishinaabemowin, -ban or -ba is a preterit suffix that is added to a noun stem to indicate a past state, absence, or loss. For example, -ban is added to a noun to indicate that the person is now deceased.
7 To be "fed" in this context means that it is the place where asemaa is put into a pipe to smoke, but it is also the sacred place where offerings are given to the Spirit of the pipe and to the Spirits or ancestors that are the intended recipient of the prayers.

References

"Akik." *The Ojibwe People's Dictionary*. Available Online: https://ojibwe.lib.umn.edu/main-entry/akik-na [Accessed 20 March 2022].

Back Roads Bill (n.d.). 'Nature Trail and Legend – Dokis – Lake Nipissing West – Hwy. 64. Cultural Trails Tell Stories: Dokis Embraces More Tourism.' *Steer to Northern Ontario, Blog*. Available Online: http://www.steerto.com/?p=685 [Accessed 19 March 2022].

Benton-Banai, E. (1988). *The Mishomis Book: The Voice of the Ojibway*. Minneapolis: University of Minnesota Press.

Blackaws, K. (2014). *Integrating the Eagles: Members of Dokis First Nation Reflect on Public Education in Ontario, 1960–1980. MA Thesis*. North Bay: Nipissing University.

Campbell, W.A. (1993).*The French and Pickerel Rivers, Their History and Their People*. Sudbury, ON: Journal Printing.

Conway, T. (2016). *Discovering Rock Art: A Personal Journey with Tribal Elders*. Garibaldi Highlands, BC: Thor Conway and Amber Conway, Inc.

Davidson-Hunt, I.J., et al. (2005). 'Iskatewizaagegan (Shoal Lake) Plant Knowledge: An Anishinaabe (Ojibway) Ethnobotany of Northwestern Ontario.' *Journal of Ethnobiology*, 25 (2), pp. 189–227.

Geniusz, M.S. (2015). *Plants Have So Much to Give Us, All We Have to Do Is Ask: Anishinaabe Botanical Teachings*. Minneapolis: University of Minnesota Press.

Glover, F. (2020). 'The Dish With One Spoon.' *The Canadian Encyclopedia*. Available Online: https://www.thecanadianencyclopedia.ca/en/article/a-dish-with-one-spoon [Accessed 24 March 2022].

Goulais, B. M'Zhaakwaat. (2022). 'Facts and Figures.' *Bob Goulais Blog*. Available Online: https://www.anishinaabe.ca/nipissing-first-nation/ [Accessed 24 March 2022].

Johnston, B. (1976). *Ojibway Heritage*. Toronto: McClelland & Stewart.

Johnston, B. (1982). *Ojibway Ceremonies*. Toronto: McClelland and Stewart.

"Kettle." (n.d.). *Encyclopaedia Britannica*. Available Online: https://www.britannica.com/science/kettle [Accessed 22 March 2022].

"Kettle holes." (n.d.). *Geography, Tutor2U*. Available Online: https://www.tutor2u.net/geography/topics/kettle-holes [Accessed 20 March 2022].

LeBelle, W.F. (2006). *Dokis: Since Time Immemorial*. Field, ON: WFL Communications.

Leclair, L. (2015). 'Kettle Point Kettle.' *Anishinabek News*. Available Online: http://anishinabeknews.ca/2015/12/17/kettle-point-kettles/ [Accessed 22 March 2022].

Miller, C. (2010). *Ogimaag: Anishinaabeg Leadership, 1760–1845*. Lincoln: University of Nebraska Press.

Noël, F. (2015). *Nipissing: Historic Waterway, Wilderness Playground.* Toronto: Dundurn Press.

Noodin, M. (2014). 'Megwa Baabaamiiaayaayang Dibaajomoyang: Anishinaabe Literature As Memory in Motion.' In J.J. Cox and D.H. Justice (eds.), *The Oxford Handbook of Indigenous American Literature.* Oxford: Oxford University Press.

"Robinson Huron waawiindamaagewin (n.d.) presents a Transcript of the Original Treaty Document." *Robinson-Huron waawiindamaagewin, Treaty of 1850.* Available Online: https://waawiindamaagewin.com/wp-content/uploads/2021/04/RHW_TreatyDocument_2020_REV4_MED-2.pdf. [Accessed 22 March 2022].

Schwabe, M. (2021). 'French River Man Discovers Geological Formation in His Backyard.' *CBC News.* Available Online: https://www.cbc.ca/news/canada/sudbury/rock-pots-backyard-monetville-1.6195634?cmp=rss [Accessed 21 March 2022].

Schwabe, M. (2022). 'Monetville Man Discovers Rock Kettle in Backyard with First Nation Connection.' *CBC News.* Available Online: https://www.cbc.ca/listen/live-radio/1-41-morning-north/clip/15868985-monetville-man-discovers-rock-kettle-backyard-first-nation?fbclid=IwAR20fMFocNjOy6tZBX7nv8151c43PTSVf_C6XverKIBJIuNADxQ5cg1umbs [Accessed 20 March 2022].

Simpson, L. Betasamosake. (2008). 'Looking after Gdoo-naaganinaa: Precolonial Nishnaabeg Diplomatic and Treaty Relationships.' *Wicazo Sa Review*, 23 (2), pp. 29–42.

Sinclair, Niigonwedom J. (2013). *Nindoodemag Bagijiganan: A History of Anishinaabeg Narrative.* Ph.D. Dissertation. Vancouver: The University of British Columbia.

"The Evolution of Canadian Tourism, (n.d.) 1946 to 2015." *Statistics Canada.* Available Online: https://www150.statcan.gc.ca/n1/pub/11-630-x/11-630-x2017001-eng.htm [Accessed 24 March 2022].

"The Kettles of Kettle and Stony Point." (n.d.). *Lambton County Museum.* Available Online:https://www.lambtonmuseums.ca/en/lambton-heritage-museum/the-kettles-of-kettle-and-stony-point.aspx [Accessed 21 March 2022].

7 Break in the Reef of Time

An Indigenous Science Approach to the Olowalu Petroglyphs on Maui

Apela Colorado and Ryan Hurd

Introduction

The petroglyph site at Olowalu, on the island of Maui is *wahi pana*, a storied place. Spanning centuries of active use, decorated boulders lay beside a flowing stream and an ancient footpath, connecting the ocean shore to the `Iao valley in the interior, where Hawai`i's historic kings and queens are interred. Contemporary accounts from native Hawaiians emphasise the regional significance of Olowalu as one of many sacred sites that are not just monuments to the past but living places to rest and exchange thoughts of Aloha with the spirits of ancestors (Anderson and Ashdown, 2016). Yet a tremendous gap exists between the indigenous Hawaiian perspective and what is seen by hundreds of non-native tourists every year. The site is mostly known as a quick stop for the tourist bucket list, easily accessible by car. Tourist guidebooks and online sites provide little context for the rock art site in relation to the land. Despite decades of attempts to protect and provide interpretation for the site – with varying levels of success – local park authorities are now more likely to visit Olowalu in response to vandalism, rather than to provide cultural stewardship.

In this chapter, Western historical accounts and folklore collected about Olowalu, also known as Pu'u Kilea, are complemented with perspectives from Hawaiian elders and Indigenous Cultural Practitioners. This multiplicity is central to Indigenous Science, which refers to the place-based, holistic, and spiritual knowledge systems and wisdom traditions of indigenous peoples (Colorado, 2014) and their methodologies (Kovach, 2010; Rowe, 2014). The mythic ties to this storied place and the web of related sacred sites on Maui invite a deepening of the tourist gaze to a "folklore-centric gaze" (Ironside and Massie, 2020): from merely observing artefacts of past lifeways, to experiencing the living, spiritual depth of the land. Just knowing the deeper stories does not appear to be enough to transform people's perspectives. Sacred sites demand more.

Site Description of Olowalu Petroglyph Complex

Located beside the trail of a mountain pass, the rock art of Olowalu adorns large boulders along a steep cliffside below a 250 ft tall cinder cone known as

DOI: 10.4324/9781003374138-10

Pu'u Kile'a. Streaming down from the hill is a finger of tulus: large, edgy boulders decreasing in size in their march to the sea. A muffled, rhythmic whoosh of distant surf can be heard off to the southwest – the navigational route that delivered Hawai'i Loa and the first Hawaiian voyagers to the island of Maui. Indeed, historic maps also mark the top of the cinder cone as a "tomb" (Lyons, 1879). Some say that Hawai'i Loa is buried on top of Kile'a, although it is not certain, as many resting places of Hawaiian royalty were kept secret so they could complete their journey, becoming part of the landscape as they spiritually support the living through the power of mana. This is the Hawaiian worldview.

The rock art site, SIPH Site-01200, features nearly 70 petroglyphs which depict human figures as well as animals and abstract designs (see Figure 7.1). Some are interpreted as Hawaiian canoe sails, others as humans, animals, and geometric patterns. Unfortunately, a sizable portion of the rock art has been permanently destroyed by vandalism, and historic fire damage has also been noted at the site (Lee-Gregg and Hammatt, 2012, p. 42). Of particular interest are temporary shelters in rock outcroppings at the bottom of Olowalu, which were used by travellers walking the Olowalu Pass trail between coastal Lahaina and Wailuku in the interior (Smith, 2011, p. 9). These two towns represented the two ruling families of Maui, with 'Iao Valley in between – an ancestral burial ground. The ancient footpath here

Figure 7.1 Petroglyphs at Olowalu Are Made by Scratching Away the Patina of the Basalt.

(Photograph by Apela Colorado, 2021).

follows Olowalu stream, which in pre-European times dropped into the ocean at Hekili Point. This original terminus of the stream, and many aspects of native irrigation and sustainable farming lands, were altered by early twentieth century sugar plantations.

In the ecological context, before European contact and subsequent colonisation – before the massacres, the whaling industry, the Irish potato trade, and the missionary schools – the landscape was compartmentalised into self-sustaining sections known as an *ahupua`a*, pie-shaped allotments stretching inland from coast to mountain top, each controlled by a sub-chief and his family, and further organised into *moku*, larger regional districts (Millerstrom and Kirch, 2004, p. 108). Each ahupua`a had everything that a village needed for a good life: access to the sea for marine resources, low alluvial fields for planting taro root, breadfruit and other crops, and rich forested slopes of sandalwood and hardwood that lead to the interior of the island (Lee-Gregg and Hammatt, 2012, p. 18). The Olowalu petroglyph site is positioned as a meeting place within this sacred ecology, a liminal space. As Jean Loubser has observed, "On the Hawaiian islands, rock art sites are known to occur along old trails, almost always at a transition point on the landscape" (2013, p. 31). Rock art is not simply placed where the rocks are; the location itself tells a story.

Tourism's Impact on Olowalu

Like in many other storied places, tourism has a complex relationship to Olowalu. Maui's economy depends on tourism. Low wage jobs, often filled by those of Hawaiian ancestry, are in abundance, and many islanders live in poverty without access to healthcare or education. In a 2004 study of sustainable tourism, this tension is acknowledged and framed as a continuation of European colonialist encroachment:

> Tourism has to be considered as part of a larger landscape of historical conditions, circumstances, events, decisions, and attitudes that have resulted in a diminished status of Native Hawaiians as decision makers in Hawai`i's economic future. In this context, tourism rises as a present-day flashpoint on a long trail of historical disappointments.
>
> (Knox et al., 2004, p. 1)

Case-in-point: thousands of tourists stay every year in an oceanside resort, unaware that those who make their coffee and change their linens are descendants of Hawaiian natives whose graves were disturbed in the 1980s to build the hotel. Many native Maui residents will not set foot inside the building as it is considered a living, unhealed desecration.

Just down the road, the Olowalu Petroglyphs have not fared well as park protectors made various attempts to promote and protect the sacred site. In the late 1960s, the Department of Land and Natural Resources (DLNR) erected concrete stairs to make it easier to view the petroglyphs. Unfortunately, this only promoted increased vandalism of the site in the decades that followed, including graffiti and permanent damage to the ancient rock art, as tourists and locals would carve their own initials into the stones (Uechi, 2021). The stairs were eventually dismantled, but never completely cleaned up, so large chunks of concrete remain at the site. Active promotion of the site was dropped, and it underwent a quiet period of neglect.

In 1999, a revitalisation of Olowalu petroglyphs and 74 acres of surrounding landscape was envisioned by the non-profit Olowalu Cultural Reserve. For nearly a decade, the land was converted to traditional uses, including farming and fishing, accomplished by weekly community workdays, educational talks, and fundraising. Central to this vision was "bringing back the concept of sanctuary to Hawaiian culture and redeeming the powerful legacy of Olowalu as a functioning pu'uhonua" (Smith, 2011, p. 12). A *pu'honua* is a place of peace, a sanctuary. Historically, this was a place where transgressors of Hawaiian law could find refuge without quarrel (Kirch, 1996, p. 10). All of the a'hupua of Olowalu – from reef to mountain top – were pu'honua. By organising community labour to work the lands, removing invasive vegetation, planting native plants, and restoring the Lo'i (terraces for taro), tourists and locals alike were invited to reconnect spirit to the landscape.

While Olowalu Cultural Reserve's organisation has since dissolved, this ecological tourism approach continues with the help of other organisations, such as Maui Cultural Lands, Inc., and Kipuka Olowalu, which has been funded by the Worldwide Indigenous Science Network. Ecological tourism can be a transformational experience for volunteers, but the disconnect between the tourist paradigm of "viewing" a site and an indigenous perspective that values participating with the landscape is immense. During an interview, Director of Maui Cultural Lands Ekolu Lindsey stated:

> Most visitors know nothing about conservation, culture, or respect. They come from all over the nation. How do I reach out to people who don't understand? [Yet] After they come and spend time working on the land, pulling weeds, they say they had no idea how important these lands and cultural sites are to indigenous people. I don't take them to the petroglyphs and heiau [temples] before they have worked on the land […] A restorative justice guy came here. He had no knowledge of the trees, waters, nothing. In 30 hours of work with us he learned to connect and how pieces are connected. At the end, he was a changed person. People leave fulfilled. Total cultural immersion on multiple visits grounds people.
>
> (personal communication, 2022)

Kainoa Horcajo, co-founder of Kipuka Olowalu, also described the transformation of volunteer participants, who in October 2021 began ecological restoration work in Olowalu Valley. As reported in Maui News, Horcajo commented,

Break in the Reef of Time 113

It was like watching "Extreme Makeover: Olowalu Edition." Just seeing things, that this is an overgrown area you could not see through, to lo'i running with fresh water and taro growing out of it and native plants – it was amazing [...] Between the smiling plants and the smiling faces it's been really rewarding.

(July 17, 2021)

Despite the success of this ecological approach to tourism and community involvement at Olowalu, the central rock art site still remains vulnerable to the actions of the very tourists who seek to connect with Maui's rich history. One recent reviewer on a popular tourist website writes:

While the petroglyphs are cool and great for the kids to see, this hike sucks. It's an old road, with barbed wire on one side, foul smells wafting over it, and other unpleasantness as well. If you want to see the petroglyphs, just drive up there.

(Alltrails.com, 2021)

Most tourists simply do not make time for immersion experiences, especially if work is involved. Lindsey affirmed this typical touristic attitude: "Lots of visitors are coming to see the site, more than ever. They come, look, and leave. I invite them to help with the lo'i [...] but no one comes" (2022).

The urgency of the need for further protection of Olowalu, as well as other sacred sites on Maui, can also be seen in a vandalism case from November 2021, in which several hundred paintballs were shot at the cliffs of Olowalu at close range. Dozens of petroglyphs were damaged, some beyond repair (Maui News, July 8, 2021). The vandalism shocked the island, but residents organised quickly for a clean-up effort, including stakeholders at Kipuka Olowalu. The spotlight of the news story allowed officials, many of whom have native ancestry on Maui, to discuss the significance of the rock art. Hinano Rodrigues is History and Culture branch chief of the DLNR and also a descendant of Chief Kamakakehau of Ukumehame:

Making a rock carving into basalt is hard work. So that person had a reason to do it. And so if we lose the petroglyph, we lose the thought that a human being hundreds of years ago actually made that petroglyph, and thus we lose an identity and a connection to a place and people.

(Maui News, July 8 2021)

Hawaii State DLNR Division of Conservation and Resource Enforcement (DOCARE) Lieutenant John Yamamoto commented, "It's kind of hurtful to see [...] so much historical value, the culture through here, the great battle down here, the significance of it all. It's just sad" (Hawaii Star, July 7, 2021). This mention of "the great battle" refers to the Olowalu Massacre of 1790, resulting in hundreds of deaths of Hawaiian men. Katherine Smith tells this story well:

114 *Apela Colorado and Ryan Hurd*

> At Honua'ula in 1790, a skiff and its watchman were taken from the American merchant ship *Eleanora*, and Captain Metcalf shot cannon at Honua'ula. Afterwards, Hawaiian traders he held on board revealed that the thieves fled to Olowalu for safety. Then *Eleanora* sailed to Olowalu in pursuit. Ali'i Wahine Nui Kalola, who understood the gravity of guns aimed at her village, immediately proclaimed a "Mai'u Mae" (wilted grass) kapu, requiring all men to remain where they were (literally standing in one spot) for three days. The kapu effectively stopped all canoes from leaving shore, and she hoped this "cooling down" period would avoid confrontation. Despite Kalola's wise management, on the fourth day Simon Metcalf lured all trading canoes to one side of his brig and fired cannon filled with nails and scrap metal, killing over one hundred, and wounding another two hundred innocent Hawaiians. Aside from the horrific bloodshed, Metcalf's violation of the sanctity of Olowalu forever broke Hawaiians' faith in pu'uhonua.
>
> (Smith, 2011, p.12)

Olowalu, well known as a place of refuge, was exploited during combat to lure traders to their deaths. The historic breaking of pu'uhonua resonates through mythic time. What is more, the Hawaiians are killed by the same objects which were the reason they "stole" the skiff in the first place – metal nails. (We must always place the "stealing" by indigenous peoples in quotations, when of course the colonial situation is a much vaster theft.) That the battle is mentioned so quickly in a television interview as a primary reason for the site's importance speaks to the living wound that it represents. Mythologist and ecopsychologist Craig Chalquist suggests that local folklore, and especially repetitive motifs, are key to a site's living presence. "Folklore is at least in part the dream of place and can be listened to as such. Ignored as such, it becomes dangerously, possessively re-enacted" (2007, p. 58). The attack of the site by paintballs could be seen as just such an unconscious reenactment of the Olowalu Massacre. The mythic repetition here is that European objects are weaponised against native sovereignty: iron nails, valuable for building stronger canoes and homes, placed in the cannons in the 1790 massacre, and paint, which can create art but here covers up and even destroys the ancient sacred petroglyphs.

The Creation Myths

Although noted since the days of Captain James Cook, the Hawaiian creation chant, *The Kumulipo*, was revitalised as a cultural act of resistance by Queen Lili'uokalani, the last sovereign monarch of the Hawaiian Kingdom. After she abdicated her throne in 1895, and during the annexation of the Hawaiian Islands, Queen Lili'uokalani was placed under house arrest, confined to a few rooms in what had been her palace. Under these conditions, she transcribed, translated into English, and published *The Kumulipo*, bringing into literature an oral tradition that she had learned from her great grandmother (Beckwith, 1951).

Break in the Reef of Time 115

In English we designate *The Kumulipo* as a chant, but it is truly a song of ancestral remembrance, including thousands of members of the Hawaiian royal family, charting their divinity and interconnection with the natural world. The song begins with darkness and heat, and later illustrates how all the creatures arose from the sea, starting with the coral that composes the reef. Here are the first six lines of Folklorist Martha Beckwith's translation of the central creation story, Chant 1, of *The Kumulipo*, which shows how important dualisms, as well as the subversion and integration of dualisms, are to Hawaiian cosmology:

> O ke au i kahuli wela ka honua
> At the time when the earth became hot
> O ke au i kahuli lole ka lani
> At the time when the heavens turned about
> O ke au i kuka'iaka ka la
> At the time when the sun was darkened
> E ho'omalamalama i ka malama
> To cause the moon to shine
> O ke au o Makali'i ka po
> The time of the rise of the Pleiades
> O ka walewale ho'okumu honua ia
> The slime, this was the source of the earth.
> (Beckwith, 1951/2008)

Unlike the massive sites on the Big Island, oral folklore of Olowalu on the island of Maui was not formally recorded in the eighteenth or nineteenth centuries. Smith simply reported, "the meaning and intent of these drawings has been lost" (2011, p. 7). Rodrigues commented in a recent newspaper article that officially the park service is not certain of the age of the petroglyphs or their meanings. "We really don't know. A lot of the petroglyphs were not done as a composite that may reflect a story," he said. "A lot of them were done just as one petroglyph by itself. I have a feeling the petroglyphs were not made to tell a story but to tell about people that lived there" (Uechi, 2021). This authoritative perspective is mirrored in the current interpretive signage of Olowalu, faded and bleached by the sun, reading only that "The numerous images shown here tell a story and provide us with a glimpse into the community of pre-contact and historic Olowalu," followed by the guidance, "DO NOT climb on the rocks" (Olowalu Petroglyphs sign).

Indigenous Views of Sacred Sites

The word "Olowalu" is usually translated into English as "many hills" (Pukui and Elbert, 1986). However, Smith explains that Olowalu can also mean

> multiple sounds occurring at once, or a din, such as drums beating, dogs barking, or chickens crowing at the sun. La'amaikahiki, who is credited

with bringing the drum to Hawaii from Tahiti in the eleventh century, is called, '*O ke aliʻi ke olowalu o ka pahu o Hawaiʻi*.' "The aliiʻ is the rumble of Hawaiʻi's drums."

(2011, p. 3)

The kaona, or hidden meaning, understood by only cultural Hawaiians fluent in their language, refers to the synchronisation of voices, not just a din, but a reverberation or resonance. This multidimensional definition is a theme that emerges in relation to the rock art site at Olowalu, providing a potential clue as to how this site still speaks.

Not all is lost. Hawaiian Elder Hale Makua gave generously of his time and wisdom to not only renew the traditional spiritual practices of his Hawaiian people, but also to share his teachings with students and seekers from other cultures and traditions. Presented here are some of his thoughts on sacred sites:

> In ancient times of the ancestors, the sacred sites were treated with reverence and humility. These places possess the spiritual power of the ancestors; but these designated areas were more than what the eye perceives. It tells me who I am, who my extended family is, and it gives me my family history, history of my clan, and the history of the people itself.
>
> Approach the sacred sites with appropriate sensitivity, thoughtfulness, and humility. Those who visit and pay these sites the respect and deference they deserve, whether they are native Hawaiian or not, will benefit from the experience of communing with the ancestors, learning the functions, and absorbing the spiritual power of the sacred site. Study, observe, and appreciate, for these sites are part of spiritual wisdom.

(personal communication, 2001)

Makua visited the Olowalu petroglyphs with one of us (Apela Colorado) before he died tragically in a car accident in March 2004. Visiting the site with a Hawaiian elder opened new vistas of experience, and the experience reverberated in future visits to the site.

I, Apela Colorado, am an indigenous Oneida woman. Our tribal name means the long living rock. We say the rock carries the story of life because life begins with the rock. For years I had been studying the rock carvings of the Pacific Northwest. Those situated in the tide lines were often navigational guides (Colorado, 1980). I was captivated by the thought that petroglyphs strewn across the Pacific constituted a gigantic interlocking data bank, not only for seafaring but also for other kinds of travel. From my Native ceremonial background I knew inherently that knowledge would not only come in terms of facts but also in visceral communication.

I have come to Olowalu many times to establish a relationship with the site, and to understand my strong pull to a location deemed so important by the ancients. The site looks like it could use some care. Standing alongside my open

Break in the Reef of Time 117

car door, I glance down at my tote bag to make sure I have my water bottle, salt, awa [ceremonial tea], everything I need to enter the Olowalu petroglyph site.

Arriving at the first and smallest boulder, looking ahead towards the mountain pass, I take in the length and breadth of the site, deceptively small, just 300 ft, beginning to end. It is early in the morning but already the temperature nears ninety degrees. Slowly, gently, I return the car door to its frame. Instantly, in the length of time it takes for the soft thud to reach my ears, an all-embracing and enveloping holographic reverberance of the car door closing wraps around me. I stand on sacred ground. Walking from the car towards the tulus, strange acoustic phenomena continue. My rubber slippers hitting the gravel sound like gunshots and serve to heighten awareness of the preternatural stillness.

Laying down a line of sea salt as Maui Kahuna, Auntie Mahilane Poepoe, taught, I look down the road, up to the mountains, call out my name, explain my relationship to this site, through my husband's Hawaiian family and my Oneida Native American ceremonial ways and asked permission to enter.

Here at the first carving, it is hard to make out, but with concentration I can dimly see the image of a man holding a crescent with a couple of circles at his feet. Looking at the rock like an old friend, tender memories well up of standing here with esteemed, beloved, Hawaiian kahuna Hale Makua.

On that visit, Mr. Makua had agreed to stop by the site on his way to the airport. He just had a few minutes, but it was enough. I could not make sense of what it communicated and wanted his help. He glanced at it for less than a minute and responded, "It's about time," and identified the crescent and circles as moon phases. As he spoke a curious thing happened. The rock message, previously as impenetrable as its basalt composition, suddenly became inter-dimensional. Two, then, three petroglyph men, then more and more, to infinity, cascaded down from the top to culminate in the image I had been able to identify. The moon symbols also multiplied, not just in number but in telescoping layers. Cultural knowledge is revelatory – I could literally see what Mr. Makua was saying.

I visit the site again. This time I am accompanied by three traditional healers. Each one contributes a story. As I look at the rock face I notice the lower boulders streaming down towards the ocean become darker as they approach the sea. The place where the rocks begin to lighten, I see the petroglyph figure: an ancient ray headed spirit. When two worlds meet, memorable things happen, power is passed from one to another. I see something with newfound certainty: that the journey to Olowalu Petroglyphs, the walk from the sea to the mountains, can be experienced as a geophysical embodiment of the Hawaiian creation chant. We have a chance to revitalise the site, to renew the cycle of life. As Mr. Makua has said, *it's about time*.

Geomythic Appraisal of Pu'u Kilea

Dr. Colorado's embodied experience and personal revelation at Olowalu brings hope and a chance of renewal. First, we remember that the site is not just about visual images placed on stone, but is a living habitat that speaks to visitors today. In the Hawaiian indigenous context, Olowalu is placed in between two worlds, and as such the responsibility of humans is to maintain the *pono* (balance) of the boundary zone, between the sea and the cliffs, the light and the dark, the ancestors and the living, the lower and upper worlds. Binaries like these are central to Hawaiian cosmology. Once recognised, the liminality of Olowalu – as a storied place that plays with and possibly integrates these binaries – can be communicated to visitors to foster deeper listening and participation while traversing the site. From a Hawaiian perspective, conflict and parties engaged in it are often dual aspects of the same supernatural being. In this way, supernatural and secular conflict can be creative and life sustaining forces (see Figure 7.2).

Secondly, the strong echo effects at Olowalu are not accidental but central to the power of the locale, as the geophysical context of the slopes of Pu'u Kilea has changed little over the millennia. The stream still flows past the petroglyphs, bringing a rich life-giving and acoustically dynamic dimension to Olowalu as the water's sounds are folded over by the bouldered slope and set to the distant heartbeat of the ocean waves. The deeper, hidden, significance of Olowalu as meaning "synchronised voices" comes back into focus, as rock art sites are often placed in boundary zones along waterways, drawing

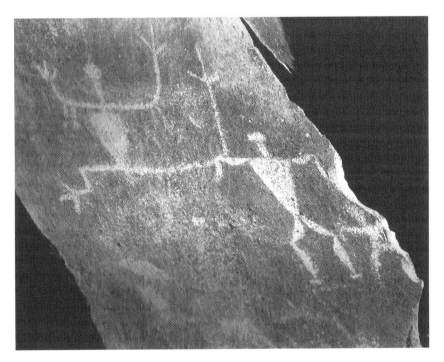

Figure 7.2 Petroglyphs with This Characteristic Filled in Triangular Torso Are Dated from AD 1650 to the Modern Era (Patterson, 2002).

(Photograph by Apela Colorado, 2021).

power from consciousness-altering acoustic features and creating watery soundscapes (Devereux, 2007; Garcés and Nash, 2017), as well as functioning as territorial markers (Millerstrom and Kirch, 2004). Acoustic physics researcher John Stuart Reid suggests that the tropical heat at Pu'u Kilea also contributes to the extraordinary acoustic effects of the area. The brown basalt of the boulders absorbs solar radiation and reflects the heat until that hot air meets cooler air about 100 ft above the rock face, creating refractions of sound on the flat basalt surfaces that can be experienced as sound mirage. More than a flat "echo," the effect is more like a sound bubble that envelops a person (2021, personal communication). This natural priming for altered consciousness is an invitation for prayer and remembrance, especially if visitors are given guidance through ceremony, led by an indigenous sacred site guardian (Colorado and Hurd, 2018).

Thirdly, from a geomythical or terrapsychological perspective (Chalquist, 2007; Vitaliano, 2007), Pu'u Kilea represents a cosmic opening between worlds that parallels the break in the reef directly below the cliffs, which gives canoes safe harbour. These features are the geological dimensions of Olowalu's folkloric expression into human consciousness as a place of sanctuary and rest, a meeting ground to meditate and exchange thoughts of Aloha with the ancestors. These enchantments of the landscape can be lifted into site interpretation materials, deepening ecological participation and hopefully even changing tourist behaviour by generating new energy for grassroots, community-led site protection (Ironside and Massie, 2020, p. 9).

Finally, Colorado's insight into Olowalu petroglyphs as an invitation to enter the Hawaiian creation story deserves more discussion. When Queen Lili'uokalani became a prisoner of the American government, she gave voice to her ancestors by publishing *The Kumulipo*. This is the model for reclaiming Olowalu from the cycle of negativity that currently holds sway in the folkloric remembrance. Placing Olowalu back into its ecological context can be felt and lived out by walking the walk: by walking up from the ocean and moving up the hill in a creative enactment of Hawaiian cosmology. Life begins in the sea, lower forms appear and evolve into greater complexity, forces of nature manifest, and so do human beings. Grounded in the creation myth, site visitors can walk into sanctuary and into creativity, so they are in relationship with the site for purposes that are life giving and affirming, rather than destructive and death affirming. As Hakea Makua has said, "Only when a kanaka maoli (native) gains spiritual wisdom is the ancestral and spiritual sense of place reactivated. Spiritual knowledge and the sacred sites are ancestrally related, thus spiritual strength connects to the ancestral guardians" (2001). Creativity is a meditation, a prayer: centring, focusing, and teaching how to let go.

Perhaps by limiting access to the Olowalu Petroglyphs to hikers, rather than vehicles, the site could be re-enchanted as a functioning pu'uhonua, protecting the site from fast-food visitors who do not have the time or intentionality to participate more fully with Olowalu's presence. Deepened by folkloric narratives, this restorative act makes sacred the mundane task of

120　*Apela Colorado and Ryan Hurd*

hiking to the Olowalu site, and recasts the walk as a journey within the break in the reef of time. This simple proposal is in line with other contemporary rock art management plans that have successfully re-focused the quality of visitor interactions, as well as cut down on vandalism and littering (Whitley, 2011, p. 190). While Maui's development remains uncertain and bristling with competing economic visions, restoring the hallowed places or *wahi pana* is critical to the future of Maui's self-identity in the twenty-first century.

References

Anderson, M. and Ashdown, I.A. (2016). *The Storied Places of West Maui: History, Legends, and Placenames of the Sunset Side of Maui*. Lahaina: North Beach-West Maui Benefit Fund Inc.

Chalquist, C. (2007). *Terrapsychology: Reengaging the soul of place*. New Orleans: Spring Journal Books.

Colorado, A. (2014). 'Scientific Pluralism.' In F. David Peat (ed.), *The Pari Dialogues: Essays in Indigenous Knowledge and Western Science*, Volume 2. Pari, Italy: Pari Publishing.

Colorado, A. and Hurd, R. (2018). 'To Re-enact Is to Remember: Envisioning a Shamanic Research Protocol in Archaeology.' In D. Gheorghiu, G. Nash, H. Bender and E. Pásztor (eds.) *Lands of the Shamans: Archaeology, Cosmology & Landscape*. Oxford: Oxbow Books, pp. 258–270.

Devereux, P. (2007). *Stone Age soundtracks: The acoustic archaeology of sacred sites*. London: Vega.

Garcés, S. and Nash, G. (2017). 'The Relevance of Watery Soundscapes in a Ritual Context.' *Time and Mind*, 10 (1), pp. 69–80.

Hawaii Star (2021). 'Ancient Hawaiian Petroglyphs Damaged.' Available Online: https://www.hawaiistar.com/2021/07/maui-olowalu-petroglyphs-damaged/ [Accessed 15 March 2022].

Ironside, R. and Massie, S. (2020). 'The Folklore-Centric Gaze: A Relational Approach to Landscape, Folklore and Tourism.' *Time and Mind*, 13 (3), pp. 227–244.

Kirch, P.V. (1996). *Legacy of the Landscape: An Illustrated Guide to Hawaiian Archaeological Sites*. Honolulu: University of Hawai'i Press.

Knox, J., et al. (2004). *Planning for Sustainable Tourism. Part IV: Socio-Cultural & Public Input Study. Volume III: Socio-Cultural Impact, Native Hawaiians*. Honolulu: Department of Business, Economic Development & Tourism.

Kovach, M. (2010). *Indigenous Methodologies – Characteristics, Conversations, and Contexts*. Toronto: University of Toronto Press.

Lee-Gregg, T. and Hammatt, H. (2012). *Consultation Plan for Assessing Potential Cultural Impacts for the Proposed Olowalu Town Master Plan Olowalu Ahupua'a, Lāhaina District, Island of Maui TMK*. Wailuku: Cultural Surveys Hawai'i, Inc.

Lindsey, E. (2022). Personal communication with Apela Colorado, March 22, 2022.

Loubser, J. (2013). 'A Holistic and Comparative Approach to Rock Art.' *Time and Mind*, 6 (1), pp. 29–36.

Lyons, C.J. (1879). 'Coastline of a Part of Olowalu and Ukumehame, West Maui.' Reproduced in T. Lee-Gregg and H. Hammatt (2012). *Consultation Plan for Assessing Potential Cultural Impacts for the Proposed Olowalu Town Master Plan Olowalu Ahupua'a, Lāhaina District, Island of Maui TMK*. Wailuku: Cultural Surveys Hawai'i, Inc, p. 27.

Makua, H. (2001). Personal Communication to Apela Colorado, May 31, 2001.

Millerstrom, S. and Kirch, P.V. (2004). 'Petroglyphs of Kahikinui, Maui, Hawaiian Islands: Rock Images within a Polynesian Settlement Landscape.' *Proceedings of the Prehistoric Society*, 70, pp. 107–127.

Olowalu Petroglyphs, comment by poster on February 21, 2019. *AllTrails.com*. Available Online: https://www.alltrails.com/trail/hawaii/maui/olowalu-petroglyphs [Accessed 10 November 2021].

"Olowalu Petroglyphs" Sign. Department of Land and Natural Resources, Maui. Viewed January 2022.

Patterson, C. (2002). 'Parallels in Hawaiian Ethnography and Petroglyphs: Utilizing Gesture, Posture and Proxemic Arrangements.' *Utah Rock Art*, 22, pp. 11–41.

Pukui, M. Kawena and Elbert, S.H. (1986). *Hawaiian Dictionary*, revised ed. Honolulu: University of Hawai'i Press.

Reid, J.S. (2021). Personal communication to Apela Colorado, 2021.

Rowe, G. (2014). 'Implementing Indigenous Ways of Knowing into Research: Insights into the Critical Role of Dreams as Catalysts for Knowledge Development.' *Journal of Indigenous Social Development*, 3 (2), pp. 1–17.

Smith, K. Kama'ema'e (2011). *Pu'uhonua: The legacy of Olowalu*. Olowalu, HI: Olowalu Cultural Reserve.

Site of Olowalu Petroglyphs Shot with Paintballs: Officials Seek Information in Vandalism Case (2021). *Maui News*, July 8. Available Online: https://www.mauinews.com/news/local-news/2021/07/site-of-olowalu-petroglyphs-shot-with-paintballs/ [Accessed 22 March 2022].

The Kumulipo. A Hawaiian Creation Chant (1951/2008). Translated and edited with commentary by Martha Warren Beckwith. Chicago: University of Chicago Press with interlinearization by David Stampe. Available Online: https://blogs.ksbe.edu/adakina/files/2008/02/kumulipo-text.pdf [Accessed 22 March 2022].

Uechi, C. (2021). 'Managing Editor. Nonprofit Plans to Restore Vandalized Olawalu Petroglyphs.' *Maui News*, July 17. Available Online: https://www.mauinews.com/news/local-news/2021/07/nonprofit-plans-to-restore-vandalized-olowalu-petroglyphs/ [Accessed 22 March 2022].

Vitaliano, Dorothy (2007). 'Geomythology: Geological Origins of Myths and Legends.' In L. Piccardi and W.B. Masse (eds.), *Myth and geology*. Special Publications, 273, pp. 1–7.

Whitley, D. (2011). *Introduction to Rock Art Research*, second edition. Walnut Creek: Lost Coast Press.

8 Creating *La Cuna del Folklore Nacional*

The Colonisation of Indigenous Celebrations, Legends, and Landscapes in Nicaraguan State Heritage Tourism

Paul Edward Montgomery Ramírez

Introduction

Resistance is a foundational theme within the storybook of Nicaragua, both in its histories and in other cultural expressions. It can be found in the imagery of national heroes like Andrés Castro who, after his rifle failed to fire at the Battle of San Jacinto, continued to fight against the filibuster William Walker by throwing rocks at the Estadounidense invaders. It is encompassed in the nearly legendary figure Augusto César Sandino, whose revolutionary struggle against Estadounidense imperialism was immortalised by the *Frente Sandinista de Liberación Nacional* (FSLN). It echoes in the dying words of Leonel Rugama, made famous during the Revolution against the Somoza dictatorship, "*¡Que se rinda tu madre!*" (Francis, 2012). This theme of anti-imperial struggle is one that continues to hold currency today, both against foreign powers and the policies of the controversial Ortega presidency.

After the Revolution and the political loss of the Sandinistas in 1990, Nicaragua struggled to recover financially and internationally. The Chamorro presidency's austerity measures, currency devaluation, and wage stagnation led to civil unrest and strikes (Chavez Metoyer, 2000, pp. 5, 90–91). Policies and foreign assistance reduced the country's inflation and private companies increased their interests into industries. And, despite the adoption of neoliberal policies and investments by the Sandinista party, re-elected into power in 2006, Nicaragua is among the most economically deprived states in the western hemisphere, with a per capita GDP of US$1,905 in 2020 (Macrotrends, 2021).

Agriculture has been the largest industry in Nicaragua; however, the service sector – especially with the inclusion of tourism – has pushed to the forefront of the state's economy. In 2017, agriculture accounted for an estimated 15.5% of Nicaragua's GDP and made up 31% of the labour force, while services made up 60% of the GDP and employed half of the country (CIA, 2021). In the nearly two decades prior to the protests and civil unrest that began on 18 April 2018, Nicaragua reported an average economic growth of 3.9% (World Bank Group, 2021a). Tourism has been among its most significant sources of growth. In 1995, the country was visited by 341 thousand people, by Ortega's return to power in 2006, a million people had toured

DOI: 10.4324/9781003374138-11

Creating La Cuna del Folklore Nacional   123

Nicaragua (World Bank Group, 2021b). The year 2017 marked the country's highest visitation numbers and longest duration: 1.96 million foreign travellers, staying on average for ten and a half days, spending around US$430 each, to a total of US$841 million – over 6% of Nicaragua's GDP (Central American Data, 2018; World Data, 2021).

Tourism can be considered an opportunity for commercial development in economically deprived regions and a pathway to conducting diplomacy (see Barankowski et al., 2019). Ecotourism, with a focus on the biodiverse landscapes of volcanoes, forests, beaches, and lagoons is an important feature of Nicaragua's tourism agenda. Cultural elements: performances, stories, music, and objects have increasingly been tapped into in an effort to generate a greater well of resources to be consumed by tourists.

Masaya is the smallest department, by area, in Nicaragua. Despite its relative size, this area, between the capital Managua, and the colonial city of Granada, is known as *la cuna del folklore nacional* (the cradle of national folklore). This designation was formally enshrined with the introduction of Law 61, which declared Masaya to be "cultural heritage of the nation" and the "cradle of popular insurrection" (Asamblea Nacional de la República de Nicaragua, 1989). The city, within a landscape of lagoons and volcanoes, holds a special position in the heritage-weaving of Nicaragua. One cannot understand Nicaragua without knowing Masaya. Its location along tourism routes has certainly facilitated Masaya as a resource, but these same resources also have a history of indigenous resistance and survivance (see Vizenor, 1999, p. vii) that has largely been whitewashed by the state for the creation of a Nicaraguan Mestizo identity.

To approach the layers of appropriation and invisibility, we must be visitors in our own right. This chapter is a tour through the author's ancestral pueblo – one taken many times. Indigenous research is inherently spiritual and ceremonial (Wilson, 2015); this tour, this procession recreated, is no different. As Kovach (2010, p. 7) wrote, 'we know what we know from where we stand.' The chapter and tour are informed by indigenous autoethnography (see Houston, 2007). It also draws parallels with Muñoz's application of serpentine conocimiento in her own tour of her homelands, whereby she understood that "all life is connected to both earthly and spiritual realms, emphasising duality, intuition, and fluidity" (2019, p. 64). It speaks to indigenous stories that have been woven into the dominant culture's mat of power, sat upon by the powerful and enjoyed by the *extranjero*.

This tour is an act of survivance, as voiced by Visenor it is "an active sense of presence, the continuance of native stories, not a mere reaction, or a survivable name. Native survivance stories are renunciations of dominance, tragedy and victimry" (1999, p. vii). It, too, is an act of indigenous re-storying, whereby the dominant narratives can be questioned and countered by indigenous understandings of heritage (Corntassel, 2009, pp. 138–139). In this tour, we approach indigenous heritages that live within the landscape of Masaya, their co-opting by state power, and a path travelling towards indigenous futures within and beyond *la cuna del folklore nacional*.

124 *Paul Edward Montgomery Ramírez*

La Tierra de Lagos y Volcanes

More than most parts of the country, Masaya embodies one of Nicaragua's monikers, the "Land of Lakes and Volcanoes," being nestled in between two lagoons and home to an extensive volcanic system featuring numerous craters and two volcanoes. Between the capital and Masaya is the Volcán Masaya: the country's first national park and one of Nicaragua's most visited sites. The primary volcano, called Popogatepe (The Smoking Mountain) in Nawat language, has a long tradition of use.

On a typical day during the peak tourist season, processions of cars line up along the Carretera 4 to Masaya, waiting to be admitted into the park (rates vary based on the time of day, who is in the cars, and where they might be from). The earliest Spanish depictions of the volcano note a pathway to the caldera. It is also in these writings and drawings that the feelings of the invaders about the site are made abundantly clear, the open caldera being called *la boca del infierno* (Hellmouth), or the "Gates of Hell" (Chicago Tribune; de Bréadún, 2006). And while many of Nicaragua's volcanos are active, Popogatepe is particularly lively, with no fewer than 42 recorded Holocene eruptive periods. The current period has been on-going (as of this writing) since 2015 CE (Bennis and Venzke, 2021). Its uniqueness has attracted curiosity from outsiders for centuries, but it is also part of a traditional, sacred landscape for the indigenous Chorotega.

The volcanic landscape is a part of the cultural foundations of the Chorotega people in the area called Diria Mankesa, translating to something along the lines of "the Land of the Highland Lords" (the Chorotega endonym, *Mankeme*, meaning roughly "lord"). Since our arrival into the sacred lands between the waters, the speakers among the many Diria Chorotega groups used the volcanic system as a place to conduct communications across all boundaries. Diplomacy between differing parties took place, and a specially elected leadership emerged from these events in the rocky landscape. Even more important than its role in political matters, the volcano also possessed an explicitly spiritual dimension. Ancestors and other powerful spirits met with guests at this site, to whom offerings were given.

Like many indigenous societies with volcanic sacred landscapes and ancestral associations, Chorotega people were accused by the Spanish of virgin sacrifice. In reality, evidence in support of such accusations is scant, though this absence of evidence is often dismissed by consideration of the destructive capacities of volcanoes (see Socha et al., 2020). Sacrifice is known in Chorotega tradition, though in the form of plants, animals, meat, crafted items, and blood, rather than killing humans. Colonial powers have painted imagery of human sacrifice with broad brush-strokes across indigenous people, to fuel ethical calls to eliminate indigenous culture and sovereignty. This "human rights" argument was made by Juan Ginés de Sepúlveda during the Valladolid Debate to support the enslavement of indigenous people (trans Menendez y Pelayo and Garcia-Pelayo, 1941, p. 155). By misunderstanding and villainising indigenous cultures, colonisation could be viewed as moral.

Creating La Cuna del Folklore Nacional   125

The major recipient of sacrifice allegations was said to be an ancient "witch" with black skin, fiery eyes, and the teeth of a jaguar who lived in a cave called Xinancanostoc ('Cave of the Bat'). Gonzalo Fernández de Oviedo y Valdez's work *Historia general y natural de las Indias, Islas y Tierra Firme del Mar Océano*, the earliest colonial writings from the region, described her as a being of immense power. Indigenous people brought her offerings inside polychrome pottery for personal healing, for fertility (personal and agricultural), protection from natural forces, and to gain divine insight. She also presided over and blessed the diplomatic gatherings of the Diria Chorotega. Among Chorotega in Guanacaste, Costa Rica, a similar figure – called Dabaiba – exists at the volcano Rincón de la Vieja (Zeléldon Cartín, 2012, p. 70). This spirit is sometimes considered in the tragic story of an indigenous "princess" called Curabanda. Outraged at her love-affair with a man (possessing a Nawat name, associated with the Milky Way: Mixcoac) from a rival community, her father hurled Curabanda's love into the volcano. Grief-stricken, she cast their new-born child into the volcano to join its father. From this, she developed great healing powers and lives eternally in the volcano. These histories highlight the long-term shared volcanic spirituality of Mankeme across communities divided by cultural and colonial borders.

These spirits in Masaya and Guanacaste are ultimately thwarted by Catholicism. Dabaiba in Guanacaste is said to have been trapped in a volcanic mudpot by a Nicaraguan priest, during the National Campaign of 1856 against the filibuster William Walker. The ancient spirit at Volcán Masaya was denounced by Oviedo and the priesthood as a "witch" and the devil, leading to the construction of a crucifix at the crater by friar Francisco de Bobadilla to exorcise the "Satanic" landscape (Viramonte and Incer-Barquero, 2008, p. 424). Afterwards it was said that the spirit announced to a gathering of Chorotega leaders that she would no longer contact or advise them while Christians remained on the land. Although this particular story ends here, the spirit's does not, but that story lays further down the path of this tour.

Bypassing the road and taking the old procession route leads to the companion of the volcano: Lenderí. A source of life and protection since the beginning, this lagoon – a deceased crater of the Volcán Masaya – is a holder of legends. The waters are said to contain multiplicities of spirits, and the indigenous community of Monimbó holds a festival called Los Agüizotes every year to convince these potentially dangerous beings to return to their world in the water. But there is an even greater spirit that is connected to the waters of the lagoon: a great serpent that is the creator and lifeforce of the lagoon. Its tears fell as rain over a powerful and magical woman and are said to have drowned a forested valley. From then on, the giant serpent was said to guard the lake and forests, and was a powerful force that humans have communicated and maintained a relationship with. While early Spanish documents do not explicitly record the serpent in the lagoon as they do the "witch" in the volcano, there is evidence of this important being in imagery from the area – prehispanic and later. A great and plumed serpent is painted

126   *Paul Edward Montgomery Ramírez*

into the cliffs of Lago de Managua, and serpentine elements mark petroglyphic works called Cailagua near Lenderí.

The great serpent of the lagoon is, by numerous accounts, no longer alive. Versions of this story are often told within a generational depth, whereby the teller's great-grandfather was a witness or participant in the slaying of the serpent. The campesino, Don Hernando recounted to the anthropologist Les Field that his grandmother's father wanted to drain a lagoon so that he could farm it. Over a particularly dry period, the lagoon shrank until only its centre-most portion remained, housing the mighty snake which he then killed, drying out the lagoon (Field, 1999, p. 196). Despite the many deaths of the serpent and the lagoon (often explained away as a "different" lagoon), Lenderí still exists, and Monimboseños still describe witnessing the serpent swimming beneath the surface or resting along the shores.

Stories like these depict either the end of a way of life or the very extinction of indigenous people and culture. The killing of the great serpent is a punctuation mark repeated over and over, declaring the death of the indigenous. Still in Masaya alone, three indigenous communities remain.

"Come Yuca"

Continuing along the edge of Lenderí, the petroglyphs called Cailagua can be found. Indigenous people fled here for protection from the destructive forces of the Spanish and the Estadounidense. The people of Masaya are nicknamed *come yuca* ("eat cassava"). This phrase about a traditional staple has a grim history.

Before the Invasion, Pacific "Nicaragua" had an estimated population of between six and eight-hundred thousand. Within a quarter century of the Spanish Invasion, 92% of that population was destroyed, with a depopulation ratio "higher than that recorded for central Mexico and the central Andean area [and] higher than the depopulation ratios [...] for other chiefdoms, such as the Chibcha" (Newson, 1987, p. 337). According to oral histories, the Spanish Invaders in the 1500s and Walker's forces aimed to annihilate the indigenous communities of Masaya. As the people sought refuge at Cailagua from the bullets and blades of invaders, their homes and fields were set to the torch. If they could not be massacred, they could be starved into extinction. While most of their crops were destroyed, the yuca survived – its edible roots safely protected underground. Eating yuca carries with it a sense of defiance against destructive forces, sometimes embodied in the saying of an indigenous person when asked how their people will survive: "We will eat yuca."

At night, the streets of Monimbó remember generational trauma given shape. People are warned not to look out of the windows at night, and to never be found on the streets in the darkest hours: that was the time of *la carretanagua*. An oxcart driven by the skeletal Muerte Quirina leads a procession of the dead through the streets. Witnessing it brings madness, illness, the loss of speech and senses; its coming brings sickness and death. As described by the anthropologist, Milagros Palma, this nocturnal horror is a

Creating La Cuna del Folklore Nacional   127

reminder of the terrors of the Spanish Invasion (1987, p. 83). With the arrival of the invaders and their oxen-led supply carts came disease, suffering, and slavery. La carretanagua and Muerte Quirina are the still-dangerous person-ifications of these traumas within the histories of the people of Masaya.

Survival against the force of *mestizaje* (a "bio-cultural" mixing project of the "indigenous" and "European" into a unique "race") takes many shapes among the indigenous peoples of what is today Nicaragua. By the end of the 1800s, members of the ladino elite – historians, sociologists, or political agents – noted the "complete disappearance" of indigenous peoples in Pacific Nicaragua (Peralta, 1893, pp. xvi–ii; Cuadra, 1981, p. 209). To foreign researchers, eager to study the "exotic," the Chorotega in Masaya were a disappointment as they "in most ways act[ed] just like other mestizos" (Adams, 1957, p. 238). By disease or mestizaje, the case was allegedly settled: the "Indian" had gone extinct. Yet, the CIA *World Factbook* (2021) estimates that 5% of Nicaragua's 6.24 million people are indigenous.

Mestizaje is a powerful myth with many captives, including Sandino him-self, who said, "I used to look with resentment on the colonising work of Spain, but today I have profound admiration for it […] Spain gave us its lan-guage, its civilisation, and its blood" (in Field, 1998, p. 437). But mestizaje did not create "a new hybrid or mestizo culture that marries the best of two different civilisations [but] plainly and simply […] a Western model" (in Field, 1998, p. 436). For the mestizo to succeed, the indigenous needed to be made "the past," both physically and culturally. Indigenous cultural trappings that would not die were outlawed, as happened briefly in the 1800s with the ritual performance called *El Güegüense* (see Montgomery Ramírez, 2021). Serpents must die – repeatedly – and volcanic spirits need to vanish.

Today, the patron saint of Masaya is a particular aspect of San Jerónimo: an ancient, white-haired and fair-skinned hermit with the powers of healing and an ability to commune with nature. He is associated with the landscape surrounding Masaya, including the volcano. This saintly man found a home left "vacant" by the departure of the black-skinned and ancient woman after her final chiding of Chorotega leaders. Multiple celebrations are held in his honour, not merely his feast day. This physical inversion has not gone unno-ticed, even by outsiders, such as Borland (2006, pp. 22–24), who noted a strong connection between the cave-dwelling hermit-saint and the ancient volcano spirit.

San Jerónimo and *El Güegüense* are both emblems of indigenous culture, hidden within the acceptable language of the Christian, the Spaniard, the Mestizo. Their masquerade has allowed for indigenous survivance, but has also placed them within the marketplace of mestizaje to be spirited away and sold.

El "Antiguo" Mercado

There are two markets in Masaya: the one that everyone goes to for their daily needs, and the "Ancient Market" where tourists are dropped off from

128 *Paul Edward Montgomery Ramírez*

their busses to buy "authentic" items like masks, stuffed frogs and lizards, ceramics replicating prehispanic design, or perhaps the figures of nude "Indian princesses." This is a go-to stop for many day-trippers to either the volcano or the colonial city of Granada. It is not uncommon for the people who arrive by tour bus to only come to the city for an hour or so with the purpose of buying a souvenir and to snap a quick photo. Tours from holidayers in Costa Rica stop to consume the culturally rich area in a whirlwind to exemplify Nicaragua as a whole. The "Ancient Market" embodies the very appropriation and consumption of the indigenous that has advanced the myth of mestizaje and the making of *la cuna del folklore nacional*.

The masked performances in honour of sacred beings have been a characteristic of indigenous Chorotega cultural practice; elements acknowledged well into the 1960s (Borland, 2006, p. 112). In the face of the nation-building myth of mestizaje, Chorotega custom was re-branded as "lo típico" (typical) culture and sold that way, domestically and internationally (Stocker, 2013, p. 160). In this way, the sacred performance of indigenous resistance – *El Güegüense* – exists in the public eye as a great work of Nicaraguan intangible heritage (officially designated as such by UNESCO in 2008), rather than a great Chorotega work (see Montgomery Ramírez, 2021). Today it and other sacred performances are staged out of time, out of location, and out of spirit for the sake of "national heritage" and tourism.

Through the myth of mestizaje, the indigenous is rendered invisible, subsumed, and re-imagined as synonymous with class. The campesino and the indigenous were the same in Sandinismo's ideologies. Anti-colonial pasts – and thereby the "Indian" – were tapped into within the language of Sandinismo. The lionisation of indigenous pasts and their resistances made contemporary indigenous people believe "that the Frente could respect our history kept our relationship with the Frente very close for a long time" (de la Concepción, cited in Field, 1998, p. 438). The Sandinista government painted the Monimboseño uprising against the Somoza dictatorship as a valiant revolutionary action, marking the community as the "cradle of popular insurrection" and declaring the indigenous Matagalpinos, who sent archers to oppose Walker, national heroes (Prensa-Asamblea Nacional, 2012). In the conflation of "race" and "class" that continued to crystallise under the Sandinistas, Monimboseño scholar, Flavio Gamboa, remarked that the FSLN "recognised the rights of Indians only on the Atlantic Coast; the costesos were against the revolution, but they got autonomy. The Indians of the Pacific were always in favour of the revolution, but they got nothing" (Field, 1998, p. 439). The dis/alignment of resistances could either push peoples into being "Indians" or reduce indigeneity to invisibility. Indigenous actions that supported the causes against William Walker and Somoza should not be mistaken as acts of national pride or of revolutionaries, but stem from a tradition of indigenous resistance against colonial forces.

The second era of the Ortega government has advanced a cultural – and touristic – policy of mestizaje, while speaking of the "indigenous," with great success. Said of the Chorotega in Costa Rica, but as applicable in Masaya:

Creating La Cuna del Folklore Nacional   129

The "success" of such assimilation projects is evident in the fact that in order to present Chorotega Indigenous imagery today, it must be done through artefacts left over from a past when Indigenous existence was undeniable, or it must follow stereotypes plain enough to be recognised as Indian in a nation whose appropriation of Indigenous traditions has rendered them ineffective at evoking recognition of their Chorotega origins.

(Stocker, 2013, p. 152)

These artefacts that "prove" indigeneity are not safe from being traded and put on elite, mestizo, display. In the same conversation with Don Hernando about the murder of the great serpent, Field was informed about the campesino's habit of selling prehispanic artefacts to tourists and mestizos willing to pay – one of several things that scandalised Field's Monimboseño companion (1999, p. 196). The looting of tangible heritage in Central America is a longstanding practice (see Whisnant, 1995, pp. 273–312; Yates, 2015). Field's companion, Flavio Gamboa, flatly told the anthropologist that: "Our campesinos don't value our past, don't value this land anymore. They are just thinking about today, about their *guarito* [rum] […] That's what *mestizaje* did to this people" (Field, 1999, p. 197). Indigenous histories of landscapes, like intangible and tangible heritages, have been worked into the fabrics of the mestizo and utilised to suit their concerns.

Popogatepe as an exploitable resource has an enduring lineage among non-indigenous people. Barely a decade after the Spanish Invasion of Mankesa, a priest descended into the crater, convinced that the lava was molten gold that could be extracted (Viramonte and Incer-Barquero, 2008, p. 425). Centuries later, in 1927, German engineers proposed a project to tap into and extract the gases emitted from the volcano for industrial use (Incer-Barquero and Le Lous, 2016). Neither of these undertakings produced their desired results. As a political and touristic resource, however, the state has found the gold that the friar sought. In peak tourist season, visitors in their thousands arrive at a space held sacred, a space once reserved for the devout expression of spirituality and diplomacy. Tourism, and particularly cultural tourism, is not apolitical or without position and charge; narratives of Volcán Masaya as a cultural resource are charged with anti-indigenous sentiment.

The monstrous image of human sacrifice at Popogatepe has been parroted in the same breath as demonisation of the violent repressions of the US-supported dictator, Anastasio Somoza, known to cast political prisoners into the volcano (see Chicago Tribune, 1990). Nik Wallenda's tightrope crossing of the crater also saw the media adopting the language of sacrifice (Haring, 2020). Critics of the government used this same language for what they saw as a publicity stunt to attract tourism back to the country, newly scarred by civil strife. This was coupled with the accusations of Rosario Murillo, the vice president/wife of the controversial Ortega presidential couple, being a "witch" among her detractors (see Redacción El Heraldo, 2015). The creation and sustaining of *la cuna del folklore nacional* was never neutral,

130 *Paul Edward Montgomery Ramírez*

but an act of mestizaje to eliminate the indigenous, harvest the most desired pieces, re-branding them for nationalist, political, and touristic markets.

La Cuna

Cultural tourism is a tool for diplomacy, instilling pride in people, and finding pathways to economic development. After the 2018 uprising, tourism evaporated in Nicaragua and poverty sharply rose across the country, its GDP decreasing by 8.8% between 2017 and 2020 (World Bank Group, 2021a). Encouraging visitors to the country is seen as a step towards stabilisation and peace. But the heritage weaving of these narratives as being "Nicaraguan" does so to the detriment of indigenous people; in *la cuna del folklore nacional* it is the Chorotega. As Stocker wrote, "history denied Chorotega identity, law imposed it and delimited it within specific places, and social science decried its authenticity" (2013, p. 160). Indigenous peoples across Nicaragua continue to resist colonisation, fight for their rights to culture and land, and combat narratives of the "vanished native."

Whereas indigenous heritages and pasts find lionisation, indigenous people find demonisation. Anti-indigenous expressions still litter the Nicaraguan phrasebook: "the Indian came out" of one who has lost their temper, one who cannot act in a proper/civilised manner is "pure Indian," and one who is ignorant is called a local slang for "Indian"; *jincho* (García Bresó, 1992, p. 126). Monimboseños are still equated with monkeys or vermin as insults. Indigenous people in Central America live shorter, less healthy lives, with less access to wealth and education; only around 5% of indigenous people in Nicaragua complete secondary education (UNPFII, 2009, Ch. 5; 2017, p. 121).

Article 31.1 of the United Nations Declaration on the Rights of Indigenous Peoples (UNDRIP), which the Ortega government voted in agreement to, guarantees indigenous peoples the rights of control over their intellectual property and cultural elements. Earlier, in the 2001 case of the *Mayagna (Sumo) Awas Tingni Community v. Nicaragua*, the Inter-American Court ruled that

> the close ties of indigenous people with the land must be recognised and understood as the fundamental basis of their cultures [...] relations to the land are not merely a matter of possession and production but a material and spiritual element [...] to preserve their cultural legacy and transmit it to future generations.
>
> (UNPFII, 2021, p. 4).

Despite legal adoptions, application has been lacking. Ramírez Plata's great serpent story is a parable about following demagogues and the exploitation of the natural world (2015, pp. 74–83). This is a pointed comment about the controversial oceanic canal project forwarded by the Ortega presidency and a Hong Kong-based company, despite outcry on environmental, sovereignty,

Creating La Cuna del Folklore Nacional   131

and human rights grounds. The canal would have displaced some 80% of the indigenous Rama population and endangered the lifeways of neighbouring communities (Cupples and Glynn, 2018, pp. 44–48). Nicaraguan tourism and politics may claim to admire indigenous people, but action says otherwise. Indigenous people remain forced into the margins of a country itself in a marginalised position within the Global South. This state cannot endure so long as there are ears to hear and eyes to read indigenous stories from indigenous mouths and hands.

Nicaragua needs indigenous people and heritages. Santos Román Mercado Méndez, representative of the indigenous community of Monimbó, reminds us that while Masaya might be *la cuna del folklore nacional*, that folklore was born in Monimbó (in Falla Sánchez, 2013, p. 453). It is a message that must be kept in mind when considering cultural projects in Nicaragua and beyond. Indigenous people are foundational to the state of Nicaragua, without whom there would be no "Nicaraguan" masterpieces of intangible heritage, and narratives of resistance to colonial forces would be strikingly threadbare. As indigenous heritages continue to be woven into the tapestry of modern "Nicaragua," in both cultural expression and in legal frameworks, there is an opportunity to be found in undermining the colonial power of the mestizo, of the "Nicaraguan" (Cupples and Glynn, 2018, p. 11). It must be recognised that Nicaragua is a colonial entity to the indigenous people who call the land home. After five centuries of occupation and colonial violence, the indigenous people of Mankesa remain. While this cradle was crafted to carry a "Nicaraguan" offspring, its source is the water of Lenderí and the rocks and smoke of Popogatepe. As settler states continue to grapple with their inheritances, it will not be denied any longer that the future is indigenous. Our stories and faces will be known.

References

Adams, R. (1957). *Cultural Surveys of Panama, Nicaragua, Guatemala, El Salvador, Honduras*. Washington, DC: Pan American Union.

Asamblea Nacional de la República de Nicaragua (1989). *Ley que declara la ciudad de Masaya patrimonio cultural de la nación*. Available Online: http://legislacion. asamblea.gob.ni/normaweb.nsf/9e314815a08d4a6206257265005d21f9/21bef946f 8d71e41062570a100583311?OpenDocument [Accessed 16 March 2022].

Baranowski, S., Covert, L., Gordon, B., Jobs, R., Noack, C., Rosenbaum, A. and Scott, B. (2019). 'Discussion: Tourism and Diplomacy.' *Journal of Tourism History*, 11 (1), pp. 63–90.

Bennis, K.L. and Venzke, E. (2021). 'Report on Masaya (Nicaragua).' *Bulletin of the Global Volcanism Network*, 46 (6). Available Online: https://doi.org/10.5479/si.GVP. BGVN202106-344100 [Accessed 16 March 2022].

Borland, K. (2006). *Unmasking Class, Gender, and Sexuality in Nicaraguan Festival*. Tucson: University of Arizona Press.

Central American Data (2018). *Nicaragua: Tourists Staying Longer*. Available Online: https://en.centralamericadata.com/en/article/home/Nicaragua_Tourists_Staying_ Longer [Accessed 16 March 2022].

132   *Paul Edward Montgomery Ramírez*

Chavez, M.C. (2000). *Women and the State in Post-Sandinista Nicaragua*. Boulder, CO: Lynne Rienner Publishers.

Chicago Tribune (1990). 'Volcano Park Offers Rest to War-Tried Nicaraguans.' *The Baltimore Sun*. Available Online: https://www.baltimoresun.com/news/bs-xpm-1990-10-28-1990301037-story.html. [Accessed 10 February 2022].

CIA (2021). *CIA World Factbook*. Washington, DC: United States Government Publishing Office.

Corntassel, J. (2009). 'Indigenous Storytelling, Truth-telling, and Community Approaches to Reconciliation.' *ESC: English Studies in Canada*, 35(1), pp.137–159.

Cuadra, P.A. (1981). *El nicaragüense*. Managua: Ediciones El Pez y El Serpiente.

Cupples, J. and Glynn, K. (2018). *Shifting Nicaraguan Mediascapes: Authoritarianism & the Struggle for Social Justice*. Cham, Switzerland: Springer.

de Bréadún, D. (2006). 'Volcano Rumbles in Laid-Back Land with History of Revolutionary Eruptions.' *The Irish Times*, 20 February. Available Online: https://www.irishtimes.com/news/volcano-rumbles-in-laid-back-land-with-history-of-revolutionary-eruptions-1.1017872 [Accessed 16 March 2022].

de Peralta, M. (1893). *Etnología centro-americana: Catálogo razonado de los objectos arqueológicos de la República de Costa Rica*. Madrid: Hijos de M. Gines Hernández.

Falla Sánchez, R. (2013). 'Testimonios: Pueblos originarios en la centroamérica contemporánea.' *Anuario de Estudios Centroamericanos*, 39, pp. 413–458.

Field, L. (1998). 'Post-Sandinista Ethnic Identities in Western Nicaragua.' *American Anthropologist*, 100 (2), pp. 431–443.

Field, L. (1999). *The Grimace of Macho Ratón*. Durham, NC: Duke University Press.

Francis, H. (2012). '*¡Que se rinda tu madre!* Leonel Rugama and Nicaragua's Changing Politics of Memory.' *Journal of Latin American Cultural Studies*, 21 (2), pp. 235–252.

García Bresó, J. (1992). *Identidad y cultura en Nicaragua: estudio antropológico de Monimbó*. Cuenca: Ediciones de la Universidad de Castilla-La Mancha

Ginés de Sepúlveda, J. (1941) *Tratado sobre las Justas Causas de la Guerra contra los Indios*. Mexico DF: Fondo de Cultura Económica.

Haring, B. (2020). 'Volcano Live!' Sees Nik Wallenda Appease the Gods – And Anger Some Fans.' *Deadline*, 4 March. Available Online: https://deadline.com/2020/03/volcano-live-nik-wallenda-appeases-gods-angers-fans-1202874833/ [Accessed 16 March 2022].

Houston, J. (2007). 'Indigenous Autoethnography: Formulating Our Knowledge, Our Way.' *Australian Journal of Indigenous Education*, 36, pp. 45–50.

Incer-Barquero, J. and Le Lous, F. (2016). 'Mitos, leyendas y verdades del volcán Masaya.' *La Prensa*, 4 September.

Kovach, M. (2010). *Indigenous Methodologies: Characteristics, Conversations, and Contexts*. Toronto: University of Toronto Press.

Macrotrends LLC (2021). 'Nicaragua GDP 1960-2021.' Available Online: https://www.macrotrends.net/countries/NIC/nicaragua/gdp-gross-domestic-product [Accessed 16 March 2022].

Montgomery Ramírez, P.E. (2021). 'The Deer & The Donkey: Indigenous Ritual & Survivance in Nicaragua's *El Güegüense*.' *Latin American Research Review*, 56 (4), pp. 919–933.

Muñoz, M. (2019). 'River as Lifeblood, River as Border: The Irreconcilable Discrepancies of Colonial Occupation from/with/on/of the Frontera.' In L. Tuhiwai Smith, E. Tuck, and K.W. Yang (eds.), *Indigenous and Decolonizing Studies in Education*. Abingdon: Routledge, pp. 62–81.

Creating La Cuna del Folklore Nacional   133

Newson, L. (1987). *Indian Survival in Colonial Nicaragua*. Norman, OK: University of Oklahoma Press.

Palma, M. (1987). *Senderos miticos de Nicaragua*. Bogotá: Editorial Nueva América

Prensa-Asamblea Nacional (2012). *Indios flecheros de Matagalpa, declarados Héroes Nacionales de la Batalla de San Jancinto*. Available Online: https://noticias. asamblea.gob.ni/asamblea-nacional-declara-heroes-de-la-batalla-de-san-jacinto-a-los-indios-flecheros-de-matagalpa/ [Accessed 16 March 2022].

Ramírez Plata, R. (2015). *Masaya: una mujer dos historias*. Miami, FL: Publicaciones Entre Líneas.

Redacción El Heraldo (2015). 'Pareja presidencial de Nicaragua figura en 'Brujos del poder.' *El Heraldo*, 29 April. Available Online: https://www.elheraldo.hn/mundo/pareja-presidencial-de-nicaragua-figura-en-brujos-del-poder-GGEH835553 [Accessed 16 March 2022].

Socha, D., Reinhard, J., and Chávez Perea, R. (2020). 'Inca Human Sacrifices on Misti Volcano (Peru)' *Latin American Antiquity*, 32 (1), pp. 138–153.

Stocker, K. (2013). 'Locating Identity: The Role of Place in Costa Rican Chorotega Identity.' In M. Forte (ed.), *Who Is an Indian? Race, Place, and the Politics of Indigeneity in the Americas*. Toronto: University of Toronto Press, pp. 151–171.

UN Permanent Forum on Indigenous Issues (UNPFII) (2009). *State of the World's Indigenous Peoples*. New York: United Nations.

UN Permanent Forum on Indigenous Issues (UNPFII) (2017). *State of the World's Indigenous Peoples, Vol 3, Education*. New York: United Nations

UN Permanent Forum on Indigenous Issues (UNPFII) (2021). *State of the World's Indigenous Peoples, Vol 5, Rights to Lands, Territories and Resources*. New York: United Nations.

Viramonte, J.G. and Incer-Barquero, J. (2008). 'Masaya, the "Mouth of Hell," Nicaragua: Volcanological Interpretation of the Myths, Legends and Anecdotes.' *Journal of Volcanology and Geothermal Research*, 176, pp. 419–426.

Vizenor, G. (1999). *Manifest Manners: Narratives on Postindian Survivance*. Lincoln: University of Nebraska Press.

Whisnant, D.E. (1995). *All that is Native and Fine: The Politics of Culture in an American Region*. Chapel Hill: UNC Press Books.

Wilson, S. (2015). *Research Is Ceremony: Indigenous Research Methods*. Halifax, NS: Fernwood.

World Bank Group (2021a). 'The World Bank in Nicaragua.' Available Online: https://www.worldbank.org/en/country/nicaragua/overview#1 [Accessed 16 March 2022].

World Bank Group (2021b). 'International Tourism, Number of Arrivals – Nicaragua.' Available Online: https://data.worldbank.org/indicator/ST.INT.ARVL?end=2019& locations=NI&name_desc=false&start=1995&view=chart [Accessed 16 March 2022].

World Data (2021). 'Tourism in Nicaragua.' Available Online: https://www.worlddata. info/america/nicaragua/tourism.php [Accessed 16 March 2022].

Yates, D. (2015). 'Illicit Cultural Property from Latin America: Looting, Trafficking, and Sale.' *Countering Illicit Traffic in Cultural Goods: The Global Challenge of Protecting the World's Heritage*. Paris: International Council of Museums, pp. 33–45.

Zeléldon Cartín, E. (2012). *Leyendas ticas*. San Jose, Costa Rica: Editorial Costa Rica.

9 Wildness Makes This World

Matthew Cowan

As an artist who is engaged with folklore and its performance rituals, especially "Wildman" characters as they appear in traditional folk rituals across Europe, I am particularly interested in the connections between wildness, folklore, and the marking of place. This led to a recent artistic survey of wildness and its connotations in Seinäjoki, Finland in the exhibition *Wildness Makes This World*, at Kunsthalle Seinäjoki, which took place from 9 December 2020 to 6 March 2021.

My pathway as an artist has usually been to seek out folklore and traditional customs and their practitioners, and through these encounters and exchanges reflect and present them in artistic documents, as a way of understanding and re-considering how folklore impacts our lives. My approach is as both an insider and an outsider – as on one hand I have a background as a folk dancer performing English Morris dances and Mummers plays, but on the other hand, I am operating as a contemporary artist in the world of contemporary art, a milieu that comes with its own set of rituals, frameworks, and contextualisation.

Artistically, I seek those things where I might encounter spectacle and wonder as a folk performer myself, often through the act of putting on a mask or a costume and performing. But it is also about the opportunity to understand how folklore is connected to tradition and its strong thread of connection to the local. These things – the transformations that costumes and masks offer, the kinds of meanings that are produced by this sense of tradition and the logic of place – are continually at play in my art practice.

Digging deeper, I find it is always the process of the disruption of order and the folkloric chaos of costumed performances that interests me. I think primarily of "wildman" traditions such as Strawbears (*Strohbären*) and Maymen (*Maimänner*) in Germany, the Burryman and the Jack in the Green in the UK, and many more folk devils and wild beasts and their annual appearances in carnivals and calendar rituals throughout Europe. These customs often involve a central character – a wildman bringing a sense of focus, danger, chaos, and joyous unpredictability to a community event (Forth, 2007). Such folk rituals create a moment of spectacle that unfolds as chaotic and wild in marking meaning in place between audiences and participants. They disrupt the everyday through their performance in a way that Terry

DOI: 10.4324/9781003374138-12

Eagleton links to a process of carnavalesque deconstruction, where chaos and disorder indicate a state of being, a wildness that defies meaning (Eagleton, 2019, p. 27). This combination of elements – of a performative folk tradition involving costumes, an audience, and a spectacle is one sense of invoking the wildness that I am interested in; however, I also seek to explore other understandings of wildness, that can take place in the everyday.

A traditional characteristic of wildness was evident in customs such as the Strawbear and the Mayman, which were the protagonists of a previous exhibition of mine, *The Scream of the Strawbear*, presented at Kunsthalle Giessen in 2019. Both the Mayman and the Strawbear are wildmen at the centre of village-level community celebrations in Hesse, and after the exhibition was completed I reflected on the essential wildness of these traditions. What was this chaos that they performed and enacted? What did people gain from the experience of observing the spectacle year after year, of participating in the tradition as both performers and audience, and remembering it from years gone by? I began to understand that this kind of wild disruption is an essential community focus.

My interest in this folkloric wildness, then, comes from accessing the communal instinct for chaos and spectacle. I became interested to test this definition against others' ideas of what it could mean. I wanted to understand people's experience of wildness in other senses – including the experience of nature, but also reaching into more psychological and communal experiences.

The invitation to make an exhibition project with Kunsthalle Seinäjoki provided the perfect opportunity. In this Finnish context I was interested in the kinds of wildness that could be translated as "*raivoisuus*," which evokes the wildness and unpredictability you might find in a wild animal, as well as "*jylhyys*," which is evokes more of the grandeur of the natural environment. Discussing these translations with a group of people living close to Seinäjoki, whilst exploring landscapes, buildings, and environments both in and around the wider region of South Ostrobothnia, became an important part of the process of making the exhibition.

As an artistic researcher, there is always the question of how the process of working artistically is attempting to *make-sense-of*. In this project, I saw that there was a chance to bring many different perspectives and experiences together as a way of reflecting. The result was an artistic survey, making sense of wildness through the experience of many. Personal folkloric memories, stories, and experiences of place were shared and presented alongside an understanding of the wildness connected to them, and the role that wildness has played in having an impact on memory and understanding.

Standard definitions of wildness often separate the idea from the realm of nature itself, thereby defining it as a process, a quality, or a mode. It can then usually be thought of in one of two ways. Firstly, that wildness is *another*, something that represents a threshold, and secondly, that wildness is a tonic, or a state of being or place that people are drawn to, that might provide insight (Cookson, 2011, p. 188). Both of these ideas or approaches, however, rely on accepting that wildness is something that is beyond being totally

136   Matthew Cowan

understood, described, or made tangible, and this might explain why it is that wildness is both an attractive and a dangerous state to seek out.

In Francis Alÿs' video *The Nightwatch* (2004), in which he releases a fox into the National Portrait Gallery in London to roam the galleries, and Mark Wallinger's *Sleeper* (also 2004), in which he himself nocturnally roams the Neue Nationalgalerie in Berlin in a bear costume, animal wildness acts, amongst other things, as a symbolic disruptor of convention and a metaphor for art's fascination with animal chaos and imagery. Works like these give an idea of the connotations that artworks might draw from wildness and its symbolic power as a connection to other possibilities for inhabiting familiar worlds.

William Cronon suggests that wildness "can be found anywhere" (Cronon, 1996, p. 24). Such a statement appeals to the sense that wildness is not simply related to nature, or the wild animals we might encounter in nature, but really belongs to a psychological state of being. It is like a mode that we slip into through experience of a situation or environment. Through observation and reflection of such experiences we can unlock this mode, and its qualities.

The artworks that were included in the final presentation of *Wildness Makes This World* sought to bring together these different ways of under-standing wildness and its psychological modes of being. As an artistic pres-entation, the exhibition had the chance to dwell on the intangibility of the experience of wildness from a multitude of perspectives and mark the knowl-edge of these experiences through connections to place, which was in the case of this exhibition Seinäjoki and the wider region of South Ostrobothnia. As the exhibition developed it became clear that the artistic potential for dealing in imagination was uniquely suited to presenting this work. It had the oppor-tunity to connect with the intangibility of the wildness at the heart of the show, whilst suggesting that memory and experience were the essential cur-rency of how we come to know wildness.

Usually, my collaborative practice is with experts or special practitioners of folklore and with historical museums. However, my process in approach-ing *Wildness Makes This World* was to open up this collaborative way of working to people from many backgrounds, including a small orchestra and the Seinäjoki Museums. This way of working was rewarding and interesting for me as I had to firstly re-understand my status as an outsider – as an artis-tic "expert" – in order to have conversations with participants. The questions I asked were not only specifically about the expert knowledge of others, but also about personal understandings, experiences, and skills.

The initial stage of the process was to work with a group of 12 people who lived in the city of Seinäjoki and the surrounding region, in order to mark places that defined wildness for them personally or communally. The product of these conversations between myself as an artist researcher and each partic-ipant was an artwork that was included in the final exhibition. These art-works connected people's experience of wildness with points of folklore and personal significance. The title of the exhibition project takes up William Cronon's suggestion that wildness is able to be found in many places, but also suggests that it has a productive effect on us. The exhibition surveyed the possibility that wildness could be a mode of being that we experience at particular times and places, and that these experiences can produce deep personal meaning. It was a collective presentation that approached the concept of wildness as it relates to the folklore of everyday life, place, and memory and an attempt to articulate this as an exhibition.

Conversations with each participant unfolded in different ways over the course of the year preparing for the show. Some referred me immediately to specific places in the landscape, while others offered many options to define an understanding of wildness. Overall, options for producing work with most people did not finalise until close to the time of presenting the exhibition. As a visitor to Seinäjoki, I was aware of my status as an outsider as I learned about the places that were important to people. Meetings with participants were social and conversational as we talked about the project. Although this working process touched on ethnographic practice with questions and field notes, it was primarily a process that was always openly moving towards the production of artistic works. Sometimes there were stories from childhood, and sometimes there were discussions about what feelings or emotions were stimulated in certain places. Over time we came to an agreement about a place that represented wildness for each participant and then we worked on a process of documenting, and sometimes performing in, these places with images and video.

People were incredibly generous with their time and their reflections. Everyone considered the wildness of place and the phenomena that best evoked a definition of wildness for them. What emerged through the discussions and collaborations were universal commonalities: childhood nostalgia, family memories, sites where adrenaline is experienced, and a sense of connection to points in the landscape were all strong factors in understanding wildness.

The artworks that were finally presented in the exhibition visually connected wildness with points of folklore and personal significance. Works were identifiable in the exhibition notes through referring to each participant by their first name, the place and in some cases a further explanation.

Mauri brought me to a large glacial rock on his land. Local mythology declares that on midsummer evenings it splits in half and the devil emerges from within. He told me about the seasons he has spent with the rock since he was a child, and I climbed up his handmade wooden ladder to inspect the rock itself and the view from the top. We made a video of him singing a folk song next to a campfire he lit under the rock and the wooden ladder was later integrated into the exhibition presentation (see Figure 9.1).

Sanna led me through a forest to a cave where she revealed that she had located the site of a seventeenth-century hiding place for persecuted witches. It had taken her a long time to research and pinpoint from various historical sources, but she now leads participants in communal drumming workshops there. We made a video where she animated the space, also lighting a fire, burning incense, and playing drums.

Figure 9.1 The Stone on Mauri's Land that Splits at Midsummer to Release the Devil. (Photograph by Mika RintaPorkkunen).

Juha raced his motorbike around a motocross track that sat next to a sand quarry, adjoining his family farm. He pointed out many spots that he had spent time at as a teenager, all connected to times in the past where motorbike racing was an escape and a pastime. In many places, there were various pieces of junk, old car parts, and trash that had at some point been dumped in the landscape, all of which were slowly being overcome by nature. It had long been a place of freedom for him as a teenager. Alongside groups of friends they raced each other and worked on their motorbikes. For the exhibition, we made a video of Juha "flying" over some of the jumps and borrowed one of his motocross bikes as part of the installation.

Kirsi collaborated with her horse Nella in making a feathered costume. This costume, constructed from a long red banner of chicken feathers, was wrapped around the horse's belly and we made portraits of him in the forest. Later we strung the long line of feathers between two trees at Läntineva, near Ylistaro, a peat swamp near to where Kirsi had previously lived. The swamp had been a site rich in bird life and Kirsi had ridden there often. Since it has been drained and the forest cut in order to be used by a power company, most of the birdlife is now absent. The act of hanging the feathered red ribbon marked her experience of the loss of this environment and the birds that had lived there.

Mannar and Tuomas took me to the art centre in nearby Lapua. The centre contains a theatre, library, museum, and gallery space and is built on the

Wildness Makes This World 139

site of an old ammunition factory. Their family stories about visiting the centre and the history of how it had transformed the site gave rise to a family portrait, taken in the museum, using costumes, and an old painted photographic studio backdrop.

On Miri's farm were many small ponds on which she set sail tiny birchbark boats, constructions that she had learned to make as a child. We discussed her childhood memories and made a video as she set the boats afloat, while she was wearing a mask, also fashioned from birchbark. In the video Miri does not speak, but is re-performing the playfulness of childhood in the forest, a nostalgia for chance and possibility.

Laure guided me to Lauttajärvi, near Ilmajoki, the site of a lake that was unsuccessfully drained some decades ago. This partial drainage has resulted in a landscape that remains an open space with a surface that ripples and undulates when you walk on it. Laure's nostalgia for motorbike riding and walking through this scenery from his childhood was re-performed by jumping from a ladder into the ground with rubber boots on, and watching the ripples dissipate through the surface grasses and reeds.

A bird-watching tower on the outskirts of Seinäjoki was a site for Maryna. An immigrant to Seinäjoki, over years the tower had become a meditative site for her to return to again and again. The strong impressions of nature and solitude were important to Maryna and our collaboration focused on the tower as a site of reflection for her. We literally represented this contemplative process with an image of Maryna holding a mirror in the landscape, framing the tower itself.

There were many more special places and conversations had over the course of the project. Each participant carefully and graciously uncovered points and places of wildness through conversations and discussions as we worked towards the exhibition. As already noted, universal commonalities emerged through the discussions and collaborations, with regular themes returning in participant's responses, including childhood nostalgia, family memories, sites where adrenaline is experienced, and a sense of connection to certain features in the landscape.

The second part of the project was a collaboration with the Seinäjoki Museums. In the same way that I had asked the individual participants in the project to consider what a psychological approach to wildness might mean to them, I asked the museum to consider their own collection from this curatorial perspective. From this starting point we discussed a range of items that might be possible to include in the exhibition. These included archive images as well as artefacts relating to natural history, agricultural history, and local landmarks. In the end we included a number of stuffed animals, handmade tools, and other implements relating to farming and fire fighting.

Thirdly, the collaboration involved the Laitakaupungin Orkesteri (LKO), a group of professional musicians based in Seinäjoki. I had asked them to consider wildness from their perspective as professional musicians. Together with some field recordings of my own, each member of the LKO contributed new tracks to the resultant soundscape. We worked on producing an LP over the

140 *Matthew Cowan*

course of the year, and the final recording included the traditional Finnish instrument kantele and vocals that imitated traditional Finnish cow calls. This recording was the soundscape present in the exhibition, as well as being an LP published on the Sibelius Academy Folk Label.

The fourth element of the exhibition came directly from my own artistic response to working with this material from participants, the Museum, and the LKO. I included new "wildman" costume works as the idea of performing, or inhabiting, wildness is – from my artistic perspective – one way of making sense of it. I took up many of the motifs present in the rest of the show – acts of making fire, drumming, and walking all had their own wildman costumes. The installation and exhibition room itself could be read as a theatrical stage, including a soundscape. In this way the artistic material became animated and the sounds in the exhibition room provided a sense of movement and motion to the static presentation of artefacts and artwork. There was an interesting tension between the drama of these sounds and new costume works, its potential for fiction and the real places, spaces, experiences, objects, and historical artefacts that were presented in the show. In my own interpretation, this filled in the intangible quality that wildness has, a quality linked with experience, but also with dreams.

Visitors entered the exhibition hall and encountered the installation and sculptures all around them (see Figure 9.2). At certain points the soundscape rose and fell as they moved around the space. There was a lot of material present in the exhibition, collected from all of the participants, and although the exhibition guide provided a sense of order in what was present, there were many ways to experience the installation. The wildman figures could be seen as gatekeepers to the installation, but as you re-experienced them or passed them on your way out of the show, you might also notice that they are responses to other material in the exhibition. There was no chronology or hierarchy of value to the objects, images, and videos that were presented; rather, they were arranged through aesthetic and visual logics. In some parts of the exhibition the lighting was particularly strong, giving shadows and depth to the works and objects and emphasising performative and theatrical narratives.

In the past, my collaborative practice has been with experts and special practitioners of folklore and with historical museums. However, in this project I opened up this way of working to a collaborative and participatory practice, with people from many backgrounds, including the Laitakaupungin Orkesteri orchestra and the Seinäjoki Museums. With this way of collaborating, exploring, and understanding the place in which I was working, the Kunsthalle itself also became a key partner in mediating translation and practical support for the project. Their role was crucial as they introduced me as an artist and utilised their networks in order to invite people from their region to participate. Also essential was their support with the added pressure of the pandemic year in 2020. They helped to manage photographers and videographers to work with me from a distance, as it was not possible for me to travel from Berlin until it was time for the final installation.

Figure 9.2 Wildness Makes This World, Exhibition View, 2021.
(Photograph by Jenni Latva).

Wildness Makes This World also influenced the Kunsthalle itself to reflect on its own wildness of place. In the catalogue, director Sanna Karimäki-Nuutinen considered the site of the exhibition, the institution itself, in terms of its own wildness and its place as a site of power (Cowan et al., 2020). Quoting the Finnish Nigerian writer Minna Salami's book *Sensuous Knowledge* (2021), she placed the institution in a framework of power that branches out from a core, a central wild point from which influence can spring. This balancing point between nature and culture is where the opportunity to influence and provide agency emerges. It places people at the centre of the institution and reflects the idea that people *are* the wildness.

As Sanna also points out, the exhibition presented a selection of places that dealt with continuity – places that were far off in time or isolated, and yet were always there. This is a mode of wildness that can be accessed again and again like a wellspring. It is clear that many participants in the exhibition returned to strong memories related to place and experiences from their past, even from childhood, that for them related to wildness. On reflection this should not have been a surprising discovery. I had thought that the experience of wildness would be something that brings a sense of the here and now for people, that experiencing wildness would connect people to place, and connect them to themselves. This was certainly the case, but it also has had the effect of becoming deeply rooted in memories of these experiences.

This quality of nostalgia for wildness is something that I think is at the heart of the reasons for the recurring annual calendar of folk traditions that sparked my questioning of wildness in the first place. Having the chance to

142 Matthew Cowan

invoke, repeat, and replay the experience on a regular, annual, community-based cycle not only reinforces connections to place and community but also reinforces the fact that wildness is a necessary and fruitful element of such rituals and celebrations. The exhibition suggests that even on a personal level wildness is an essential element of rejuvenation. It seems that the urge to discover and experience aspects of wildness is almost innate for humans.

Nearly everyone would have found material in this exhibition that would resonate with them as an understanding of what wildness could be. My role as an artist has been to present the material as an exhibition – placing objects, artefacts images, and other elements together to experience them as a set of examined, considered, and remembered materials. It was important to be able to give the opportunity to audiences to understand all of these sensory points of view aesthetically, in the same room at the same time.

Despite the intangibility of the wildness at the heart of the exhibition, *Wildness Makes This World* did not attempt to define wildness; rather, it suggested that knowing wildness when you experience it is part of human experiences such as childhood nostalgia, family memories, and sites where adrenaline is provoked. The folklore that develops alongside these experiences of wildness has deeply personal links to place and community and helps to reinforce the experience of wildness as a state of being.

References

Alÿs, F. (2004). *The Nightwatch*. Single channel colour video. 6:17mins. London: In collaboration with Rafael Ortega and Artangel.

Cookson, L.J. (2011). 'A Definition for Wildness.' *Ecopsychology*, 3 (3), pp. 187–193.

Cowan, M., Elfving, T., Karimäki-Nuutinen, S. and Teitti, E. (2020). *Wildness Makes This World*. Seinäjoki: Kunsthalle Seinäjoki.

Cronon, W. (1996). *Uncommon Ground: Rethinking the Human Place in Nature*. New York: W.W. Norton & Co.

Eagleton, T. (2019). *Humour*. New Haven: Yale University Press.

Forth, G. (2007). 'Images of the Wildman Inside and Outside Europe.' *Folklore*, 118 (3), pp. 261–281.

Wallinger, M. (2004). *Sleeper*. Single channel colour video. 154mins. Berlin: DAAD.

10 Tasting the Intangible

Examples of Communication from Sápmi

Kajsa G. Åberg and Doris A. Carson

Tourism in the North: A Role for Heritage

Food holds a symbolic status but is also a tangible way to communicate local values and ways of life linked to geographical factors (Bessiere and Tibere, 2013). In local food traditions, culture and nature are united in inseparable ways: available crops and game, methods for hunting, foraging and harvesting, traditions regarding preparation of meals and preservation are all formed based on local circumstances that also reflect a society's relations to, and influences from, other communities. This chapter focuses on Västerbotten, a region in northern Sweden where the role of food as a bearer of heritage, lifestyle, and nature's impact on human livelihood is well illustrated. In particular, the long, dark winters and nomadic lifestyle of the indigenous Sámi population, dependent on reindeer herding, have called for special techniques to harvest and preserve food. Those techniques are based on the relations between people and the spirit of life found in nature. The Sámi approach to food has been formulated as one to *use without consuming* and to *use all parts of what has been foraged* – animals as well as vegetation. In essence, never leave less than you found (Harnesk, 2020).

In peripheral, sparsely populated parts of the North, tourism is by now an established strategy to counteract the process of declining services and employment (Hall and Jenkins, 1998; Lundmark, 2006). It is a strategy that often creates seasonal activities concentrated in and around a handful of remote resorts and urban hubs, but also has the potential to address more general issues related to the attractiveness of places (Byström and Müller, 2014). As many products in tourism are available to permanent residents as well, the strategic work aiming at enhancing tourism consumption is part of a broader aim to attract both residents and investors, an aspect found in the national as well as regional strategies for development (Regeringskansliet, 2021; Region Västerbotten, 2021).

A major challenge for tourism in regions like northern Sweden is linked to their remoteness from markets and their need to develop unique and attractive pull-factors to overcome distance (Prideaux, 2002). The more unique and place-based an asset is, the more likely it is to catch attention, and indigenous culture and heritage have been used in many northern destinations as

DOI: 10.4324/9781003374138-13

one such asset for destination marketing (Viken and Müller, 2017). However, commercialisation of natural and cultural assets needs to avoid "disneyfication," where the original asset is so much adapted to a perceived demand that it loses its initial worth and uniqueness (Cohen, 1993; Cooper et al., 2019). This is especially crucial in the context of indigenous populations whose heritage may be entangled in historical and present conflicts and who have experienced highly questionable treatment. On the other hand, there are potential positive economic effects, interconnected with social, psychological, and political impacts (Cooper and Hall, 2007). Communicating and developing products based on cultural aspects can have beneficial effects on local community building, knowledge sharing, and pride among indigenous stakeholders and communities (Smith, 2003; Leu, 2018).

Tourism offers a vehicle to turn elusive cultural values and immaterial aspects into commercial products and facilitate the consumption of culture and heritage, with food being a good example (Hjalager and Richards, 2003; Pettersson et al., 2005). The global organisation World Foodtravel Association, which offers programs for developing food as an attraction to increase sales and strengthen local produce, states that food tourism is "the act of travelling for a taste of place in order to get a sense of place" (World Foodtravel Association, 2022). What, where and how to eat is, according to trend reports published by Visit Sweden, increasingly important to consumers beyond those labelled as "foodies," that is individuals with special interest in food and meals (Visit Sweden, 2020; UR, 2021). The act of eating while travelling for leisure is turning from a necessary or coincidental activity into a motivational driver.

Developing local tourism and food products under local control has often been a challenge in remote and sparsely populated areas (Koster and Carson, 2019). Many places in northern Sweden have historically evolved around the activities and investments of external actors. Mining, hydroelectricity, and forestry are prime sectors that have extensively changed the landscape and livelihoods in the region over the past centuries. They have enabled overcoming logistical challenges and paved the way for tourism development, in some areas leading to the co-existence of these sectors (Byström, 2019), but a certain dependence on external investors and entrepreneurs has often remained, even in tourism. Yet, the view in tourism development on the landscape as an attractive pull factor and a resource for small-scale local development is a reversal from its previous role as a bulk resource export commodity to be extracted and sent away. Sometimes hidden within this changing discourse from extractive to attractive industries are the views and development priorities of the traditional indigenous inhabitants, the Sámi, who found their way to Västerbotten long before the industrialised establishments of the 1800s.

This chapter is an exploration of how Sámi heritage may fit into the general reasoning around place-based assets in the tourism context, with food as a selected case. Sámi culture may be seen as one of the unique features of the region, distinguishing it as an "exotic remote" destination (Koster and Carson, 2019), encouraging visitors to travel far in a spatial as well as socio-cultural sense. However, the cases chosen for this chapter are not necessarily physically distant from their audience or consumers. The cultural centre Tráhppie is located in the city of Umeå, and the organisation Slow Food Sápmi is a virtual network with representation at the Svenska Samernas Riksförbund (National Association of the Sámi People in Sweden, SSR) office in Umeå, both targeting their activities to residents of the city and the wider region, as well as more distant visitors. This somewhat reflects the broader visitor economy in Västerbotten, which is dominated in numbers by intra-regional and domestic visitors, unlike in other Arctic regions that rely more heavily on international markets (Region Västerbotten Turism, 2021). Apart from a few popular tourist hotspots in the inland mountain region, much of the county's tourism and hospitality industry is concentrated in the cities along the coast, together with around two thirds of the county's population, and increasing temporary visitor populations such as students (Carson, Prideaux and Åberg, 2020). The term "tourism" is therefore used in this chapter more to label the activity than the audience, as not all visitors or consumers discussed are spending time away from their home region. Still, Sámi heritage and specific Sámi tourism products have so far mostly been associated with the more peripheral inland and mountain areas, even though many Sámi today live in the cities (Hudson et al., 2019). As such, making traditional heritage and cultural products accessible in the cities offers opportunities for new locally-controlled development, with local Sámi actors and organisations establishing bridges between traditional and contemporary lifestyles and mobilities, as well as dispersed producer networks, whilst taking advantage of growing urban markets.

Commercialising Culture and Life

As soon as something is presented as a product it evolves from its original state into something different. The crucial question is: how much is adapted, and who is in control of the change? This relates to a discussion of authenticity, control and power found in research regarding indigenous tourism in general, and Sámi tourism in particular (see Hinch and Butler, 1996; Leu, 2018; De Bernardi, 2020). In such reasoning on how products are performed, both time and place are underlined as crucial aspects for consideration. The temporal side relates to how traditions may be both old and a vivid part of the present (de la Barre and Brouder, 2013). De Bernardi (2020) and Jamal and Hill (2004) suggest labelling this a "living heritage" – one that aims to integrate both past and present, and acknowledges the interaction in the context of tourism and the communication surrounding it. This suggests a need to keep the heritage evolving whilst maintaining its authenticity, in what Verran (2002) calls post-colonial moments. The spatial aspect is crucial not only due to the place-based nature of defined cultures, but also because there are ecological considerations that need to be made (Ironside and Massie, 2020). In the case of Sámi themed products, this may be illustrated by how certain plants may no longer be plentiful due to climate change, and some

146   *Kajsa G. Åberg and Doris A. Carson*

even need to be avoided in spite of their prominent role in traditional Sámi cooking. In line with Kramvig and Førde (2020), this chapter considers interactive products and situations as tools to share and enhance knowledge and understanding in a way that creates possibilities for discussion and interaction, rather than by exotifying and distancing the performance from the audience or consumer. Whether or not tourism offers such a tool for gaining control and counteracting expropriation, as well as for facilitating a diversified economy, has been debated (see Whitford and Ruhanen, 2016; Viken and Müller, 2017). There is no single answer to this, but findings from the literature suggest that beside the economic aspects, the sociocultural function of tourism as a channel for knowledge and the creation of understanding about past and present aspects of Sámi culture and life is being acknowledged (Leu, 2018). As with all human interactions, generalisations need to be complemented by closer looks. In each specific situation, the entrepreneur, or guide, is the main mediator who steers the selection of what to include and how. Quinn and Ryan (2016) present an extensive list of aspects within this gatekeeper function. Among them are not only the selection of mode and content, but also how the consumers are choreographed through the story, led to preferred versions subject to the storyteller's own taste, agenda, and abilities.

Materialising the Intangible: Storytelling and Food

By stating a geographical origin, a food brand can be experienced as more interesting and attractive (Sadovska et al., 2019; Kreuzpointner and Bathurst, 2021). The story created by connecting a product to a place can be laden with further details to enhance the preferred message. Mossberg and Johansen (2006) present examples of how hotels and restaurants can formulate stories about localities and individuals and communicate them through marketing, but also physically through interior design, menus, and other aspects of the visitors' experience. Less tangible aspects can also be formulated and expressed, as in the case of cultural heritage or in storytelling that embraces the complexity of a whole destination. This is illustrated by the growing interest in visiting Sweden based on aspects related to food. Among the key factors is the appreciation of the Swedish natural environment as being clean, thus resulting in healthy produce in a country known for its modern industries. Swedish food is, according to this notion, based on traditional techniques used with a modern twist (Visit Sweden, 2020).

Storytelling techniques and performances entail communication beyond what is expressed in words. It awakens senses in the audience and the more senses that are triggered, the more engaged the audience will be. Food is thus well suited as a tool to enhance the experience of a storytelling situation, as it offers potential to engage several senses simultaneously. Likewise, a meal can be upgraded to a "meal experience" by adding elements of storytelling. In Sápmi, the oral tradition is ancient in contrast to the written form which developed quite late. This has created a lack of documented recipes. The initiative of Slow Food Sápmi described below is therefore one way to formulate communal stories and aid actors in developing their own communication, but also, and not least, it is a vital contribution to the preservation of traditional knowledge.

Storytelling and oral traditions have been explored in Swedish folklore research mainly within the field of ethnology (Arvidsson, 1999). Sámi studies are today found in research centres where several expressions of lifestyle and historic contexts can be merged to create a holistic understanding of how nature, culture, and spirits are, and have been, interacting. Those cross disciplinary centres address the whole living area of the indigenous Sámi people, Sápmi, which covers parts of Norway, Sweden, Finland, and Russia and transcends several national borders. As other indigenous groups, the Sámi people have lived in the same area prior to, through, and after colonisation and the establishment of national borders. The indigenous aspect is expressed by the group having a language, customs, and culture that differs from the surrounding population, which is regarded as the majority society, i.e. Swedish national society (Samiskt informationscentrum, n.d.).

The subsuming of Sápmi under the national states has caused much disruption of the Sámi lifestyle, resulting in suppression and discriminating treatment. In the Swedish part of Sápmi, there are five varieties of Sámi language, with a geographical pattern of units that stretches in the east-west directions. The Sámi population in Sweden has maintained a large share of reindeer husbandry alongside a nomadic lifestyle based on the seasonal migration of reindeer between grazing areas (Samiskt informationscentrum, n.d.). By the late seventeenth century, the rights of free movement and expression of faith and culture had been extensively reduced by the Swedish king and national state, and it was not until the 1960s that the Sámi language was allowed and reintroduced in school (Samiskt informationscentrum, n.d.). In the act on National Minorities and National Minority Languages in 2010, the right to learn, use, and develop both the language and culture is protected. This underlines the crucial aspect of strengthening knowledge-based initiatives related to communicating commercial products based on Sámi traditions and current lifestyles.

The Case of Tráhppie

Tráhppie is a Sámi cultural centre located in the city of Umeå, next to the regional museum of Västerbotten county. The cultural centre is run by Såhkie, Umeå Sámi Association, a member organisation open to all who share the values of the association. Såhkie is a virtual hub for information on Sámi events and culture, while Tráhppie serves as a place for information and interaction. The building contains a large room entailing a café, bookshelves with Sámi literature, and showcases displaying craft and produce for sale, as well as temporary exhibitions relating to Sámi handicraft and life.

Såhkie arranges diverse events with Sámi themes, all striving to establish Tráhppie as a meeting place. Sámi creators may perform readings from books, arrangements based on the music tradition joik, as well as seminars

148   *Kajsa G. Åberg and Doris A. Carson*

hosted by Várdduo, the centre for Sámi Research at Umeå University. A recurring arrangement is the weeklong event Ubmejen Biejvieh, the Sámi week when several actors arrange events around Umeå that relate to the fact that Umeå is, and has long been, an important place in Sápmi. Other recurring arrangements at Tráhppie are the get-togethers for Sámi seniors organised in cooperation with the municipality, offering an opportunity for older Sámi people to meet and talk about their shared history and life in their Sámi language.

The communication of folklore is performed in several ways by Tráhppie, the most obvious being public events where information is shared by oral presentations. The interior design is chosen based on the national colours of Sápmi, and as far as possible by Sámi creators and materials found in the region. The culture is, thus, visible and tangible, and Tráhppie can be said to actualise the concept of an experience-room where a chosen story or message is performed by all objects (Mossberg and Johansen, 2006). Among the products showcased and sold in Tráhppie are food produce from Sámi producers from all parts of Sápmi, or at least based on ingredients found in traditional Sámi cooking, such as fish and wild berries. The function of food and meals as communicators of folklore and lifestyle is also found in the small café. Besides offering meals with clear connections in name and recipes, there are also products common in Swedish cafés but made with elements of Sámi produce, such as reindeer meat on the bread gáhkku, which would elsewhere be a toast with ham from pork. Likewise, the menu is based on Sámi eating habits, which in turn mirror access to fresh and conserved food, based on the time of the year. This opens up a dialogue between the guests and staff in a mutually relaxed situation, and connects them to seasonal cycles through food.

According to Tráhppie's business manager, the current kitchen only allows for simple cooking, preventing operations from expanding, despite frequent inquiries for larger dinners and catered events. The Department of Food, Nutrition and Culinary Sciences at Umeå University arranged a series of seminars in November 2021 focusing on Arctic and Sámi food and nutrition together with the University's Sámi and Arctic centres. Further development of this collaboration is desired, such as letting students produce full meals at Tráhppie as part of their education in cooking and meal design. Overall, the potential held by students in Umeå as a substantial market (currently around 35,000) has been noted by the manager, as many of them experience Umeå from a visitor's perspective and look for place-based experience products. According to the manager, the refurbishing of the kitchen was a key priority which would allow for further development of Tráhppie as a place for initiating, performing, and communicating Sámi lifestyle, history, folklore, and traditions. A vision shared by Såhkie is to be able to strengthen the economic part of the operations enough to allow for generous opening hours, which could attract a broader group of visitors. The manager shared the vision of Tráhppie being the preferred place for the nearby university's students to spend their days studying while being in a place where Sápmi is experienced both physically and in more intangible ways.

This presents possibilities for further discussion and, thus, deepens the general understanding and insights gleaned about the Sámi worldview for visitors. Food would in this way be a tool, or medium, that enables stories to be told, as well as enhancing the experience of visitors through sensual triggers such as taste, smell, and texture. Tráhppie, as a cultural centre, would be a centralised hub that enables physical encounters with a diverse target group – local inhabitants as well as tourists and the in-betweens, e.g. university students – as well as being an ambassador, and distribution or marketing platform, for the many small and dispersed and remotely located producers and operators.

The Case of Slow Food in Sápmi

The slow food movement, organised within the global network Slow Food International, connects grassroots actors in more than 160 countries. It consists of local associations interested in more sustainable food production, stating its aim as being to "prevent the disappearance of local food cultures and traditions, counteract the rise of fast life and combat people's dwindling interest in the food they eat" (Slow Food International, digital). This resonates well with the work of the Sámi organisations that build on a holistic view of the conditions set by nature as an approach to life, as well as to businesses and expressions of culture. In 2009, a Sámi branch of Slow Food International was initiated, followed by a vision for Sámi food formulated on behalf of the Sámi parliament by Slow Food International, SSR, and Sámij åhpadusguovdásj (the Sámi centre for education) (Slow Food International, 2022). This was done to link the initiative to national strategic work focusing on food during 2010–2014, resulting in a document from the government in which Sámi food traditions were presented as being of culinary interest when profiling Sweden as a "new country of food" in Europe (Johansson, Norman and Norrman, 2010).

Slow Food Sápmi is also in close cooperation with the initiative Indigenous Terra Madre. The aim is to institutionalise the indigenous aspects of Terra Madre within the Slow Food Movement. Slow Food Sápmi started off the engagement by arranging and hosting the first conference for indigenous peoples in Jokkmokk in northern Sweden in 2011, followed by stating the organisation's work for indigenous peoples' rights to their land, waters, food culture, language, identity, and protection of their culinary traditions (Slow Food Sápmi, 2022a). Slow Food Sápmi includes areas in Sweden, Norway, Finland, and Russia, and works to strengthen Sámi food entrepreneurs through collaborations and activities. Many of the operations are financed through project funding and relate to developing and spreading knowledge, something that is especially needed as the written version of the Sámi languages is a quite recent development, meaning that much traditional knowledge is at risk of being lost with the individuals who bear it. A milestone in this was the book *Taste of Sápmi* (Harnesk, 2020), first released by Slow Food Sápmi in 2014. It presents basic facts about Sámi heritage, history, and

150 *Kajsa G. Åberg and Doris A. Carson*

traditions together with recipes and has received a number of international awards. One extraordinary part of the book is that its content was created through workshops and dialogue with individuals who are active within cooking and culinary research, but also senior people in the Sámi community who are bearers of intangible knowledge that has never been written down.

The idea behind Slow Food Sápmi is to augment products with details about heritage and origin, as well as the producers' background. In this way the producers become bearers of knowledge and ambassadors for Sápmi. This is a strategy in line with reports regarding trends and interests in food tourism presented in the Visit Sweden Trend report 2020 (Visit Sweden, 2020). However, as stories spread – and there is an increased interest in local produce and small-scale food entrepreneurs, as well as in the Arctic region as a destination – the original message and meanings risk being modified and even exploited. To counteract this, and to provide Sámi food entrepreneurs with guidance, Slow Food Sápmi published a comprehensive folder of material focusing on communication about food called *Communication as a Path Towards Business Goals: Food Communication that Changes Sápmi* (Slow Food Sápmi, 2022b). It was produced with the support of the Pawanka Fund, Indigenous Ways of Knowing and Learning, and directed to businesses working with Sámi food. The material contains four manuals with text, images, and videos that address different aspects of indigenous values and how to handle heritage in commercial communication. The manuals are focused on food but incorporate the aspects in ways that make this material relevant for entrepreneurs in many different areas. The material is free to access and available from the webpage of Slow Food Sápmi (https://www.slowfoodSápmi.com/matkommunikation-som-forandrar-Sápmi/).

Although structured for self-study, representatives of the organisation suggest that there is potential for much more impact and wider usage, as the material could also be used in workshops and other interactive activities.

Conclusions

So, can heritage be experienced through food? Based on the evidence discussed here, the answer is yes. In a Norwegian Sámi context, as described in Kramvig and Førde (2020), there is an understanding that nature is culture and there can be no separation between them. Eating something foraged in that area would, thus, mean that one would physically be consuming heritage, in line with Kramvig and Førde (2020, p. 35): "The clear distinction between the past and the present is dissolved by the tactile investigation of an object." The case of Tráhppie illustrates the tactile experience of heritage through the experience-scape – with furniture, food, and other items – but also the importance of accompanying such physical communication with explicit information. For example, Tráhppie offers the Sámi bread gáhkku which can be experienced as chewy by new tasters. However, when accompanied by an explanation that the bread was carried around in bags in nomadic times and therefore needs to be like this in order not to dissolve, the experience may be quite different. In this sense, the display of food and traditions creates a link to, and understanding of, the natural world, as the local lifestyle makes the limitations and possibilities of nature easily understandable to visitors. As the Sámi lifestyle has evolved within the limits of what can be consumed without hampering natural regrowth, consuming tourism products based on this holistic view indeed offers an opportunity to create and spread understanding of nature.

An interlinked question here is: can a place be experienced through food? Again, when understood through the material referred to in this chapter, the answer is yes. Local produce is a manifestation of the local natural environment: light, humidity, ecosystems, as well as culture – that is, what and how to eat. As in the Norwegian example, one could, thus, claim that nature and culture cannot be separated, and neither should food be separated from place or culture. By embracing specific local characteristics, one may produce tourism experiences that transcend the boundaries between "food tourism" and "heritage tourism" and create experiences that are fit for a new, more complex era of tourist experiences. This is in line with Ironside and Massie's (2020) proposed evolution of Urry's (1990) tourism gaze into a folklore-centric gaze (2020), where the needs of the production site are prioritised rather than those of consumers.

As illustrated by the examples in this chapter, communicating intangible aspects of culture through food is an opportunity to engage visitors in local heritage and the natural environment – even when communicating from a distance, as in the case of the Slow Food Sápmi manuals. In the increasing competition between destinations uniqueness is desirable. The potential risks of commodifying tradition and folklore are obvious, but what would the alternative be? Due to restructuring and reforming the landscape, sources for income are needed and the lure of Sámi themes may not only attract Sámi entrepreneurs. Thus, the growing interest in local heritage, uniqueness of places, and perceived potential gains from the experience industry may be forming a situation where the Sámi theme, traditions, and cultural expressions will inevitably be commercialised. By establishing their role as bearers of the Sámi theme, actors such as Såhkie and Slow Food Sápmi may aid individual Sámi entrepreneurs in protecting their assets – material as well as intangible – from being violated, as well as informing non-Sámi actors of vital aspects of Sámi culture to take into consideration.

By underlining the potential for spreading knowledge and understanding, the positive side of using heritage and folklore in tourism may be understood and strengthened. However, this needs to permeate not only activities in the private and idealistic sector, but also public sector strategies. The seminars referred to earlier, co-arranged by Sámi organisations and departments at Umeå University, were a much-appreciated event in terms of information. However, the fact that the Swedish government (which runs the university) has a dark history in terms of relations with the Sámi population should not be ignored. By joining efforts, troublesome aspects may be addressed together with reasoning, building on the gains from an increased understanding of a

152 Kajsa G. Åberg and Doris A. Carson

living indigenous culture. The international event Gourmand and Hallbars Awards was held in Umeå in June 2022, and in the program a dinner was served by, and in, Tráhpphie. The venue was selected in connection with the award-winning cookbook, but not least because of its renowned abilities to combine long traditions and modern aspects in gastronomy. Heritage and folklore were, thus, not added as a flavour to the program, but essential parts of it that cannot be separated from the place and its produce.

Acknowledgement

The authors would like to thank Licelott Omma and EllaCarin Blind, representatives of Tráhppie, Såhkie and SSR, for their collaboration and support in writing this text.

References

Arvidsson, A. (1999). *Folklorens former*. Lund: Studentlitteratur.

Bessiere, J. and Tibere, L. (2013). 'Traditional food and tourism: French tourist experience and food heritage in rural spaces.' *Journal of the Science of Food and Agriculture*, 93 (14), pp. 3420–3425.

Byström, J. (2019). *Tourism Development in Resource Peripheries: Conflicting and Unifying Spaces in Northern Sweden*. Doctoral dissertation. Umeå: Umeå University, Department of Geography.

Byström, J. and Müller, D.K. (2014). 'Tourism labor market impacts of national parks.' *Zeitschrift für Wirtschaftsgeographie*, 58 (1), pp. 115–126.

Carson, D.A., Åberg, K.G., and Prideaux, B. (2020). 'Cities of the North: Gateways, competitors or regional markets for hinterland tourism destinations?' In L. Lundmark, D.B. Carson & M. Eimermann (eds.), *Dipping in to the North: Living, Working and Traveling in Sparsely Populated Areas*. Singapore: Palgrave McMillan, pp. 285–310.

Cohen, E. (1993). 'The study of touristic images of native people: Mitigating the stereotype of a stereotype.' In D.G. Pearce and R.W. Butler (eds.), *Tourism Research: Critiques and Challenges*. Abingdon: Routledge, pp. 36–69.

Cooper, C. and Hall, C.M. (2007). *Contemporary Tourism*. Abingdon: Routledge.

Cooper, E.A., Spinei, M. and Varnajot, A. (2019). 'Countering "Arctification": Dawson City's "Sourtoe Cocktail".' *Journal of Tourism Futures*, 6 (1), pp. 70–82.

De Bernardi, C. (2020). *Authenticity as a Compromise: A Critical Realist Perspective on Sámi Tourism Labels*. Doctoral dissertation. Rovaniemi: University of Lapland, Faculty of Social Sciences.

De la Barre, S. and Brouder, P. (2013). 'Consuming stories: Placing food in the Arctic tourism experience.' *Journal of Heritage Tourism*, 8 (2–3), pp. 213–223.

Hall, C.M. and Jenkins, J. K. (1998). 'The policy dimensions of rural tourism and recreation.' In R. Butler, C.M. Hall and J. Jenkins (eds.), *Tourism and Recreation in Rural Areas*. Chichester: Wiley, pp. 19–42.

Harnesk, V. (2020). *Taste of Sápmi*. 4th edition. Slow Food Sápmi.

Hinch, T., & Butler, R. (1996). (Eds.) *Tourism and Indigenous Peoples*. 1st edition. London: International Thomson Business Press.

Hjalager, A.M. and Richards, G. (2003). *Tourism and Gastronomy*. Abingdon: Routledge.

Hudson, C., Nyseth, T. and Pedersen, P. (2019). 'Dealing with difference: Contested place identities in two northern Scandinavian cities.' *City*, 23 (4–5), pp. 564–579.

Ironside, R. and Massie, S. (2020). 'The folklore-centric gaze: A relational approach to landscape, folklore and tourism.' *Time and Mind*, 13 (3), pp. 227–244.

Jamal, T. and Hill, S. (2004). 'Developing a framework for indicators of authenticity: The place and space of cultural and heritage tourism.' *Asia Pacific Journal of Tourism Research*, 9 (4), pp. 353–372.

Johansson, S., Norman, T. and Norrman, M. (2010). 'Matlandet ur ett regionalt perspektiv.' Report RA 10:13. Jönköping: Jordbruksverket/Swedish Board of Agriculture.

Koster, R.L. and Carson, D.A. (2019). *Perspectives on Rural Tourism Geographies.* Cham, Switzerland: Springer.

Kramvig, B., and Førde, A. (2020). 'Stories of reconciliation enacted in the everyday lives of Sámi tourism entrepreneurs.' *Acta Borealia*, 37(1–2), pp. 27–42.

Kreuzpointner, T., and Bathurst, M. (2021). 'Geografiska matvarumärken – en accelererande kraft för lokal mat.' Report OVR594. Jönköping, Sweden: Jordbruksverket/Swedish Board of Agriculture.

Leu, T. C. (2018). 'Tourism work among Sámi indigenous people.' Doctoral Thesis, Department of Geography and Economic History. Umeå: Umeå University.

Lundmark, L. (2006) 'Restructuring and employment change in sparsely populated areas. Examples from northern Sweden and Finland.' Doctoral thesis, Faculty of Social sciences. GERUM, Department of Social and Economic Geography. Umeå: Umeå University.

Mossberg, L., and Johansen, E. N. (2006). *Storytelling: Marknadsföring i upplevelseindustrin.* Lund: Studentlitteratur.

Pettersson, R., Svensson, B., Grundberg, J., Nordin, S., and Grängsjö, P. (2005). *Målkonflikter mellan natur, kultur och turism i hållbart utvecklingsarbete.* Östersund: ETOUR, European Tourism Research Institute.

Prideaux, B. (2002). 'Building visitor attractions in peripheral areas—Can uniqueness overcome isolation to produce viability?' *International Journal of Tourism Research*, 4 (5), pp. 379–389.

Quinn, B., and Ryan, T. (2016). 'Tour guides and the mediation of difficult memories: The case of Dublin Castle.' *Ireland. Current Issues in Tourism*, 19(4), pp. 322–337.

Regeringskansliet (2021). *Strategi för hållbar turism och växande besöksnäring. (National Strategy for Sustainable Tourism).* Stockholm: Regeringen.

Region Västerbotten (2021). *Besöksnäringsstrategi för Västerbotten. Remissversion mars 2022.* Umeå: Region Västerbotten Turism.

Region Västerbotten Turism (2021). *Besöksnäringen är viktig för Västerbotten.* Umeå: Region Västerbotten.

Sadovska, V., Mark-Herbert, C., Ferguson, R., and Ekelund Axelson, L. (2019). Marknadsföra MER (-) värden. LTV-fakultetens faktablad 2019:9, SLU Alnarp/Swedish University of Agricultural Siences, Alnarp, Sweden.

Samiskt informationscentrum (n.d.). *The Sámi – An Indigenous People.* Kiruna/Östersund: The Sámi Information Centre, Sámi Parliament.

Slow Food International (2022). Web platform for organisation Slow Food International, information published in section 'about us'. Available Online: https://www.slowfood.com/about-us/ [Accessed 1 March 2022].

Slow Food Sápmi (2022a). Web platform for organisation Slow Food Sápmi, information published in section 'om oss'. Available Online: https://www.slowfoodSápmi.com/om-oss/ [Accessed 1 March 2022].

154 *Kajsa G. Åberg and Doris A. Carson*

Slow Food Sápmi (2022b). Web platform for organization Slow Food Sápmi, material published in section 'matkommunikation-som-forandrar-sapmi'. Available Online: https://www.slowfoodSápmi.com/matkommunikation-som-forandrar-Sápmi/ [Accessed 1 March 2022].

Smith, M. K. (2003). *Issues in Cultural Tourism Studies*. Abingdon: Routledge.

UR (2021) Måltidsturismens platser, filmed seminar 2021-11-04 arranged by Várdduo – Centre for Sámi research, Arcum - Arctic Centre, and Department of Food, Nutrition and Culinary Sciences, at Umeå University, Sweden. Available from UtbildningsRadion (Swedish Educational Broadcasting Company): https://urplay.se/program/226231-ur-samtiden-Sámisk-och-arktisk-gastronomi-maltidsturismens-platser [Accessed 5 March 2022].

Urry, J. (1990). *The Tourist Gaze: Leisure and Travel in Contemporary Societies*. London: Sage.

Verran, H. (2002). 'A postcolonial moment in science studies: Aalternative firing regimes of environmental scientists and aboriginal landowners.' *Social Studies of Science*, 32 (5–6), pp. 729–762.

Viken, A. and Müller, D.K. (eds.) (2017). *Tourism and Indigeneity in the Arctic*. Bristol: Channel View Publications.

Visit Sweden (2020). Trend rapport 2020 Måltidstrender [Trend report 2020 Food trends].' Stockholm: Visit Sweden. Available Online: https://corporate.visitsweden.com/kunskap/maltid/trendrapport-maltidstrender-2020/ [Accessed 5 March 2022].

Whitford, M. and Ruhanen, L. (2016). 'Indigenous tourism research, past and present: Where to from here?' *Journal of Sustainable Tourism*, 24 (8–9), pp. 1080–1099.

World Foodtravel Association (2022). Web platform for organisation World Foodtravel Association. Available Online: https://worldfoodtravel.org/ [Accessed 5 March 2022].

Part III

Reimagining Folklore in a Globalised World

Tourism, Placemaking, and Re-enchantment

11 A City Made of Stories

Re-enchantment and Narrative Placemaking in Madrid

Leticia Cortina Aracil

The Oblivion of Madrid's Folklore

Madrid, capital of Spain, is one of the main destinations for urban tourism in Europe, receiving both national and international visitors throughout the year, given that its cultural profile – counting more than one hundred museums that include those of the Golden Triangle of Art – does not make its appeal dependent on seasonal conditions. Despite this cultural impulse, the city does not appear to stand out for its folklore and deeply rooted traditions; rather, it feels like a modern and multicultural metropolis, defined by its great institutional and economic apparatus. Notwithstanding, the verifiable history of Madrid goes back to the eighth century (earlier even, the legends say), and it is pervaded with meaningful landscapes and historic sites that, hidden behind the contemporary hustle and bustle of the city, often pass unnoticed. This historical development, of remarkable intensity since the Royal Court settled there in 1561, was naturally partnered with the development of local folklore and traditions.

Most of Madrid's popular customs are related to, or find justification in, the particular religious sphere that for centuries permeated everything in the region and, initially, they were not much different to those of other territories of Castile. With the settlement of the Royal Court in the *Villa*, however, differences arose with respect to the folklore of nearby areas according to this new role. For instance, as far as celebrations are concerned, there was such an increment that in 1643, by means of an unsuccessful apostolic brief, the festive calendar was instructed to be reduced to 21 official celebrations (Montoliú Camps, 1990, p. 15). Even if this instruction had been observed, the celebration days of the patron saints of different districts and trades, *romerías* (local pilgrimages), seasonal fairs and *verbenas* (festivals), neighbourhood devotions, and many other festive occasions would have to be included as well.

It cannot be said that this popular dimension has been overlooked since few places in Spain have been more thoroughly documented than Madrid, from representations in the popular arts to official chronicles. Furthermore, history shows how this popular sphere tends to prevail by force of custom, or by the weight of the significance attached to its expressions, against the attempts at regulation or prohibition by the authorities, although not without

DOI: 10.4324/9781003374138-15

158   *Leticia Cortina Aracil*

being affected by them.[1] The consequence of this is a particular balance – that could be called "organic" – between the popular and the institutional.

In spite of this, there was a rupture in the balance during the period surrounding the Civil War (1936–1939). A large part of popular practices throughout Spain had to be discontinued or were forced into secrecy with the prohibition of public manifestations of religiosity during the Second Spanish Republic (1931–1939) and the religious persecution that followed (Martín Rubio, 2001, pp. 82–85; Moral Roncal, 2012, pp. 47–48). In addition, over the course of the conflict there were successive prohibitions regarding celebrations, the best-known case being that of the carnival by the Nationals in 1937, which continued into the Franco regime, although it was gradually reborn unofficially in most of Spain before the dissolution of the regime in 1975.

Nevertheless, it was not by the force of the authorities that so much of Madrid's popular lore and celebrations came to an apparent end. Proof of this is that other regions of Spain preserved their traditions and folklore despite the controls imposed on them. The singularity of Madrid compared to other regions is that in the post-war period it experienced an exceptionally large urban development. The first consequence of this was the accelerated destruction of historical environments – which had been taking place since the nineteenth century (confiscations, wars, modernising impulses, etc.). This led to the disappearance of geographical features, buildings, and green spaces with folkloric relevance associated with the city (slopes, streams, hermitages, picnic areas, etc.), which were replaced by the building of residential neighbourhoods and modern structures. Similarly, cars took over the roads, hindering their use by pedestrians, and even more so for the pilgrimages, processions, or parades that typically moved through them.

Notwithstanding, the chief cause behind this change was the immense demographic growth produced by a population shift to Madrid from other parts of the country[2] precisely in a period in which numerous local traditions were no longer being perpetuated consistently. This propitiated the inaccurate belief – now held in other parts of Spain – that Madrid lacks popular traditions of its own.

From the 1970s, coinciding with an increase in the percentage of native Madrilenians, an interest in the local culture arose that led to a new appreciation of traditional spaces of local history. As a consequence, an effort to promote popular festivals and traditions was undertaken. This was complemented with the touristic boost experienced by Spain from 1960 onwards, that required a response to the interest of foreigners for Spanish culture, marking the beginning of outreach work specifically aimed at visitors from abroad. These recovery initiatives had irregular results in Madrid as a consequence of not being grounded in popular knowledge, or demand, but as part of promotional work by the City Council. This was done through programs of celebratory activities (concerts, fireworks, competitions, etc.), often far detached from the original motivations of those traditions, chiefly associated with a religiosity now uncomfortable to the secular politics of the organisers and promoters.[3]

A City Made of Stories   159

Expanding on these difficulties, it must be considered that "folklore" is not widely understood as a field of study in Spain,[4] standing indeterminate between history, religious studies, and ethnography. Thus, tour guides with an academic profile often address this sphere superficially, tending towards sensationalistic, or non-rigorous, narratives. Despite this, the legitimisation of folklore as an important part of the historical and social scene, and as a meaningful part of the culture, has been a priority of this researcher's work as a tour guide in Madrid, leading to the realisation that it has a particular importance when it comes to placemaking.

It has been found that there is a substantial difference in the way in which travellers connect with Madrid as a *place*[5] when this dimension is accurately included. Compared to tours focused exclusively on data (whether historical, architectural, political, etc.), or those that, at the expense of accuracy, seek to provoke the visitor with outlandish anecdotes, the knowledge and understanding of local folklore prominently elicits in the tourist a sense of *authenticity* that redounds to an experience of intimacy with the place that does not occur otherwise. It is understood that this happens because folklore conveys in a privileged way the *intrahistory* of the place, in the sense in which the concept was formulated by the philosopher Miguel de Unamuno (1986, p. 33), as the history of the anonymous people that, while never reflected in the officially recorded history, sustains the latter as its living core.

Furthermore, participation in this dimension also affects the experience of time. When engaging with folklore, an intellectual and emotional connection is made with these anonymous people from the past, which not only partially satisfies the scholarly concern of people who sign up for a historical tour but also favours a connection with the surrounding space as a place shared with these past people in their daily lives, despite their distance apart in time. This is more pronounced when the folklore in question is of a ritual nature.

Beyond the Obstacles: How to Share Tradition in Rootless Times

In the context of tourism, storytelling is the main means by which to endow a particular landscape with meaning and historical significance. This is especially true before a diverse and globalised audience, with disparate backgrounds and whose prior knowledge of a subject cannot be taken for granted because, often, they share no ties with the place. Based on the experience of this research, narration as a means of dissemination has to fulfil four conditions to be successful in the aforementioned way.

The first is to rely on the present and effective landscape that surrounds the narrative action, to carry out a sensory integration that helps an enhanced perception of the place, of its current configuration as well as of what it may show from its past. Our bodies are the most inescapable bond that unites us to the place where we stand, and a central part of the guide's job here is to draw the audience's attention to this, and help it focus on what is relevant to the folklore being shared. This shapes a sense of the space in which one is physically present that goes beyond taking it as a mere framework of an

160 *Leticia Cortina Aracil*

action or event but revealing it as the scenario that enabled a particular historical experience. Attending to this physical and sensorial aspect as a constitutive part of the narrative action has a grounding effect that often goes unnoticed, or is taken for granted.

The second condition is of an academic nature, consisting of a rigorous and complex knowledge of the folkloric content to be communicated. This requires specific study and research that goes beyond merely reproducing popular sayings and generalisations (time and again hoaxes), actively avoiding explanations prejudged from contemporary sentiment. Commonly, due to the aforementioned blurred character of the notion of folklore, this is neglected and, when tourists inquire about these aspects, the guides only provide explanations distorted by their biases or funny legendary justifications known to be false, on the understanding that it is not a topic deserving of greater efforts.

The third condition is ethical. It is related to the previous condition as it consists of being respectful of these views and traditions. Sharing, or subscribing to, them in a personal capacity does not follow from this, but it is impossible to access the interest and experiential value of folklore when considering it from a position of condescending superiority (such as presenting it as superstition, or as ignorant extravagance), or seeking to justify them based on ideologies alien to their nature. Nor should such stories be told without regard for the life experience and worldviews of those who formulated this folklore, kept it alive, and transmitted it. This is, by far, the most important approach in order to achieve a sense of authenticity, because the respect shown by the guide invites the audience to honestly consider it beyond their preconceptions.

The last condition is of a technical nature, and it applies to presentation and good communication techniques that are appropriate to the guide's role as narrator and storyteller.

When these four conditions are met the result is a well-constructed story, grounded both in the known, or learned, history of the area, and the immediate experienced reality. Through this the listeners establish a participatory relationship with the environment where they are found, which considers the spatial and the emotional, the sensory and the intellectual in an integrated manner, enabling them to get in touch with the experiences of everyday people that inhabited that place before them. This generates an enchanted perception of the environment that, in general, is characterised as being awe-inspiring. This enchanted perception is understood in opposition to the sociological notion of disenchantment – the historical process by which the world, and human experience, becomes progressively inscribed within the interpretive paradigm and strategy of experimental science and rational dominance at the expense of everything that would not fit said model (Jenkins, 2000, p. 12). Therefore, rather than some*thing* to use, a location is revealed as some*where* to be – a tangible term of a significance attested by those now unreachable preceding lives, through which that place was endowed as such. This is abundantly clear when the folklore has a non-materialistic, magical, or miraculous substratum that sets it apart from the secular everyday experience of most contemporary societies.

In accordance with what has been stated, three cases pertinent to the folklore of Madrid – which appear in this researcher's repertoire as a tour guide – will be shown next, outlining how these conditions apply in each example, and their impact on the audience according to feedback that tourists themselves have provided about their experience.

A Case of Forgotten Lore: A Ghost Story

Madrid is considered to be one of the most haunted capitals in Europe, and yet ghost tours are not particularly popular there. Nevertheless, there are a number of spooky stories shared with diligence, standing out among them are those that have the beautiful *Plaza de Oriente* as their scenery. This square, which extends between the Royal Palace and the opera house, is said to be inhabited by a ghost.

Word has it that when King Philip V commissioned the construction of the Royal Palace, he wanted the greatest palace in the world. The King entrusted the works to the Italian architect Filippo Juvara, which his apprentice, Juan Bautista Sachetti, took over after his death. At the end of the construction, worried that Sachetti could in the future build a palace that might surpass his own, King Philip asked him to give up architecture in exchange for a luxurious room for life in the magnificent palace. Sachetti refused, so the king ordered his eyes gouged out and his tongue cut off, but still gave him the promised room. Locked inside his own masterpiece, Sachetti died of grief, unable to cry or to weep. Yet, ever since, in the silence of the night, his ghost can be seen wandering through the square, letting his bitter fate be known. This legend is then supported by a tangible fact: Among the human heads embellishing the frontispieces over some windows there is one of man with a vacant stare that opens his mouth as if to show its empty inside; that was Sachetti's room, whose face appeared there at the moment of his death.

Despite the fact that this popular story can be counted as part of this city's contemporary folklore, it is historically false from beginning to end.[6] This is something made known to the audience in a deliberately anticlimactic manner after the tale is told by progressively transforming the narrative tone from an historical chronicle to that of a horror story.

It may seem contradictory to what has been said here to present the audience with a story that not only is known to be false but which even the guide does not pretend to be true. Regardless, the narration is carried out in the context of an explanation of the square's historical context, accounting for its age and relevance, highlighting its changes over time and providing an abundance of details that contribute to a sensory assessment of the space. The story itself is based on elements of the present landscape, helping the visitor to look at it in a renewed way, and excuses the contribution of a multitude of data (the great dimensions of the palace, the names of the architects, the dates, etc.), that will later serve to show the falsehood of the story.

162 *Leticia Cortina Aracil*

In addition, this story creates an aura that not only samples the intensity with which ghost stories and legends of bewitchment have arisen in this enclave over the centuries – evidence of the retention by the collective memory of an otherwise forgotten fact, which can then be revealed to great effect: that they are standing on the oldest known necropolis in Madrid, the Muslim cemetery known as *Huesa del Raf*, and perhaps even a Jewish cemetery of a later period as well (Andreu and Paños, 2012).

Thus, it becomes clear that this story did not arise here by chance, but rather as a remnant of the memory that this used to be a place inhabited by the deceased. It is revived by bonding with the surrounding monumental architecture. Contrary to the usual effect of demystification with which revelations are usually made, this one elicits a sense of wonder at the invisible that suddenly takes on a presence that allows the tourist to connect with the historical substratum, participating in the surrounding landscape, overt or implied.

A Case of Surviving Folklore Bearing Witness to Disappeared Elements: A Miraculous Story

The recounting of this story requires standing at the top of what is known as *Cuesta de la Vega*, the descent towards the river that for many centuries was a ravine. Although this landscape appears now significantly softened by urban action, just a few steps on this descent already allows the visitor to admire some of the impressive views, for which the enclave was selected for the erection of a fortress in the Middle Ages. Yet, to do this, one must "cross" the now disappeared gate that once stood here, the *Puerta de la Vega*, ending at the feet of the twentieth century cathedral. This is the exact location where the first known miracle in Madrid occurred: the apparition of its patroness, the Virgin of Almudena.

The story dates back to the year 711. With the defeat of King Rodrigo in the Battle of Guadalete, almost the entire Iberian Peninsula fell into the hands of the Umayyad Caliphate. Little is known about what the territory of Madrid was like back then, but it is said that a small settlement stood by the river where an image of the Holy Virgin was venerated with great devotion. Aware of the imminent arrival of the invaders, the locals decided to protect their beloved image by hiding her in a wall, leaving two lighted candles as a last gesture of devotion. Over the centuries the memory of this hiding spot was forgotten, but never so the legend of the concealed image, which passed from generation to generation among the Mozarabic population.

In the eleventh century, when Madrid was conquered by King Alfonso VI, the King was informed of this legend, and he fruitlessly endeavoured to find the Virgin. Eventually running out of options, the monarch arranged a solemn procession of prayers to request the image to show herself. When this procession descended through the *Puerta de la Vega*, suddenly, a fragment of the defensive wall crumbled, revealing the much-sought-after image wrapped in the light of two candles. The King gave this image the name of *Santa*

María La Real (Saint Mary the Royal), but the people of Madrid called her *Virgen de la Almudena*, the Virgin of the walls of the citadel.

This story, which has foundational significance for Madrid insofar as it inaugurates its Christian period, is intimately linked to the defensive walls, of which only scattered fragments remain to be found in the most unlikely places. The narration requires drawing attention to the orography and its relevance, and to the original layout of the medieval enclosure, and provides an introduction to the socio-political situation of the time. Through this story the audience is led to perceive the geographical space occupied by the old town as a place transverse to time in meaningfulness through specific historical content. Correspondingly, it allows for an understanding of the emotional weight associated with the modern buildings surrounding the tourist; prominently, the Emir Mohamed I park, which holds the best-preserved remains of the original wall, the Cathedral of Almudena – erected there as the site of the miracle – and the Royal Palace, which occupies the enclave of the first medieval fortress.

In addition, this is a miracle story, these being the most abundant and best documented wonder tales from Madrid. It elicited a lively devotion for the Virgin in the area, witnessed through the centuries, as attested by legends, attributed miracles, a multitude of artistic expressions, themed sweets, and numerous popular traditions that can be seen today, highlighting her feast day on 9 November. Through it, the tourist, religious or not, is provided with a foundation to contemplate these places and the associated devotions in a participatory way, rather than as an external observer, since they have "pilgrimed" through the relevant enclaves, becoming narrative witnesses of the miracle and of what it has meant for the Madrilenians for centuries.

A Case of a Tradition Adapted to Meaningfully Include the New Urban Environment

The *Entierro de la Sardina* (Burial of the Sardine) is a traditional mumming event held in various parts of Spain that marks the passage from Carnival to Lent. It consists of a parade that parodies a funeral procession and culminates with the incineration of the effigy of a sardine. Contrary to other similar rites, such as the Shrovetide, or the *Mardi Gras*, this one is controversially performed on Ash Wednesday.

Despite its current diffusion, everything points to Madrid as the birthplace of the tradition. The popular legend, albeit unlikely, tells that the origin of this custom dates back to 1768 when, a decaying batch of fish arrived among the stocks commissioned for the city markets in anticipation of Lenten fasting, filling the city with a terrible stench. To deal with this problem, an edict was published on Ash Wednesday ordering the burial of said consignment by the banks of the river.[7] The gesture has been perpetuated ever since as a celebration, turning it into the popular carnival that has been held continuously throughout the history of this city.

164   *Leticia Cortina Aracil*

The celebration was affected by the ban on carnivals during the Spanish Civil War. Yet, in 1952, the antiquarian Serafín Villén clandestinely revived the tradition through the creation of a brotherhood called the *Alegre Cofradía del Entierro de la Sardina* (Merry Brotherhood of the Burial of the Sardine). From that moment on, and despite the prohibition, the Brotherhood continued to publicly perform the ritual year after year. Even so, this mumming was enacted in a way that diverted remarkably from those recorded in earlier times.

The new parade shares with the old one having the area of *El Rastro*[8] as its starting point, moving from there to the forests and meadows on the other side of the river in a pilgrimage aimed to enact the abandonment of the civilised world of men for the wilderness of nature. The border character of this area defined the original carnival, but the relative location of this neighbourhood has changed dramatically since the eighteenth century, and even more since the beginning of the twentieth. It has gone from being a working-class neighbourhood perched on the hill overlooking the greenery on the other side of the river to being absorbed by the city centre. In addition, the other side of the Manzanares River has now been taken over by residential districts and the green areas that survive now do so as urban parks. Successfully reviving this carnival called for the incorporation of that new geography in a meaningful way, an adaptation that happened spontaneously.

Now, the mumming is made up of two parts. The first one takes place at daytime as a parodic funeral procession through the historical centre of the city, making stops at century-old taverns along the way. The second is carried out at sunset, moving into a nature-scene to stage the incineration and burial of the sardine.

This change was not cosmetic, but profoundly affected the contemporary significance of the mumming. The Burial was born as a popular celebration when this qualified it as an uncouth festival, of a rustic and unrefined profile, which consisted precisely of one last histrionic escape from the constraints of civilisation through the symbolic abandonment of the city for wild nature. When the new Brotherhood inherited the old celebration it underwent a substantial change, which followed from having been revived from a different motivation: the aesthetic longing for historical ritual, relying mostly on oral tradition and popular memory.

A decisive element in these changes was the transformation that the notion of "the popular" has undergone in the contemporary urban world, ceasing to mean what belongs to the lower classes to now refer to something that, due to its age, is endowed with greater originality and authenticity. Consistently, the Burial of the Sardine has gone from being reviled by the institutions to being assisted by them.

Explaining this festival to visitors requires a previous walk through this quarter that brings forth the aforementioned characteristics and historical peculiarities that gave rise to this ritual, drawing special attention to how the former liminal character of the area endows it still with a somewhat mysterious atmosphere, highlighted by the multitude of antique shops. Furthermore,

A City Made of Stories 165

the colourful display of this festival promotes a spontaneous sensory immersion that, complemented with an explanation of the regalia and small ceremonies that make it up, engenders an impression of wonder. The sensation commented on by the tourists is that of an initiatory effect by which they go from "watching the burial" to feeling that they "participated in the burial." This often moves the tourist into taking proactive roles, such as going out to dance with the brothers, or pretending to cry uncontrollably for the deceased sardine.

The Desire for a Place

It can be stated uncontroversially that the deep motivation of much tourism is the desire to know a place. But this is not an academic, intellectual knowledge that the interested party could pursue at a theoretical level by means such as the study and consultation of data. It is an experiential type of knowledge, which makes it essential to travel, to *be* there. Furthermore, tourism like this develops place-based knowledge in ascendancy over other types of knowledge by becoming "knowledge of something experienced."

This is in fact the root of tourism as a phenomenon which, long before today's mass travel, emerged in the context of the Romantic Grand Tour. This was a journey through marked enclaves of Europe that, for around two centuries, was undertaken by young men from wealthy families, and it was understood as an essential experience to complete their education and their passage to maturity (Redford, 1996, pp. 15–16). These voyages not only generated the first travel literature linked to leisure and enjoyment – among which were some of the earliest travel guides – but also a literature of great emotion in which the travellers relate their individual experiences of these different places and their transformative value, which ranges from the strictly emotional experience to an intellectual transformation; such as J.W. Goethe's *Italian Journey* (1816/7). These diaries and sentimental records not only give an account of what happens to their authors during the journey, but also show the experiential intention that underlies the decision to undertake them and their hopes about their destinations.

Today's travelling frequently does not have such a demanding economic and vital cost, but this does not detract from the fact that tourists choose to sacrifice their time and money, sometimes both in great quantity, moved by the desire to obtain this particular knowledge of a place.

Expectations about a place can be as diverse as the travellers themselves, but it seems fair to say that the place is perceived as endowed with a particular allure, or enchantment, which is expected to challenge intimate aspects of those who become involved with it, or bring about a sense of fulfilment.[9]

Certainly, such expectations are not without criticism. For many tourists this search is specified as another consumer experience in which the tourists perceive themselves, implicitly or explicitly, as having been awarded a special concession that exempts them from adapting their behaviour to that of the culture that receives them, expecting, rather, that they will be provided

166 *Leticia Cortina Aracil*

with their desired experience, for which they have paid. This approach has not only devalued tourism in the eyes of many, often taking on pejorative connotations, but also negatively affects the places themselves, transforming them into theme park scenarios, shaped by foreign expectation, that become unliveable for its inhabitants. Spain resents this enormously given that it is often known abroad through cartoonish images that border on the grotesque; in this we find the root of the growing anti-tourism movements (Hughes, 2018).

Places need to be lived in, and uninhabitable places quickly become non-places that lose the authenticity from which that sought-after charm is born. Thus, the most authentic tourism is not driven by a mechanism of consumption, but rather seeks to propitiate an encounter with the life that through history shaped these places. When a culture focuses on welcoming a deeper desire for encounter with a place, rather than selling itself as a market product, then tourism can become something nurturing for that culture.

In this sense, folklore is an irreplaceable expression of the inner life of a culture and its people that does not manifest through demographic, geographic, or economic analyses. Generally strange and disconcerting for those alien to it, being able to communicate to an audience with depth and rigour the intimate aspects that animate this folklore is equivalent to sharing a secret with them, revealing for them something that they would not have been able to learn had not they travelled there. This connects them as individuals with profound features of that desired place.

Conclusions

The cases presented in this chapter show the effect of turning a visit to a particular location into an experience that provides a peculiar knowledge of place, which arouses in the audience a feeling of intimacy with it. This invites the tourist to become involved with the inner life that is manifested in the experience as someone who is privy to something secret about it, shared only by its closest inhabitants.

It is remarkable how people find a special kind of connection with what is revealed to them; as a form of joy or satisfaction that turns those things described as "secret," "mysterious," or "enigmatic" into the enchanting. Notwithstanding, the daily life of most contemporary societies appears to be governed by the myth of the disenchantment of the world, and these revelations, discoveries, and unmaskings are implicitly expected to have a disappointing effect. Folklore, despite everything, is elusive. These three cases were selected because, in a remarkable and systematic manner, they produce in the visitor an effect contrary to disenchantment, such as the evocation of a sense of wonder, fascination, or excitement (even in disbelief), all of which are associated with the desire to know a place more and better.

The characteristic narrative action by which this is conveyed is the instrument that introduces the visitor to a city on a level that is much deeper than a sheer excuse to seek an accumulation of activities different than those available at home. Through these stories Madrid appears as a place that is attested as habitable, capable of giving a profoundly significant response to the desire that motivated the tourist to become a visitor.

Notes

1 A good case of this is the evolution of the *Corpus Christi* procession in different parts of Spain (*e.g.* Sanz, 2007).
2 For instance, in 1970 the population of Madrid was 3,121,000 inhabitants, from among them 1,545,000 were originally from other parts of Spain and had moved in within the previous 50 years (Montoliú Camps, 1990, p. 16).
3 It is relevant in this context how the traditions that survive by their own strength and more faithfully to their historical style are those more directly linked to religious worship and devotion, particularly, Easter processions and the celebration of the patron saints of the neighbourhoods.
4 In its general use, the term is associated narrowly to regional dances and it is applied to those things that are bizarre or caricatured.
5 "Place" is here understood as those physical spaces that can be, following Heidegger, *inhabited* (Acevedo Guerra, 2017), lived-in in a way through which they become intrinsically embedded with meaning.
6 This is a local variation of an unknown origin of a story told about many impressive constructions around the world, such as the Taj Mahal in Agra or St. Basil's Cathedral in Moscow.
7 Regarding the historicity of this origin, see Cortina Aracil, 2021.
8 *El Rastro* is the neighbourhood born around a slaughterhouse inaugurated in 1497 that has become the most popular flea market in the country, standing out for its antique dealers and artisans.
9 A proof of this aspiration is the existence of the Paris Syndrome, a collection of physical and psychic affections produced by a disappointment of the high expectations with which the city is visited.

References

Acevedo Guerra, I. (2017). 'El habitar como ser del hombre, según Heidegger.' *Hermenéutica Intercultural*, 28, pp. 189–197.

Andreu, E. and Paños, V. (2012). 'Nuevas propuestas de ubicación espacial de la judería medieval de Madrid: evidencias arqueológicas.' *Revista Historia Autónoma*, 1, pp. 53–72.

Cortina Aracil, L. (2021). 'The Merry Mourning: The festival of the Burial of the Sardine in Madrid.' Paper presented at International Mummers Festival Symposium, 4 January 2021.

Hughes, N. (2018). '"Tourists go home": Anti-tourism industry protest in Barcelona.' *Social Movement Studies*, 17 (4), pp. 471–477.

Jenkins, R. (2000). 'Disenchantment, enchantment and re-enchantment: Max weber at the millennium.' *Max Weber Studies*, 1 (1), pp. 11–32.

Martín Rubio, A.D. (2001). 'La persecución religiosa en España (1931–1939): una aportación sobre las cifras.' *Hispania Sacra*, 53 (107), pp. 63–89.

Montoliú Camps, P. (1990). *Fiestas y tradiciones madrileñas*. Madrid: Sílex.

Moral Roncal, A.M. (2012). 'Anticlericalismo y poder: la desacralización de las calles y los espacios públicos durante la Segunda República.' *Hispania Sacra*, 64 (1), pp. 47–68.

Redford, B. (1996). *Venice and the Grand Tour*. New Haven and London: Yale University Press.

Sanz, M.J. (2007). 'La procesión del Corpus en Sevilla: influencias sociales y políticas en la evolución del cortejo.' *Ars longa: cuadernos de arte*, 16, pp. 55–72.

Unamuno, M. (1986). *En torno al casticismo*. Madrid: Alianza Editorial.

12 The Folklore of the Subterranean
The Spectres of the Underground in Dudley Tourist Sites

Sian Macfarlane

Introduction

In the introduction to his evocative "Walks in the Black Country," American Consul Elihu Burritt, writing in 1868, introduces a Black Country of two halves, one above ground, one below

> [...] the better half, the may be, faces the sun; but the richer half, averted thence, looks by gaslight towards the central fires. If that subterranean half could be for an hour inverted to the sun; if its inky vaults and tortuous pathways, and all its black-roofed chambers could be but once laid open to the light of day, the spectacle would be a world's wonder, especially if it were uncovered when all the thousands of the subterranean road-makers, or the begrimed armies of pickmen, were bending to their work.
>
> (Burritt, 1976, p. 1)

The underground is a curiously fertile place for the imagination. From HG Wells' Morlocks to the well dwelling character in Haruki Murakami's *The Wind Up Bird Chronicle*, literature is populated by depictions of an imagined life underground. Our relationship to the world below the surface is further explored in the mythologies of the underworld found in almost every culture (Wallace and Hirsh, 2011). Further to this, recent scholarly enquiry has highlighted the importance of looking both *through* as well as *at* landscape, to consider the verticality of place particularly with regard to the subterranean (Endfield and Van Lieshout, 2020). The Black Country, from the Kinver Rock Houses, whose last inhabitants vacated in the mid-twentieth century, to the extensive labyrinths of manmade tunnels that make up the Dudley canal tunnels, offers up much to be found below the surface.

There is no greater place to illustrate these complex relations between the resources of deep time, the men and women who made a living from them, and the folklore that sprang from these relationships than at Wren's Nest Nature Reserve, a Silurian seabed from 440 million years ago. Recently awarded UNESCO world heritage status as part of the Black Country geopark (Dudley Metropolitan Borough Council, 2020), it is one of several geo-sites

DOI: 10.4324/9781003374138-16

170 *Sian Macfarlane*

across the region, including the Dudley Tunnel and Caverns, after a sustained campaign by local advocates (Black Country Global Geopark, 2022). The former limestone mine site sits near to Dudley Canal Tunnel Trust, a network of underground tunnels, open to the public for boat tours, and the Black Country Living Museum, where buildings from across the Black Country are brought brick by brick, and preserved.[1] Nearby sits Dudley Castle, dating from around 1070 (Durkin, 2019), within the grounds of Dudley Zoo. Purportedly one of the most haunted castles in the United Kingdom, this tourist destination offers an instructive counterpoint to the adjacent destinations of the museum and canal tunnel complex. This chapter will offer a comparative analysis of these tourist destinations and the different ways in which the folklore of the location and region is communicated in each place, considering the folkloric traditions themselves, before exploring how they are communicated through translation in the locations. This is achieved through research in the field, with local people and museum and tourist site staff.

There will be a focus on the supernatural folklore of the region in reference to its industry, and how the production of spaces of industry, the underworld caverns, and tunnels of transportation compared to the comparatively more easily accessible, overground structures of Dudley Castle and Black Country Living Museum.

In this way it is hoped that a further understanding of how folklore can be utilised within modern day tourism can be engendered, considering the opportunities that folklore might offer the subterranean sites of Wren's Nest and Dudley Tunnel. Alongside these considerations will run a recognition of the tensions that inevitably lie within the use of the vernacular and the hidden stories of history, with their origin/provenance either partially understood or lost completely.

The History of Mining in Dudley and the Black Country

The region known as the Black Country is an area in the Midlands loosely defined as the four Metropolitan District Council areas of Dudley, Sandwell, Walsall, and Wolverhampton. There has been mining within the region of Dudley since the thirteenth century, and very possibly earlier (Palmer, 2007). It is, however, in the eighteenth and nineteenth centuries that the numbers of miners rapidly increased (Palmer, 2007). Much of this activity was due to the abundance of coal in the South Staffordshire coalfield, with a nucleus around the Dudley area, where outcrops of limestone are also to be found (Raybould, 1973). At Dudley, lime was quarried and mined, with the local supply of limestone deposits at Dudley Castle Hill, Wren's Nest, and Sedgley creating a virtual monopoly of lime to be exploited and used in the blast furnaces.

The building of the canal system was largely responsible for the widespread growth of industry in the eighteenth century, a general trend across the United Kingdom that was in evidence in the Midlands. However, the relative elevation of Dudley proved problematic (Parsons, 1986). To solve this, a tunnel was completed in the late eighteenth century to pass underneath Dudley, linking canal

The Folklore of the Subterranean   171

systems either side (Wolverhampton Arts and Culture, 2010; Dudley Canal and Tunnel Trust, 2021). In 1805 a canal was driven to reach the working face of limestone at Wren's Nest, East Mine, allowing for far easier transportation of mined limestone, with further waterways subsequently driven further westward, linking Seven Sisters mines about ten years later (Wolverhampton Arts and Culture, 2010; Dudley Canal and Tunnel Trust, 2021).

The systems by which the mining industry were organised led to entrenched abuses of power by those with authority and ran on what was known as the "butty" system.[2] Miners were paid in "truck" rather than more widely recognised currency, a company store system which could only be spent in pubs and shops owned by the mine, paying inflated prices for low-quality items. The work was highly dangerous with a high mortality rate. In 1863, the death toll ran at around 800 per year in the Black Country according to the *Edinburgh Review* (1863 cited in Palmer, 2007, p. 104). Safety provisions were inadequate, with those in power failing to provide life-saving apparatus, to save costs and maximise the profits of the mine (Palmer, 2007). It was a harsh and unforgiving climate in which a strong sense of place and community grew, particularly in Dudley and Tipton, where the tourist locations and sites of particular interest for this chapter are to be found.

The Industrial, the Rural, and the Folkloric

Folklore customs and beliefs are more often than not associated with rurality (Davies, 1971, p. 80). Thus, it may seem counterintuitive to explore the rich histories and vernacular cultures of the industrial Black Country. However, this industry rapidly emerged in the eighteenth and nineteenth centuries from agricultural land, still visible in places well into the 20th century (Wise, 1953). Significant changes occurred in the lifetime of its inhabitants, who experienced the death of the rural, as this description outlines:

> Amidst these flaming, smoky, clanging works, I beheld the remains of what had once been happy farmhouses, now ruined and deserted [...] They had in former times been surrounded by clumps of trees; but only the skeletons of them remained, dead, black, and leafless.
>
> (Nasmyth and Smiles, 2011, pp. 133–134)

In the case of mining, work involved a constant battle with unfavourable underground conditions, hindered by inadequate safety defences. Rock might produce sparks on impact, with the potential to cause fire, the threat of damp,[3] of rockfall, of flooding, a constant threat to life. Others have noted how professions where the workers are pitted against "Nature" can be the conducive conditions for folkloric beliefs to be fostered, the threat of injury and death causing a reliance on such beliefs (Davies, 1971, p. 80). The Black Country miner's protection against such dangers were traditions and home-spun defences of a superstitious bent. In these circumstances, the Black Country proves to be rich in folklore of ghosts and superstition, charted in

172 *Sian Macfarlane*

many locally conceived books (Palmer, 2007; Poulton-Smith, 2008; Homer, 2017; Edwards, 2018).

Collected in Palmer's book *Folklore of the Black Country*, one such example of the superstitions of mining communities was recorded in 1901 by Amy Lyons in her book *Black Country Sketches*. Transcribing from a board in the Cockfighter's Arms in Wednesbury she captures the following guidance:

YE COLLIERS' GUIDE OF SIGNES AND WARNING

1st, - To dream of a broken shoe, a sure sign of danger.
2nd, - If you mete a woman at the rising of ye sun turne again from ye pit, a sure sign of deathe.
3rd, - To dream of a fire is a signe of danger
4th, - To see a bright light in ye mine is a warning to flee away.
5th, - If Gabriel's hounds ben about, doe no worke that day.
6th, - When foule smells be aboute ye pit, a sure signe that ye imps ben annear.
7th, - To charme away ghostes and ye like: Take a Bible and a key, hold both in ye right hand, and saye ye Lord's Prayer, and they will right speedily get farre away.
(Lyons, 1901 cited in Palmer, 2007, pp. 112–113)

Signs of ill portents were many, with variations seen, much of the lore focusing on the collier's travels to the pit and sunrise. An account from 1926 mentions colliers refusing to continue to the pit if a cross-eyed person, or wooden legged man, was met on the way (Palmer, 2007, p. 114). GT Lawley, who did much to capture Bilston history, records the following from 1711:

Some colliers going to work in Mr Peroehouse's Colliery at Moorfield, near Ettingshall, met a woman. As it was sunrise they became alarmed, and some of them turned back. Several others went to work laughing at such fears. In less than two hours an explosion of fire-damp occurred and a man was killed.
(Edwards, 2018, p. 28)

Alongside this preoccupation with omens that foretold bad luck was a lore of the underground as a space for spirit, devil, and imp (Davidson and Duffin, 2012; Edwards, 2018). The devil haunted the shafts of disused mines (Palmer, 2007, p. 114). Knockers, a type of mischievous mine-dwelling fairy or spirit, were to be found in the Black Country, as elsewhere (Awal, 2022). These spirits were known to make knocking noises to warn miners of danger, sometimes taking offence and hiding clothes and artefacts (Edwards, 2018). Alongside these tales, belief in the returning spirit of those killed in the mines abound, contributing to a custom whereby work was suspended in a pit where a fatal accident had occurred until after the funeral (Palmer, 2007, p. 114). To counter these threats underground, "white witches" were called on, to advise on protective actions (Edwards, 2018, p. 29).

The Folklore of the Subterranean 173

Similar superstitions of ill-omen and mine-dwelling spirits are to be found in other mining communities, such as in Wales (Davies, 1971). Miners were known to travel for work, perhaps contributing to a transmission of folkloric belief, with tales crossing narrative categories and geographies, morphing and organically changing through their transmission (Ben-Amos, 1971, p. 5). Whilst many of the beliefs have equivalents elsewhere, they have a distinctive version in the Black Country, contributing to a sense of placemaking through shared beliefs and the traditions of the workers.

Wren's Nest

Wren's Nest is a national nature reserve to the North-West of Dudley centre. The limestone mines are scheduled ancient monuments, representing some of the best examples of the mining heritage in the United Kingdom. The site has a dual significance, also recognised for containing fossilised remains of the sea-beds from the Silurian period of rare quality (Harrison, 2016).

The social history, the industrial history, and the geology of the site are intimately entwined; the area sitting within the urban sprawl of the Black Country. Graham Worton, Keeper of Geology at Wren's Nest, marks an evocative continuum from geology and deep time, to the present, the every-day sights of the town "bursting with geological information" (Worton, 1995, p. 108). The need to understand the earth for the purposes of industrialised mineral exploitation created the conditions for the growth in geologic study (Mikulic and Kluessendorf, 2007). This occurred in a period that saw a huge rise in fossil interest. With intimate knowledge of the rock, miners supplemented their incomes through the selling of fossils. This offered local men one of the few means at their disposal to make real money, paid as they were in "truck."

Dudley's most famous offspring, "the Dudley Locust" (Calymene blumenbachii), is a fossil of huge scientific significance, key in the understanding of the trilobite. For a time, all trilobites were named Dudley Fossils (Mikulic and Kluessendorf, 2007). The fossil itself has been adopted as a mascot by the town, appearing on the town coat of arms, removed, before a local endeavour to reinstate it. At one point in 2005 two notable examples were stolen from Dudley Museum. The theft mobilised a huge local effort for their safe return, showing the strength of feeling and local identity associated with "The Dudley Bug," as it is now known (Worton, 2005).

Roderick Murchison[4] wrote the definitive study of the Silurian period, *The Silurian System*, based largely on his research in Dudley (Murchison, 1839). Visiting Dark Cavern,[5] on the Wren's Nest site, in 1839 and 1849, he gave a public address, by gaslight, with an estimated 15,000 people in attendance to hear of the geology of the area, a striking example of early geo-tourism[6] (Black Country Geological Society, 2022). In reference to these two public speeches, the Black Country Geological Society states, "these remarkable events have since become part of both local and scientific 'lore'" (Black Country Geological Society, 2022).

174   *Sian Macfarlane*

The most prominent cavern on the Wren's Nest site, the Seven Sisters Gallery,[7] was in-filled with removable loose material to limit further deterioration of the remaining pillars (Mellor, 2021), described by Graham Worton as a "gentle engineering intervention to return this mine in the future to a future potential for geo-tourism" (Wolverhampton Arts and Culture, 2010). In 2008 funding allowed renewed access to the viewing areas of Seven Sisters mine entrance to be installed and much needed improvements to the site were made (Dudley Metropolitan Borough Council, 2022b). Near the entrance to the Seven Sisters Cavern lies a public artwork including a Murchison quote, recognising the role "the labours of practical men" have had in revealing the geologic significance of the site (Murchison, 1842, p. 2). Geology and wildlife leaflets are available to orient visitors, with "Hunt the Dudley Bug" guided walks offered by arrangement with the wardens.

Alongside this on-site provision, the history of the miner's relationship to mineral and fossil is told through the work of the Keeper of Geology, Graham Worton, and colleagues, who bring to life the rich social history and relationship between human and rock through local events and talks.[8] There is an absence of folklore belief and tradition, supernatural tale, or evocation of the ways in which miners protected themselves in their precarious roles in any of these materials, and whilst it is hard to disentangle the beliefs of limestone quarrymen and miners in contrast to their colliery peers, there is much potential in these strands of folklore to bring to life the stories of the men that worked the limestone. The overall effect is that, at present, the folklore of the Wren's Nest site is inaccessible to the site visitor. The wider stories and lore of the mining traditions of the area are well-told through literature on the broader region and its traditions, explored in the previous section, but the specifics of *this* site's lore, in comparison to others, remain largely elusive.

Dudley Canal and Tunnel Trust and the Supernatural

A present-day visit to the Dudley Tunnels reveals an active tourist destination offering regular boat trips into the tunnel system. The very existence of the tunnel complex is contingent on huge local effort from the 1950s to the 1970s to save the tunnels that were in danger of being closed (Dudley Canal and Tunnel Trust, 2021). From the time of widespread mining onwards there was a common belief that spirits were to be found underground (Edwards, 2018). There are great many examples of sightings and happenings, unexplained by conventional means, related to the tunnel system (Homer, 2017, p. 30). One references a mouth-organ-playing boy on a boat, lost overboard, heard by men staffing the tunnel system. Groups of school children were known to make use of an unloaded boat at the Tipton end of the Tunnel in the holidays, and the spectre was attributed to such an event. This ghostly occurrence was reported in the Dudley Herald, with a Mr. Price subsequently coming forward to say that the spectre of the organ player was his brother, Ned (Dudley Herald, 1978a, 1978b; The Legger, 2001). This story highlights the informal usage of the tributaries by the community, a common occurrence

The Folklore of the Subterranean   175

in its history. In the late 1990s there was a resurgence of interest in the ghostly appearances in the tunnels and caverns, with a clairvoyant employed to explore historic sightings (Hasan, 1999).

The use of the supernatural within tourism is a recognised methodology for increasing interest and participation, with many institutions incorporating such lore into wider programmes of activity (Mathe-Soulek, Aguirre and Dallinger, 2016). Evening ghost boat trips were offered over Halloween in 2001 (Express and Star, 2001a). The materials presented on the trips, collated by Trust archivist James Brookes, are unfortunately lost to time. Reported in the local newspaper, they were related to incidents of murder and drownings in the tunnel system since the eighteenth century (Express and Star, 2001b). This communication of the localised instances of ghost encounters has not sustained into the present day, however, with no organised mention of these spectral sightings to be found in present tunnel tourist provision. Whilst Halloween is a notable time to feature such local lore, there is a need to cater towards family groups. Thus, provision has featured universally recognised stories. In 2022, the tunnels hosted a pirate-themed Halloween event, for example (DCTT, 2022).

In general terms, present-day tunnel trips give a sense of the working conditions of the people who mined and traversed these dark tributaries, with projection and models along the route to evoke the sound and light, and the human endeavour. However, there is little mention of the ghosts and lore of old in the provision.

Dudley Castle and Supernatural Tourism

The 2001 ghost tours of the tunnels garnered national interest in the spectral in relation to the Dudley tunnel complex, leading to *Most Haunted Live at Halloween* being broadcast from the grounds of the neighbouring Dudley Castle (The Legger, 2002). The tunnel system reaches as far as the castle, though it is now inaccessible. There is a perceived nucleus of spirit activity centred on the Dudley area, the Castle viewed as the most haunted building in the region (Poulton-Smith, 2008, pp. 33–49). A trip into the tunnels and Singing Cavern was featured as part of the four-hour live broadcast.

Since then, other events have capitalised on the supernatural, examples including a Paranormal Evening hosted by spiritualist medium Craig Morris in 2018. Presenter-led talks during October half term 2021 also included material on the castle ghosts (Dudley Zoo and Castle, 2018, 2021). The site has also teamed up with the company Haunted Happenings[9] to deliver ghost hunts throughout the year, but particularly at peak calendar moments around Halloween and the winter months (Haunted Happenings, 2022). Other companies, Haunted Houses, Haunting Nights, and Haunted Adventure, all offer Dudley Castle Ghost Hunts (Haunted Adventure, 2022; Haunted Houses, 2022; Haunted Nights, 2022).

During *Most Haunted Live*, a well-known ghost, The Grey Lady, was evoked (Antix Productions, 2001). This spectre is reported widely in the ghost

176 *Sian Macfarlane*

writings around the site and is purported to haunt the castle after having died in childbirth (Poulton-Smith, 2008, p. 33; Homer, 2017, p. 32). Through the exploration and invocation of spectres of the past, a present-day audience can gain some insight into the harsh realities of childbirth in historic times, soliciting universal and relatable themes for an audience, that of childbirth and loss. In 2014, a digital photograph taken by a visitor went viral, shared across the globe, as it appeared to show a ghostly presence in a doorway in the castle, accompanied by a child, identified as the Grey Lady (Dudley Zoo and Castle, 2014).

Ancient castles or ruins, of which Dudley Castle is both, often lay claim to visitations from the afterlife (Thompson, 2010). Whilst the provision within a visit to the zoo would rarely be the primary motivator for visitors to Dudley Castle, the specialist ghost hunting events are specifically aimed at an audience interested in the spectral. These events represent an additional revenue stream for the venue and companies that provide such tours. While the details of the histories of those that haunt the site, such as Dorothy Beaumont, The Grey Lady, are included in literature surrounding the event, and no doubt incorporated into the evenings themselves, the focus is on the activities of ghost hunting, vigils, séances, glass moving, table tipping (Haunted Happenings, 2022), to create a sense of possibility and enchantment (Holloway, 2010). Whilst the details of the lives and conditions behind these spectral events are not the primary focus, they are still worthy of serious consideration, and explanations of activity that include historically accurate information would be a great benefit (Holloway, 2010).

Black Country Living Museum

The fourth and final case study in this chapter concerns the Black Country Living Museum, or BCLM, which sits on a site over 26 acres, the Dudley Canal and Tunnel Trust sitting adjacent. The idea for the site coincided with the closure of the last coal mine in the region in the 1960s, with the first visitors welcomed on-site in 1978, growing to 250,000 visitors per year by 1985 (BCLM, 2022b). The origins of the museum are contingent on the region's industrial heritage. The museum is populated with houses brought from the region, and live demonstrators, who bring the past to life through performance and interaction.

The site holds a great number of disused mine shafts, most of which have been filled in. The drift mine, a visitor attraction, functions as a vital part of the living museum, with an underground component that is currently being reviewed for renovation and safety. The above ground section is accessible, and home to regular gas demonstrations, and evocative tales of the hardship the colliers of the region faced. According to Tom Dipple, Programme Development Manager, the ethos of the museum – "real lives, real stories" – infuses all interpretation and programming in the museum. Halloween is recognised as a key moment in the diary of the museum, offering an opportunity for special bookable events for a family audience. It is a popular fixture where the ticketed events invariably sell out. Museum staff member Tom and researcher Nadia Awal mention that while it could be said that Halloween programming offers an opportunity to be more creative with the character design and narrative of the provision, the ethos still holds that the generation of material still needs to have a basis in research and fact.

The *Hauntings and Happenings* programme for October half term of 2020 demonstrates how researchers at the museum translate existing folkloric material into museum programming. The tale of the White Rabbit was adapted for presentation at the mine and colliery. White Rabbit was a wizard-like person who could solve problems of the spectral kind (Edwards, 2018, pp. 29–32), referencing the "wise-men" or "white witches" that would be called on for protective actions. The adaptation the museum made was to incorporate the idea of a miner having died, the fellow miners refusing to continue work until the body had been buried, an idea based on research (Palmer, 2007, p. 114). White Rabbit was called to exorcise the spirit, with a character "Caggy," brought in to perform the exorcism, aligning with the original tale (Edwards, 2018). The presentation involved holding a bible and a key in a particular hand, reference to which can be seen in the above "Ye Colliers Guide to …" (Palmer, 2007, pp. 112–113), relaying a particular verse. These elements are to be found elsewhere (Poulton-Smith, 2008, p. 5), where the event is attributed to Bilston. Researchers at the museum use these, and other, sources, alongside their own databases and research documents to construct and deliver the story.

Nadia Awal, researcher at the museum, relays how she found the article *Marvels and Mysteries of Hell Lane*, from the Birmingham Daily Gazette of 1866, particularly instructive, becoming the basis of their planning for a "Hell Lane" element in *Hauntings and Happenings*, the inspiration for the White Rabbit's colourful costuming and other elements (The Birmingham Daily Gazette, 1866). The museum renamed the streets for this Halloween activity, using Hell Lane and the like, places not only utilised through the incorporation of myth and supernatural story from across the region, but through the local place names themselves. Nadia relays how this helped to not only orient the visitor in their wayfinding, but also to create a further layer of "placemaking," being an example of what she termed "the creative helping the practical."

Of note in this translation of folklore of the region into compelling and engaging entertainment is the audience it is aimed at. The audience plays a key role in shaping the materials of folklore, as does the manner of presentation, each change necessitating a re-presentation, an adaptation of the material (Ben-Amos, 1971, p. 4). Nadia talks of how they considered using the tale of "the white lady" (Homer, 2017, p. 22; Gilbert, n.d.), a mother who killed her own children through desperation, her ghost purportedly haunting Coseley tunnel. This was rejected on grounds of appropriateness for a family audience. Thus, the retelling could be said to be compromised, partial, on the grounds of audience, the stories that relay the sometimes-harsh realities of the past are often tricky to translate to family audiences.

178 Sian Macfarlane

Contemporary Tourism, Folklore, and the Dudley Landscapes

The folklore of the Black Country region, focused on the Dudley area, has a rich and evocative history, with many strands of mining folklore to be discovered. Subterranean Dudley, revealed in its industrial past, plays an important part in the identity of the region, and there is a great deal of local pride and feeling entwined within it. From the saving of the Dudley tunnels to the local response to Murchison in the 1800s, and the theft of fossils in 2005, locals feel an attachment to their subterranean histories.

Over the four sites considered in this chapter, differences in folkloric presentation, communication, and dissemination can be seen.

The BCLM uses folklore as a tool for placemaking, for forging a regional identity through the reformulation of existing lore from the region in "an environment where they can see, smell, hear, touch and taste history" (BCLM, 2022d). Here, the fact that the museum is a conglomerate of buildings from across the region is a big advantage, as it can be selective, and draw from a range of folkloric instances and traditions. One potential issue with this is that the specificity of the lore becomes somewhat muddied and hard to decipher; it being difficult to tell a folkloric tale from say, Sedgley apart from one from Wednesbury. One successful strategy that the museum has used to counter this is to use the street names associated with these specific events, evoking place, and therefore placemaking, through reference to source geographies, creating new geographies, whereby Hell Lane (from Bilston) sits next to Devil's Elbow Bridge (Wednesfield), but nonetheless, keeping the relationship between event and place largely intact. This could be said to contribute to a "mythico-history," "to see stories of people's own lives melt into the general theme of a collective narrative" (Malkki, 2012, p. 56), the authentic translation of folkloric content from the region being of benefit in helping to forge a collective sense of Black Country identity, through vibrant character-based enactments. In turn, this solidifies the idea that folk narratives have the potential to "reflect the world-views of the societies that reproduce them, through the landscapes they encounter" (Paphitis, 2014, p.71).

The use of folklore at BCLM brings additional benefits, including increased visitor engagement and enjoyment and increased economic potential. However, the opportunity to offer these elements in the spaces – which must evoke these subterranean folkloric strands of history – remains elusive at present, the mine having been closed for repairs for quite some time.

In nearby Wren's Nest, where visible evidence of the geologic conditions which created the industrial boom in the region are in plentiful supply, lies perhaps the most challenging space in which to evoke a folkloric past. The underground tributaries and caverns where this folklore emerged are now inaccessible, either permanently filled in or temporarily, for their conservation. Here the folklore, if visible at all, resides in public artwork and a programme of irregular talks that bring to life the social conditions of mining. Absent in all of this is a sense of the superstition that miners used as a weapon against impending death and injury.

The Folklore of the Subterranean   179

Close by, the subterranean is accessible to the visitor in just one of these tourist locations at present, Dudley Tunnel and Caverns. There have been times in its history when boat trips considered the spectral history of the area, using it as an opportunity to garner interest, shedding light on the realities of a tunnel complex used by the locals and youth of the area – where accidents have occurred, the ghosts of those that succumbed said to haunt the canals. At present, there being no organised translation of the lore of the tunnels into the tour provision, the opportunities for placemaking through folklore and the evocation of the realities of the industrial past therefore remain a potential for future programming.

Dudley Castle is the site that has perhaps most strategically, and commercially, incorporated narratives of the supernatural into their provision. However, in the complex and evolving relationship between tourism, commerce, and folkloric material, the preservation of folklore is difficult to decode, their purpose being primarily for entertainment. While the audience at a Ghost Hunt might attend for supernatural reasons, this is not the only motivator. Within the content of the evening there is still the opportunity for reflection on the wider socio-political significance of the story/lore. The example considered here of the Grey Lady evokes the loss of a child and the precarious mortality of women in childbirth. That said, in the case of BCLM provision, there is much more room to shape a richer and more detailed presentation of lore, for example, the precarity of life in the mines, and the story of the White Rabbit, against an arguably "authentic" backdrop. These stories allow a doorway into the harsh conditions of the past. However, the tensions in creating this content for a specific family audience does mean that some of these strands cannot be fully explored, such as considering the difficult conditions of childbirth, child loss, and poverty in the story of "the white lady" (Gilbert, n.d.). The apparent contradiction, or irony, here is that in the re-enactment, which is essentially a fictionalising, there is more opportunity to explore the wider socio-political learnings that the folklore gives us, to decipher and to understand more detail from the folkloric sources. Alongside this, these events in the museum offer a place to play, as well as a place in play (Sheller and Urry, 2004, p. 1).

The developed overground landscapes and geographies of the BCLM and Dudley Castle can well accommodate and provide a home for the folklores of the region. Whether this is the case in the neighbouring Wrens Nest and Dudley tunnels is a more complex question. In both locations, folklore in a tourist setting has the potential to contribute toward the preservation of folkloric traditions that are in danger of being lost to obscurity, that in fact "tourism may, in fact, boost 'traditional' representations of place" (Kolås, 2004, p. 274).

The nature reserve presents a geopark destination where there is a constant fight to preserve it, with in-filling of caverns required to mitigate the risk of collapse. Whilst it has been noted elsewhere that folkloric tourism has the potential to put pressure on landscape, putting at risk the fragile ecologies of that which is sought out (Ironside and Massie, 2020), in the landscapes of the

180 *Sian Macfarlane*

Black Country, having been traumatised in the industrial revolution, the opposite might be true. Folklore has the potential to offer a chance for rehabilitation, playing a part in solidifying their futures, in the case of Wrens' Nest. A more visible communication of the rich folklore touched on in this chapter, of the relationship between worker and fossil, and the folklore of the caverns, would offer an opportunity to draw larger audiences to the site, thus playing a role in assuring its future and the vast sums of money needed to rehabilitate the cavern of the Seven Sisters.

This is not complacency in the face of the issues that wider tourism and commodification of folkloric culture would bring; as others have pointed out, the results of the usage of folklore within tourism are not uniformly positive, the assimilation bringing issues of dilution of the original cultural importance to the locals (Greenwood, 1989). However, acknowledging the complexity of the relationships between tourism and folklore is to recognise the myriad of opportunities that the folkloric brings, for revitalisation, participation, and play (Boissevain, 1996).

To utilise folklore more fully within the interpretive materials onsite, in the subterranean worlds under the surface of Dudley, would be where "the habitual and […] seeming mundanity of the everyday becomes marvellous, strange, and uncanny" opening new possibilities for the landscape, creating space for enchantment (Holloway, 2010). Through the folkloric this enchantment can help foster an optimistic cultural condition, aligning with the desire for accessibility, to both the cavern itself and the tunnel system, and access to the cultures of the immediate industrial past, which so define the region and identity of the Black Country (McEwan, 2008, p. 30).

These subterranean tributaries and caverns offer a fantastic example of the intermingling of the social, economic, industrial, and geologic past. The uncovering of the layers of folkloric experience in this area offers the region an opportunity to reveal the intimate socio-cultural relationships that the workers of the region have had with the geological past. Here the folklore remains inert at present, due in part to the accessibility of the caverns themselves, but rich with potential, like the very rocks that birthed the region.

Notes

1 The Black Country Living Museum is an open-air living museum where buildings are brought from across the Black Country and re-constructed carefully on-site, often brick-by-brick, to be as close to the original presentation as possible. Pubs, shops, dwellings, and industrial buildings are to be found onsite, with over 60 buildings relocated. Historic characters demonstrate what it was to live and work in the area in the industrial revolution and beyond. The museum is concerned with highlighting the social history of the men and women that shaped the region, telling the story of one of the first industrialised landscapes (Black Country Living Museum, 2022).

2 The butty system was a controversial approach that led to widespread abuse of the mining workforce. The owner of the land leased it for a royalty to a tenant. The tenant then contracted an ironmaster or butty who organised the workforce

The Folklore of the Subterranean 181

and paid the miners. George Barnsby, Black Country historian, reported that "The chief object of the butty system was to obtain coal at the cheapest cost, and pits were worked in an unskillful way to the neglect of discipline and safety precautions" (Palmer, 2007, pp.99–100).

3 Damp is the catch-all term for the gases emitted by the action of mining within the rock. Two examples are fire-damp and choke-damp. In *Underground Life*, published in 1869, the effects of fire-damp are explored by Louis Simonin; "the moment the mixed gas comes in contact with the flame of a lamp a tremendous explosion takes place, resulting from the combination of the components of the fire-damp, hydrogen and carbon ...The reaction produces an effect like the most brilliant lightning, and makes itself heard by a clap of thunder" (p.157). "No meteor, however terrible it may be supposed to be, can be compared to an explosion of fire-damp" (p.156)

4 Sir Roderick Impey Murchison (1792-1871) was a renowned Scottish geologist who turned to the new-at-the-time field of geology after leaving the army. Based on the study of Dudley fossils, his book, *The Silurian System*, published in 1839, defined the geologic period known as the "Silurian," with distinctive organic remains present (Dudley Metropolitan Borough Council, 2022).

5 Dark Cavern is Britain's largest man-made limestone cavern (Black Country Geological Society, 2022). After several roof collapses the cavern was back filled and sealed which means it is unlikely ever accessible (Dudley Canal Trust, 2015).

6 The 1839 event was described thus, "These immense caverns were illuminated from end to end; and the lights reflected from the waters below seemed in-numerable as the starry hosts. In lateral and highly arched caves, blue lights were burnt, and the whole was truly a magic illusion. The sides were lined with people, and in boats below were the members (some 300), headed by Mr. Murchison, who delivered a most animated and scientific lecture on the natural wonders by which they were surrounded. Volleys of arms were discharged with starling effect and the shouts of the multitude gave an almost superhuman sublimity to the scene, as the clouds from the artillery rolled with their thunders along the vaulted roofs" (The Literary Gazette, 1839, p. 568).

7 The Seven Sisters is a surface opening limestone cavern, possibly the last remaining in the world – formerly reaching more than 100 metres underground, in-filled to preserve it after a major roof collapse in October 2001 (Geoscientist Online, 2008; BBC Black Country, 2009). It is so named for the seven pillars that held up the roof, two now collapsed.

8 Through the work of the Friends of the Wren's Nest, West Midlands Geology Society, and Black Country Geological Society.

9 Haunted Happenings is one of the largest paranormal events companies in the UK. They run Ghost Hunts and paranormal events at sites across the UK. "We're an entertainment company so, while we don't fabricate anything, we can't profess to be experts on the paranormal. Clients come from all walks of life. Two thirds are female and, broadly speaking, want to have a paranormal experience, while the men get really interested in the evidence and the tech" (Hazel Ford, Managing Director; Macfarlane, 2022).

References

Antix Productions (2001). 'Most Haunted Live - Dudley Castle.' Available Online: https://www.youtube.com/watch?v=e4H5lk5ks28 [Accessed 15 March 2022].

Awal, Nadia (2022) 'Mining Superstitions'.

BBC Black Country (2009). 'Wren's Nest - a geological gem.' Available Online: http://news.bbc.co.uk/local/blackcountry/hi/people_and_places/nature/newsid_8388000/8388451.stm [Accessed 15 March 2022].

182 *Sian Macfarlane*

Ben-Amos, D. (1971). 'Toward a Definition of Folklore in Context.' *The Journal of American Folklore*, 84 (331), p. 3.

Black Country Geological Society (2022). 'Wren's Nest National Nature Reserve.' Available Online: https://bcgs.info/pub/local-geology/sites/wrens-nest-national-nature-reserve/ [Accessed 15 March 2022].

Black Country Global Geopark (2022). 'Sites to See.' Available Online: https://blackcountrygeopark.dudley.gov.uk/sites-to-see/ [Accessed 15 March 2022].

Black Country Living Museum (2022a). 'About Us.' Available Online: https://bclm.com/about/ [Accessed 15 March 2022].

Black Country Living Museum (2022b). 'The Museum's Story.' Available Online: https://bclm.com/about/the-museums-story/ [Accessed 15 March 2022].

Black Country Living Museum (2022c). 'The Single Largest Development in Our History; Taking Our Story into the 1940s – 60s.' Available Online: https://bclm.com/our-plans/ [Accessed 15 March 2022].

Black Country Living Museum (2022d). 'Forging Ahead.'

Boissevain, J. (1996). 'Ritual, Tourism and Cultural Commoditization in Malta: Culture by the Pound?' In T. Selwyn (ed.), *The Tourist Image: Myths and Myth-making in Tourism*. Chichester: Wiley and Sons, pp. 105–120.

Burritt, E. (1976). *Walks in the Black Country and Its Green Borderland*. Kineton: Roundwood Press.

Davidson, J.P. and Duffin, C.J. (2012). 'Stones and Spirits.' *Folklore*, 123 (1), pp. 99–109.

Davies, L. (1971). 'Aspects of Mining Folklore in Wales.' *Folk Life*, 9 (1), pp. 79–107.

Dudley Canal and Tunnel Trust (2021). 'History of the Tunnels'. Available Online: https://dudleycanaltrust.org.uk/portfolios/history/ [Accessed 15 March 2022].

Dudley Canal and Tunnel Trust (2022). 'Ahoy There Matey - Halloween'. Available Online: https://dudleycanaltrust.org.uk/events-2/halloween-3/ [Accessed 15 March 2022].

Dudley Canal Trust (2015). 'The Tunnels, Mines, and Caverns.' Available Online: https://web.archive.org/web/20150101180643/http://www.dudleytunnel.co.uk/mines.html [Accessed 15 March 2022].

Dudley Herald (1978a). 'Ghost Boat Haunting the Canal Tunnel?' 24 November.

Dudley Herald (1978b). 'Ghost Boat Prompts Some Sad Memories.' 1 December.

Dudley Metropolitan Borough Council (2020) '"We Did It!" UNESCO Geopark Status Secured.' Available Online: https://www.dudley.gov.uk/news/we-did-it-unesco-geopark-status-secured/ [Accessed 15 March 2022].

Dudley Metropolitan Borough Council (2022a) 'Geology of Wren's Nest National Nature Reserve.' Available Online: https://www.dudley.gov.uk/things-to-do/nature-reserves/wrens-nest-national-nature-reserve/geology-of-wrens-nest-national-nature-reserve/ [Accessed 15 March 2022].

Dudley Metropolitan Borough Council (2022b) 'Wrens Nest National Nature Reserve.' Available Online: https://www.dudley.gov.uk/things-to-do/nature-reserves/wrens-nest-national-nature-reserve/ [Accessed 15 March 2022].

Dudley Zoo and Castle (2014). 'Grey "ghost" in Castle Shot.' Available Online: https://www.dudleyzoo.org.uk/grey-ghost-in-castle-shot/ [Accessed 15 March 2022].

Dudley Zoo and Castle (2018) 'Date with the Paranormal.' Available Online: https://www.dudleyzoo.org.uk/date-with-the-paranormal/ [Accessed 15 March 2022].

Dudley Zoo and Castle (2021). 'Talks Return for Half Term.' Available Online: https://www.dudleyzoo.org.uk/talks-return-for-half-term/ [Accessed 15 March 2022].

The Folklore of the Subterranean 183

Durkin, A. (2019). 'A Short History of Dudley Castle'. Available Online: http://dudleycastle.org.uk/HTML/history.html [Accessed 15 March 2022].

'Economic impact of tourism – Dudley Borough 2019.' (n.d.). Available Online: http://cmis.dudley.gov.uk/CMIS5/Document.ashx?czJKcaeAi5tUFL1DTL2UE4zNRBcoShgo=kSgzXr6GUOum3exhENPcOR49hKS%2Bv9K9Rw4Dc%2BTaj8DvrMncoz2%2BVw%3D%3D&rUzwRPf%2BZ3zd4E7Ikn8Lyw%3D%3D=pwRE6AGJFLDNlh225F5QMaQWCtPHwdhUfCZ%2FLUQzgA2uL5jNRG4jdQ%3D%3D&mCTIbCubSFfXsDGW9IXnlg%3D%3D=hFflUdN3100%3D&kCx1AnS9%2FpWZQ40DXFvdEw%3D%3D=hFflUdN3100%3D&uJovDxwdjMPoYv%2BAJvYtyA%3D%3D=ctNJFf55vVA%3D&FgPllEJYlotS%2BYGoBi5olA%3D%3D=NHdURQburHA%3D&d9Qjj0ag1Pd993jsyOJqFvmyB7X0CSQK=ctNJFf55vVA%3D&WGewmoAfeNR9xqBux0r1Q8Za60lavYmz=ctNJFf55vVA%3D&WGewmoAfeNQ16B2MHuCpMRKZMwaG1PaO=ctNJFf55vVA%3D [Accessed 15 March 2022].

Edwards, C.C. (2018). *West Midlands Folk Tales*. Cheltenham: The History Press.

Endfield, G.H. and Van Lieshout, C. (2020). 'Water and Vertical Territory: The Volatile and Hidden Historical Geographies of Derbyshire's Lead Mining Soughs, 1650s–1830s.' *Geopolitics*, 25 (1), pp. 65–87.

Express and Star (2001a). 'Ghostly Canal Trips.' 8 September.

Express and Star (2001b). 'Launching the Ghost Boat.' 2 October.

Geoscientist Online (2008). 'Wren's Nest Feathered.' Available Online: https://www.geolsoc.org.uk/Geoscientist/Archive/September-2008/Wrens-Nest-feathered [Accessed 15 March 2022].

Gilbert, J. (n.d.) 'Hannah Cox (1873-1893) – The White Lady.'

Greenwood, D. (1989). 'Culture by the Pound: An Anthropological Perspective on Tourism as Cultural Commoditization.' In V.L. Smith (ed.), *Hosts and Guests: The Anthropology of Tourism*. Philadelphia: University of Pennsylvania Press, pp. 169–186.

Harrison, A. (2016). 'Wren's Nest at 60.' Available Online: https://www.geolsoc.org.uk/Geoscientist/Archive/August-2017/Wrens-Nest-at-60 [Accessed 15 March 2022].

Hasan, J. (1999). 'Ghosts 3.' Dudley Canal and Tunnels Trust Archive

Haunted Adventure (2022). 'Dudley Castle Ghost Hunts, West Midlands.' Available Online: https://hauntedadventure.co.uk/dudley-castle-ghost-hunts/ [Accessed 15 March 2022].

Haunted Happenings (2022). 'Haunted Happenings: Dudley Castle.' Available Online: https://www.hauntedhappenings.co.uk/dudley-castle/ [Accessed 15 March 2022].

Haunted Houses (2022). 'Dudley Castle.' Available Online: https://www.haunted-houses.co.uk/ghost-hunt/dudley-castle-ghost-hunts/ [Accessed 15 March 2022].

Haunted Nights (2022). 'Dudley Castle Ghost Hunt Dudley West Midlands.' Available Online: https://hauntingnights.co.uk/event/dudley-castle-ghost-hunt-dudley-west-midlands/ [Accessed 15 March 2022].

Holloway, J. (2010). 'Legend-Tripping in Spooky Spaces: Ghost Tourism and Infrastructures of Enchantment.' *Environment and Planning D: Society and Space*, 28 (4), pp. 618–637.

Homer, A. (2017). *Black Country Ghosts and Hauntings*. Birmingham: Tin Typewriter Publishing.

184 *Sian Macfarlane*

Ironside, R and Massie, S. (2020). 'The folklore-centric gaze: a relational approach to landscape, folklore and tourism.' *Time and Mind*, 13:3, 227–244, DOI: 10.1080/1751696X.2020.1809862

Kolås, å. (2004). 'Tourism and the Making of Place in Shangri-La.' *Tourism Geographies*, 6 (3), pp. 262–278.

Macfarlane, J. (2022). 'How Ghosts Became Big Business.' *Daily Mail*, 10 April. Available Online: https://www.dailymail.co.uk/home/you/article-10687515/How-ghosts-big-business.html [Accessed 16 March 2022].

Malkki, L.H. (2012). *Purity and Exile: Violence, Memory, and National Cosmology among Hutu Refugees in Tanzania*. Chicago: Chicago University Press.

Mathe-Soulek, K., Aguirre, G.C. and Dallinger, I. (2016) 'You Look Like You've Seen a Ghost: A Preliminary Exploration in Price and Customer Satisfaction Differences at Haunted Hotel Properties.' *Journal of Tourism Insights*, 7 (1), pp. 1–13.

McEwan, C. (2008). 'A Very Modern Ghost: Postcolonialism and the Politics of Enchantment', *Environment and Planning D: Society and Space*, 26 (1), pp. 29–46.

Mellor, T. (2021). 'My Involvement with Wren's Nest & Associated Locations.' *The Black Country Geological Society Newsletter*, 266, pp. 13–15.

Mikulic, D.G. and Kluessendorf, J. (2007). 'Legacy of the Locust – Dudley and Its Famous Trilobite Calymene blumembachii.' In D.G. Mikulic (ed.), *Fabulous Fossils: 300 Years of Worldwide Research on Trilobites*. Albany, NY: New York State Museum, pp. 141–169.

Murchison, R.I. (1839). *The Silurian System*. London: John Murray.

Murchison, R.I. (1842). 'Address Delivered on the First Meeting of the Dudley and Midland Geological Society.' Available Online: https://play.google.com/store/books/details?id=QB1kAAAAcAAJ&rdid=book-QB1kAAAAcAAJ&rdot=1 [Accessed 16 March 2022].

Nasmyth, J. and Smiles, S. (2011). *James Nasmyth: Engineer, an Autobiography*. Available Online: https://www.gutenberg.org/ebooks/476 [Accessed 16 March 2022].

Palmer, R. (2007). *The folklore of the Black Country*. Herefordshire: Logaston Press.

Paphitis, T. (2014). *The Place of Folklore in Archaeological Landscapes: Narratives and Identity in Medieval to Modern Britain*. Doctoral Thesis, University College London.

Parsons, H. (1986). *Portrait of the Black Country*. London: R. Hale.

Poulton-Smith, A. (2008). *Black Country Ghosts*. Cheltenham: The History Press.

Raybould, T.J. (1973). *The Economic Emergence of the Black Country: A Study of the Dudley Estate*. Newton Abbot: David & Charles.

Sheller, M. and Urry, J. (2004) *Tourism Mobilities Places to Play, Places in Play*. London; New York: Routledge. Available Online: https://ebookcentral.proquest.com/lib/uvic/detail.action?docID=199457 [Accessed 5 July 2022].

The Birmingham Daily Gazette (1866). 'Sketches of the Black Country in the olden time, No. VII. Marvels and Mysteries of Hell Lane.' 12 November.

The Legger (2001). 'The Legger,' *185* [Preprint].

The Legger (2002) 'The Legger,' *190* [Preprint].

The Literary Gazette (1839). 'The British Association. Ninth Meeting: Birmingham.' 7 September. Available Online: https://archive.org/details/sim_literary-gazette_1839-09-07_1181/page/568/mode/2up [Accessed 26 August 2022].

The Folklore of the Subterranean   185

Thompson, R.C. (2010). '"Am I Going to See a Ghost Tonight?": Gettysburg Ghost Tours and the Performance of Belief.' *The Journal of American Culture*, 33 (2), pp. 79–91.

Wallace, I.L. and Hirsh, J. (eds.) (2011). *Contemporary Art and Classical Myth*. Farnham: Ashgate.

Wise, M.J. (1953). 'The Decay of Agriculture in a Growing English Industrial Region: A Case Study.' *Agricultural History*, 27 (3), pp. 108–111.

Wolverhampton Arts and Culture (2010) *The Seven Sisters Mine, Wrens Nest, Dudley.* Available Online: https://www.youtube.com/watch?v=1rWFspg4PHc [Accessed 5 July 2022].

Worton, G. (2005). 'The Strange Case of the Dudley Bug.' *Geology Today*, 21 (3), pp. 108–109.

Worton, G.J. (1995). 'The Local Geologist 15: Geology in the Urban Wasteland.' *Geology Today*, 11 (3), pp. 108–113.

13 Ghosts, Extraterrestrials, and (Re-)enchantment

Possibilities and Challenges in Post-secular Tourism

Eva Kingsepp

Introduction

While paranormal phenomena are well established in the tourism industry in other Western countries, this is not the case in Sweden, whose official self-image has for almost a century been firmly rooted in an all-encompassing identification with modernity and values such as rationalism and materialism (Berggren and Trägårdh, 2015). Nevertheless, organised ghost walks are currently becoming increasingly popular on a local level, while UFO-related tourism is, basically, non-existent. Are ghosts and haunted houses considered more acceptable than extraterrestrials and UFOs? Notably, I do not write "belief in," as although one may be interested in paranormal phenomena; this does not necessarily include a belief in their existence. Thus, the epistemological and ontological aspects are not relevant here. Instead, my interest lies in the process when values considered socially deviant are (possibly) becoming part of "our generally accepted cultural-storehouse of 'truths'" (Sjödin, 2002, p. 84). To assess this, it is presumed that when a paranormal phenomenon is objectified through tourism, it has changed status from social deviance to social acceptance.

The paranormal and the occult have become integral parts of mainstream popular culture in the Western world (Hill, 2011; McIlwain, 2005; Partridge, 2004/2005). In many countries this has been acknowledged by the tourism industry, resulting in the phenomenon known as dark, or paranormal, tourism, offering all kinds of experiences challenging materialism and rationality (see Edwards, 2019; Hill, 2011; Meehan, 2008; Wright, 2020). The current popularity of ghost tourism suggests that belief in ghosts is today socially accepted in large parts of the Western world to an extent that it is not considered bizarre, or stigmatising, to personally participate in, for example, a ghost walk. As these are basically presenting uncanny narratives within a staged setting, questions regarding ontology or epistemology are irrelevant. In comparison, organised ghost hunts, or spending the night in a reputedly haunted house, are based on a willingness among participants to personally take part in what is claimed to include the possibility of a paranormal experience. In Annette Hill's words,

DOI: 10.4324/9781003374138-17

Ghosts, Extraterrestrials, and (Re-)enchantment 187

[t]here is a fine line between the pleasures of fear and hope in the existence of spirits [...] Whilst most people won't have an extrasensory experience, many hope to. It is this hope that makes ghost hunting much more than tourism.

(Hill, 2011, p. 106)

There are significant national differences regarding the degree to which paranormal phenomena have been commodified in tourism. For example, although ghost walks are becoming more common in Sweden, this is a fairly recent development. Moreover, with only a few exceptions (Blom, 2017; Blom and Nilsson, 2000) it is hard to find scholarly research related to dark/paranormal tourism in a Swedish context. A recent Bachelor's dissertation notes that there is "almost nothing" regarding ghost walks in Sweden (Neyman, 2020, p. 8). This suggests that although some aspects of the paranormal are currently being exploited in Swedish tourism, it may still be considered "fringe" by dominant cultural stakeholders. This chapter discusses the use of the paranormal in Swedish regional tourism, with the province of Värmland as a case study. A working hypothesis is that the tourism industry officially sanctions certain aspects of the paranormal, such as ghosts, through their deliberate use of them, while others, for example UFOs, are not considered suitable, despite their presence in mainstream popular culture.

Setting the Scene: Sweden and the Post-Secular

Sweden's official self-image has for more than a century been based on an identification with modernity and Enlightenment values, celebrating secularism, rationality, and science (Berggren and Trägårdh, 2015). Nevertheless, recent studies have indicated that around half of the country's population expresses a belief in the otherworldly. This has very little to do with traditional Christianity, but rather represents a "change in mentality," with an increasing "openness towards various new forms of paganism and esoteric thought forms" (Cavallin, 2017).[1] In a recent study based on interviews with secular middle class Swedes, David Thurfjell found a widespread kind of non-organised religiosity in today's Sweden, and an identification with virtues formerly closely associated with Christianity, such as the importance of ethics, compassion, to take care of each other, and so on. Not identifying themselves as religious, the interviewees express a "belief in something bigger," as well as an openness towards the existence of phenomena beyond the current limits of natural science (Thurfjell, 2019). Importantly, this should be regarded in comparison with the general attitude permeating official Swedish discourse regarding the paranormal, as two influential organisations, Vetenskap och Folkbildning (VoF) and Humanisterna, have for decades worked actively to shape public opinion on the otherworldly in Sweden. While VoF is part of the international sceptical movement, and primarily targets "pseudo-science," Humanisterna promotes secular humanism and opposes anything considered irrational, including religion. From this perspective,

188   *Eva Kingsepp*

research on paranormal phenomena is at best considered to be futile, simply dismissed as pseudoscience, and/or ridiculed.[2]

Both of these organisations fit very well with the official Swedish self-image as the epitome of modernity. According to Max Weber's famous theory about modernity and the disenchantment of the world (which will be discussed in more detail below), these are intrinsically related phenomena: when a society becomes modern, religious belief, as well as belief in magic and the supernatural, necessarily disappears. There is, simply put, no room for superstition in modernity. Thus, Sweden's self-identification as "the most modern country in the world" also implies that it is the most disenchanted. Nevertheless, popular culture offers another image. The next section presents an example of how the paranormal, in this case ghosts and hauntings, have been represented on Swedish television.

Disenchantment and Ghosts on Swedish Television

While the media provides much of our knowledge about the world, popular culture texts are regarded not simply as offering a reflection of contemporary society, but also as being a main source of cultural influence. Thus, the long-running Swedish reality-TV show *Det okända* (The Unknown), broadcast on one of our main TV channels, can be considered a guide to what is considered appropriate in a Swedish context. While long-running UK shows such as, for example, *Most Haunted* are largely based on spectacle, shock effects, and intensely emotional experiences (Hill, 2011, pp. 68–75; Smith and Ironside, 2022), *Det okända* downplays elements of the horrific and the exciting. The TV team's mission is to help the participants to solve a domestic issue – that of being haunted – through the help of an expert, the medium. There are only a few uncanny sequences, and there are almost never any screams or other strong shock effects. When the medium arrives, s/he will not only transform the haunted house into a more harmonious home, but also present an explanation of the phenomenon, as well as a way to handle it. Often, the inhabitants are assured that they are simply being looked after by a caring, deceased relative. The discourse acknowledges ordinary people's experiences without taking sides, combining scepticism with openness. *Det okända* also contains an element connoting more traditional scientific inquiry, as the team often – with varying degrees of success – try to corroborate parts of the unfolding narrative about the ghost through visits to historical archives.

Disturbing phenomena usually disappear after the medium's first visit, as the ghost has supposedly been helped over to the other side through a peaceful ritual. If it remains at the house, the inhabitants say that they do not get scared in the same way, "now that we know more about it." If there is a sceptic among them, he (it is most often a man) usually continues to refuse the ghost explanation, although he admits that "something" he cannot explain actually happened. He might also say that as we cannot really know anything about the paranormal, he has now become a bit more open minded towards it. Thus, there is a focus on interpreting and understanding

Ghosts, Extraterrestrials, and (Re-)enchantment 189

that somewhat downplays the intensity of the whole experience, and an overall ethical ambition to acknowledge and respect different beliefs (Kingsepp, 2012).

Popular Culture, the Paranormal, and Re-enchantment

Like "ordinary" tourism, dark/paranormal tourism is often inspired by popular culture texts. A kind of off-the-grid tourism, often called legend-tripping, targets particular locations in for example TV series about haunted houses, ancient cult places, vampires, etc. (Hill, 2011, pp. 89–107; Larson, Lundberg and Lexhagen, 2013; Smith and Ironside, 2022). The possibility of maybe oneself actually having an experience of a ghost – or, for that matter, seeing weird lights hovering in the sky – invites the individual to a type of social experience that is based on sensuous knowledge, rather than intellectual (Hill, 2011, p. 105). Still, there is a possible tension between, on the one hand, romantic folklore expressions such as enchanted forests, dancing fairies, and hauntings, and on the other hand more "suspect" areas of interest such as earth energies and ufology. Although the latter are phenomena either present in traditional folk belief or considered to be modern transformations, one might suspect that "meeting" an alien from outer space could be a considerably less attractive experience than evoking elves on a light Nordic summer's night (cf. Kripal, 2010; Kripal and Strieber, 2016). Nevertheless, many people long for encounters with the extraordinary, to personally experience feelings of magic and enchantment that are otherwise mostly associated with fantastic fiction (Hill, 2011; Saler, 2012). Accordingly, Weber's influential idea about disenchantment has been questioned:

> "Modernity" itself is just such an enchanted category that we have created. So too is the discourse of "modern disenchantment," a haunting presence that will not cease to disturb our thoughts until it is reunited with its antinomial partner, "modern enchantment."
>
> (Saler, 2006, p. 716)

Some scholars even refuse the thought that the modern world has ever lost its enchanting features (Bennett, 2001; Kripal, 2010; Landy and Saler, 2009). The appreciation of enchantment is not necessarily dependent on actual belief in, for example, the supernatural. On the contrary, it has rather been interpreted as a kind of postmodern playfulness that during the right circumstances invites experiences, actual or imagined, of phenomena otherwise banished from a materialist worldview (Bennett, 2001; Landy and Saler, 2009; Saler, 2012). In Jane Bennet's description, enchantment "entails a state of wonder [...] it is to be transfixed, spellbound" (2001, p. 5). Although she does not imply any relation to the experience of the holy or sacred, her description comes close to Rudolf Otto's classic idea of the numinous as the sudden encounter with a mystery both terrifying and fascinating (Hunter, 2021; Otto, 1958). Popular culture texts have a pivotal function, as it is here

190 *Eva Kingsepp*

that fantastic narratives, myths, and symbols used for re-enchantment are found in abundance (Moorehead and Caterine, 2019) – Lord of the Rings, the Twilight Saga, Harry Potter, Star Wars. The list of examples seems infinite, particularly when digital games and other forms of roleplay are added. Partridge (2004/2005) even proposes the term "occulture" to encapsulate the overall character of contemporary popular culture, highlighting the esoteric and spiritual roots of what has today become mainstream.

Basically, literature on the topic is divided into those who speak about a re-enchantment of the modern world (e.g., Partridge 2004/2005), and those who refer to experiences of enchantment (e.g., Bennett, 2001; Saler, 2006). In a secular/post-secular context like Sweden, it may be more appropriate to use the concept of re-enchantment, as it also implies a cultural reaction in response to rationalism and materialism (Partridge, 2004/2005). This is why I find the term re-enchantment particularly useful in a Swedish context, where the dominant worldview of disenchanted modernity is currently challenged (Cavallin, 2017; Thurfjell, 2019).

The tourist experience has many similarities to the idea of enchantment (Blom and Nilsson, 2000; Holloway, 2009; Houran *et al.*, 2020). Importantly, while popular culture in particular is providing guides for the experience of paranormal phenomena ("what do they look like and what do they mean"), tourism opens the door to possible first-hand experiences of them (cf. Kripal, 2010). While visiting a haunted house might be an experience akin to other instances of sightseeing, staying there overnight would add another level of engagement. A similar distinction may be the case regarding UFOs. The spatial and temporal aspects related to ghosts and UFOs suggest that while ghosts are place-bound – located in their haunted houses, or other specific locations – UFOs are much less predictable. In other words, although some areas are, according to contemporary folklore accounts, more frequently visited by UFOs than others, one never knows exactly where they might appear. Thus, the chances of oneself having an extraordinary experience while visiting a previous UFO sighting site are probably rather small – and the field, forest, or other location in question might in itself not be very exciting, as compared to a haunted house, a former battlefield, or other "dark places" imbued with specific cultural meanings inviting, or invoking, feelings of enchantment (see Smith and Ironside, 2022).

However, a comparison with UFO tourism in the United States suggests that while Roswell, New Mexico, is a popular tourist site, it is because of what is said to have happened there, and not because the visitors hope to actually encounter extraterrestrials when they visit (Blom and Nilsson, 2000, pp. 53; Meehan, 2008). Thus, there are two different aspects of time related to paranormal tourist experiences: at Roswell it is about transgressing the temporal border backwards, to the past, or rather to a recapitulation, a mirror, or a staging of something that took place in the past. As this past moment is being frozen in time, it is obviously not present in the way that experienced haunting is, although the latter is also (supposedly) a transgression of the temporal. If experienced, the haunting is in the present; it happens now. We

Ghosts, Extraterrestrials, and (Re-)enchantment 191

do not visit a haunted house to recapitulate the past from the safety of a temporal distance, but rather in the hope that the present might become transcendentally injected with something from the past – or at least to have a scary experience.

Notably, there are similar aspects found in certain subcultures associated with the paranormal, for example when a "normal" dowsing excursion at a specific location may for some participants develop into searching for UFO energies associated with it (cf. Kürti, 2002). However, in a Swedish mainstream context, this would be regarded as extremely deviant behaviour. In comparison, the socially "safe" visit to a haunted house would probably rather be considered eccentric, daring, or simply fun. Moreover, ghosts and hauntings are culturally well-established concepts. Using the vocabulary of social representations theory, ghosts are both named and objectified as ghosts, and we all know what ghosts *are* from popular narratives. Thus, they are in a way familiar, and especially in discourses such as that in which *Det okända* is embedded, they are made normal. The world is acknowledged as both weird and rational: as enchanted (cf Kripal, 2010; Saler, 2012).

In comparison, an interest in UFOs is often stereotypically associated with belief in little green men and conspiracy theories, which may be a reason to keep a low profile – at least in Sweden. A comparison between countries indicates that differences in paranormal tourism are often related to national and/or cultural heritage. Somewhat simplified, Britain is often associated with ghosts (Edwards, 2019), while Romania has its vampires (Candrea *et al.*, 2016; Larson, Lundberg and Lexhagen, 2013). In Iceland elves and other wonderful entities are still around (Jakobsson, 2015), and the United States offers a broad spectrum, from witches and battlefield ghosts to aliens, UFOs, and creatures such as Bigfoot (e.g., Krulos, 2018; Meehan, 2008; Thompson, 2010; Waskul and Eaton, 2018). What paranormal heritage would there possibly be for Swedish post-secular tourism to embrace?

Värmland: On Enchantment and Commodification

Located on the border between Sweden and Norway, Värmland is associated with deep forests, traditions of storytelling, and famous authors, including Nobel laureate Selma Lagerlöf, whose home Mårbacka is now a museum and one of the region's main heritage sites. Notably, much of her authorship relates to the fantastic and the otherworldly, often in a local narrative setting.[3] During the sixteenth and seventeenth centuries, Värmland was an important centre of national wealth through its numerous ironworks, where iron ore from the mines up north was refined. This was also where the so-called Forest Finns were living, originally brought to Sweden to cultivate the wilderness. Having preserved much of their old traditions, the reputation of being pagan sorcerers and witches remained well into the twentieth century (Ernvik, 1968). In contrast to Sweden's general identification with being urban and modern, Värmland's identity is founded on being rural and traditional, a borderland not only geographically, but also culturally and spiritually.

192 *Eva Kingsepp*

In other words, Värmland can be presented as a region not only of sagas and the imagination but also of magical folklore. Thus, it has a unique potential to truly enchant visitors.

Nonetheless, while there are a few local initiatives where supernatural aspects of cultural heritage are acknowledged – such as the transregional project Finnskogarna, regarding the Forest Finns, and occasional ghost-themed tours at Mårbacka – there is no official overall strategy at the regional economic tourism association Visit Värmland. When the case study for this chapter was made in 2018, Visit Värmland had an extensive guide to the region's haunted houses on their website – which provided the reason for making the study. However, as this chapter has been written in early 2022, the guide has since been removed. Another example is the municipality slogan of Sunne, where Mårbacka is located. According to the slogan, this is "sagolika Sunne." Literally translated, "sagolik" means "like a fairytale." However, a recent study shows that visitors do not find Sunne more "enchanting" than any other destination (Ryan Bengtsson et al., 2022). In fact, recent studies of Lagerlöf have chosen to highlight the author's relation to politics, gender, and early globalisation, while leaving her profound interest in the spiritual and otherworldly, including a close attachment to Theosophy, to the margins. This is also evident in the presentation of Lagerlöf on Visit Värmland's website, where she is introduced as an "influencer" of her time regarding the emancipation of women (Arenhäll, n.d.). Although a visit to Mårbacka may also offer other, more fantastic experiences, this is not what is promoted on a regional, or local, level. Thus, despite its slogan, Sunne remains disenchanted.

The Case Study: The Paranormal and Tourism in Värmland

In 2018 Visit Värmland used regional hauntings as part of their marketing. The study examined the relations between folklore and organised tourism regarding what kind of paranormal phenomena were considered useful in marketing and in place-branding (cf. Oswald, 2011). As recurring topics in regional newspapers, it can be argued that ghosts and UFO sightings are living parts of folk culture. Paradoxically, although interest in such phenomena on an individual level may be considered eccentric, or even dubious, their presence in mainstream media is socially legitimate. However, as in ghost tourism, journalists do not claim that the phenomena really exist; they are reporting about other people's experiences of them, leaving the ontological assessment to the audience. An underlying assumption for this study is provided by Serge Moscovici's (2000) theory about social representations: when we encounter an unfamiliar, often emotionally charged phenomenon, we tend to use culturally established interpretative mechanisms and frameworks to understand, and thereby to discharge, it. Such mechanisms are found in naming, whereby the phenomenon initially becomes classified, and objectification, which further transforms it into something more familiar. It can be argued that when there is a well-established narrative about a particular kind

Ghosts, Extraterrestrials, and (Re-)enchantment 193

of paranormal phenomenon, it is very probable that this will be used to make sense of experiences that seem related to it.

Newspaper Ghosts and UFOs

Before interviewing Visit Värmland, an overview was made of ghosts and UFOs in regional Värmland newspapers 2015–2018, in total 33 texts were identified. In fact, most of the 26 ghost texts were related to tourism, as when a particular house was said to be popular among visitors hoping for a spooky experience. However, the main topic was usually something else – an art exhibition, local history, a café, and so on – while the ghost was merely a curiosity in the margins. A few articles had a ghost walk/tour as their main story, focusing on the visitor experience, while one was about local ghost hunters. This was the only ghost text where epistemology was mentioned. In comparison, all the four articles about possible UFO encounters stressed the shocking, enigmatic character of the phenomena: what was this weird experience actually about? Could it really have been a UFO? Besides the descriptions of the events, there was a focus on epistemology, with representatives from the organisation UFO-Sweden acting as experts: "What was it that the woman saw that night in March, above a field near Sunne? 'Difficult to assess'[…]" (de Bouczan, 2016). Thus, the reader – and everyone else – is left in uncertainty. Notably, in the other three texts mentioning UFOs, belief in the phenomenon is explicitly referred to as irrational and/or ridiculous.

To conclude: while the ghost texts do not question the existence of ghosts as a cultural phenomenon, the UFO encounter articles highlight questions regarding ontology. In Moscovici's terminology, ghosts – "real" or performed – are both named and objectified, resulting in familiarity. It does not matter that ghosts have not been scientifically certified; they exist in our collective imagination, which is sufficient for the classification to work. In comparison, the appearance of what might be a UFO hovering over a meadow is much more difficult to name, as well as to objectify. Moreover, the persons having possible UFO experiences were all anonymous, as compared to the ghost texts, where everyone – including the ghost hunters – appeared with their names. This might support the notion of a social distinction between accounts of ghosts and of extraterrestrials.

The sample indicates that ghosts generally function as either site-bound exotic elements that possibly add extra attraction for potential visitors, or as a framework for specific events, such as Halloween or ghost walks. As the paranormal aspects are transformed into playful signs familiar from popular culture, the objectification diminishes their irrational qualities, which contributes to reducing social deviance. Although the UFO narratives also contain signifying elements anchoring them in popular culture representations, there are no signs connoting playfulness, or a light-hearted cognitive distance, in the accounts. It is hard to imagine that anyone would be inspired to visit the sites mentioned, unless extremely interested in UFO phenomena (and thus, according to many, a potential tin foil hat owner).

194   *Eva Kingsepp*

Visit Värmland's "Haunted Places" Web Project: Interviews

Visit Värmland is the region's main economic association, whose website https://visitvarmland.com includes pages for different destinations, as well as more general themes. This is the official portal for tourism in Värmland. In 2017/2018 one such theme was haunted places, with a list of 20 different locations all over the region. According to project manager Andreas Norum, there was no particular strategy behind the "Haunted Places" webpage. Linda Danielsson, who was responsible for its creation, explained that the idea was born following a sudden increase in the number of web searches through key words related to Frammegården in Skillingmark and ghosts.[4] It turned out that a young Swedish influencer couple, Jocke and Jonna, had recently published a film on their highly popular YouTube channel about their spooky experiences there, attracting young people, in particular, to search for Frammegården. The mapping of haunted places for Visit Värmland's web portal, combining Google Maps with editorial texts about each site and occasional links to short films, was a direct attempt to take advantage of this trend. It turned out to be successful: there was "a flood" of new visitors to the web site, an increase that was still to some extent visible at the time of the interview.

Nonetheless, Visit Värmland did not have a deliberate strategy to go further in using ghost tourism for attracting visitors, and there were no thoughts about working with other possible paranormal attractions from a viewpoint other than the common framework of folklore and cultural heritage. As Danielsson said, "we are still stuck in the traditional lines of thought about how to attract visitors, while we ought to think more about what the visitors as individuals are actually interested in." According to Danielsson, if it turns out that there is public interest to visit the locations of UFO sightings, or crop circles, they would possibly make use of this. Notably, she did not feel that there are any taboos related to this, as "what counts is to offer people experiences that they appreciate as memorable and enjoyable." When I asked about possible public criticism – for example by VoF and/or Humanisterna – about promoting superstition, this was not considered an issue.

A Swedish Model for the Paranormal?

Already, two decades ago, Blom and Nilsson (2000) have pointed out several places in Sweden suitable for dark, or paranormal, tourism, highlighting the wide popular interest in the fantastic, the unexplained and the spiritual, and particularly stressing the relations between media representations and the paranormal. Nevertheless, this field still seems quite unexplored by entrepreneurs. Although there are ghost walks and haunted house experiences, information about them usually requires specifically searching for them on the web, suggesting that Swedish paranormal tourism is dependent on individual enthusiasts and the level of their ambitions, as well as their economic assets. In comparison, ghost tourism in the UK gives a Swedish visitor the impression

Ghosts, Extraterrestrials, and (Re-)enchantment 195

of being an established institution, not least from the number of flyers available in hotel lobbies and advertisements in tourist guides.

It is possible that the popular Swedish reality-TV show *Det okända* has contributed to setting the national standards for the public experience of hauntings, as different kinds of powerful emotions – fear, melancholy, sadness, loss, and so on – are downplayed and combined with a rationalist, albeit ethically informed attitude, which also includes a dose of scepticism. Thus, it is not just about making people jump, as in many British or US shows. Reflecting virtues in the official Swedish self-image, the model offered by *Det okända* is rather about learning how to live peacefully together with what may be interpreted as ghosts (Kingsepp, 2012). In that way, it is possible to suggest that the show's main message is not so much about the paranormal phenomenon per se, but can rather be interpreted as an idealistic demonstration of preferable "Swedish values." Accordingly, the medium shows how initial social disorder can be turned into harmony through acceptance, openness, and dialogue, which is, basically, what is commonly known as "the Swedish model" (Berggren and Trägårdh, 2015). Obviously, this is far from the profound othering of the ghost as terrifying and alien in, for example, *Most Haunted*. Is it so that Swedish ghost tourism still has to find its own character, based on something else than simply delivering scary effects? Or are we slowly adjusting to international standards? Obviously, more research is needed.

In comparison, UFOs seem very hard to fit into the official Swedish mentality. Although one may argue that the Swedish model of tolerance should be appropriate here as well, the negative connotations with fringe culture – tin foil hats, conspiracy theories and pseudoscience – are very strong. While there are occasional media reports of possible UFO sightings, these do not seem to have inspired entrepreneurs in tourism. This would certainly be interesting to explore further as well, although that would be another type of study.

Despite being dismissed in dominant Swedish discourse as non-existent, ghosts are nevertheless a familiar part of our society, and presumably perform an important function in providing life with elements of enchantment. As the example of *Det okända* indicates, hauntings may also incite critical reflection, not only on spiritual matters, but on ethics more generally, including our relations towards other-human-beings. Together with the objectification of ghosts as a cultural phenomenon, this perspective may have contributed to establishing a socially acceptable way of relating even to "real" ghosts. However, despite a growing interest in ghost walks and visits to haunted houses, this kind of legend-tripping seems in Sweden to be dependent on the interplay between local initiatives and visitors who actively seek experiences outside the dominant rational, materialist cultural framework. The concept of re-enchantment offers one way to understand the attraction of such experiences.

Possibly, it is one thing to personally express a belief in, or openness towards, the otherworldly (cf. Thurfjell, 2019), but another to engage in performative practice. Further, the expectations and interpretations of

196 *Eva Kingsepp*

experiences related to the paranormal differ between people and may have a lot to do with how we make sense of the unknown through the use of cultural patterns, for example social representations, familiarised through popular media. There is also the question of whether one prefers authentic experiences or more playful ones. Importantly, this does not imply the endorsement of pseudoscience or anti-humanist values. As shown by several scholars (e.g., Bennett, 2001; Saler, 2012), experiences of playfulness and enchantment in modernity are, in fact, essential to being human.

Notes

1 All translations from Swedish in this chapter are made by its author.
2 Notably, there is a Swedish organization similar to the Society for Psychical Research in the UK, Sällskapet för Parapsykologisk Forskning, although it has basically no influence at all on public discourse.
3 See Wijkmark (2009) on the gothic in Lagerlöf's works. Regarding her relations to Spiritism and theosophy, see Lindqvist (1961).
4 Both telephone interviews were made 18 April 2018.

References

Arenhäll, K. (n.d.). 'Selma Lagerlöf. Författare och Nobelpristagare.' Available Online: https://visitvarmland.com/portratt/selma-lagerlof/ [Accessed 15 April 2022].

Bennett, J. (2001). *The Enchantment of Modern Life: Attachments, Crossings, and Ethics.* Princeton: Princeton University Press.

Berggren, H. and Trägårdh, L. (2015). *Är svensken människa? Gemenskap och oberoende i det moderna Sverige.* 2nd revised edition. Stockholm: Norstedts.

Blom, T. (2017). 'Falks grav: En morbid och mytrelaterad turismupplevelse i tiden.' *Geografiska Notiser*, 75 (3), pp. 105–113.

Blom, T. and Nilsson, M. (2000). *Symbolturism – Morbidturism – Mytturism. Turistiska produkter av vår tid? Arbetsrapport Nr 11. Turism & Fritid.* Samhällsvetenskap. Karlstad: Karlstad university.

Candrea, A.N., Ispas, A., Untaru, E.N., Nechita, F. (2016). 'Marketing the Count's Way: How Dracula's Myth Can Revive Romanian Tourism.' *Bulletin of the Transilvania University of Braşov Series V: Economic Sciences*, 9 (58).

Cavallin, C. (2017). 'Det postkristna Sverige i siffror.' *Signum 2*, March 2017, pp. 13–18.

de Bouczan, N. (2016). 'Såg ufo över åkern – SUNNE. Rött klot.' *Nya Wermlands-Tidningen*, 26 January.

Edwards, A. (2019). '"Do the Ghosts Roam Along the Corridors Here at Ordsall Hall?": Paranormal Media, Haunted Heritage, and Investing Historical Capital.' *The Journal of Popular Culture*, 52 (6), pp. 1312–1333.

Ernvik, A. (1968). *Folkminnen från Glaskogen: Sägen, tro och sed i väst-värmländska skogsbygder, II.* Uppsala: Landsmåls- och folkminnesarkivet.

Hill, A. (2011). *Paranormal Media: Audiences, Spirits and Magic in Popular Culture.* Abingdon: Routledge.

Holloway, J. (2009). 'Legend-Tripping in Spooky Spaces: Ghost Tourism and Infrastructures of Enchantment.' *Environment and Planning: Society and Space*, 28, pp. 618–637.

Houran, J., Hill, S.A., Haynes, E.D. and Bielski, U.A. (2020). 'Paranormal Tourism: Market Study of a Novel and Interactive Approach to Space Activation and Monetization.' *Cornell Hospitality Quarterly*, 61 (3), pp. 287–311.

Hunter, J. (2021). 'Deep Weird: High Strangeness, Boggle Thresholds and Damned Data in Academic Research on Extraordinary Experience.' *Journal for the Study of Religious Experience*, 7 (1), pp. 5–18.

Jakobsson, Á. (2015). 'Beware of the Elf! A Note on the Evolving Meaning of Álfar.' *Folklore*, 126, pp. 215–223.

Kingsepp, E. (2012). 'Medier i medier: Det okända och döden som ett annat sätt att vara.' In A. Hirdman (ed.), *Döden i medierna: Våld, tröst, fascination*. Stockholm: Carlssons.

Kripal, J. (2010). *Authors of the Impossible: The Paranormal and the Sacred*. Chicago: The University of Chicago Press.

Kripal, J. and Strieber, W. (2016). *The Supernatural: A New Vision of the Unexplained*. New York: Jeremy P: Tarcher/Penguin.

Krulos, T. (2018). 'Cryptozoology: The Hunt for Hidden Animals and Monsters.' In Waskul, D. and Eaton, M. (eds.), *The Supernatural in Society, Culture, and History*. Philadelphia: Temple University Press.

Kürti, L. (2002). 'Neo-Shamanism, Psychic Phenomena and Media Trickery.' In J. Kaplan and H. Lööw (eds.), *The Cultic Milieu: Oppositional Subcultures in an Age of Globalization*. Walnut Creek: Altamira Press.

Landy, J. and Saler, M. (eds.) (2009). *The Re-Enchantment of the World: Secular Magic in a Rational Age*. Stanford: Stanford University Press.

Larson, M., Lundberg, C., and Lexhagen, M. (2013). 'Thirsting for Vampire Tourism: Developing Pop Culture Destinations.' *Journal of Destination Marketing & Management*, 2 (2), pp. 74–84.

Lindqvist, S. A. (1961). 'Om Selma Lagerlöfs förhållande till spiritism och teosofi. Samlaren.' *Tidskrift för svensk litteraturhistorisk forskning*, 81, pp. 36–74.

McIlwain, C. (2005). *When Death Goes Pop: Media and the American Culture of Death*. New York: Peter Lang.

Meehan, E.R. (2008). 'Tourism, Development, and Media.' *Society*, 45 (4), pp. 338–341.

Moorehead, J. and Caterine, D. (2019). *The Paranormal and Popular Culture: A Postmodern Religious Landscape*. Abingdon: Routledge.

Moscovici, S. (2000). *Social Representations: Explorations in Social Psychology*. Cambridge: Polity Press.

Neyman, C. (2020). 'Den mörka turismens geografi: En kartläggning av Sveriges spökvandringar'. Bachelor's thesis. Umeå: Umeå University, Department of Geography.

Oswald, L. (2011). *Marketing Semiotics: Signs, Strategies, and Brand Value*. Oxford: Oxford University Press.

Otto, R. (1958). *The Idea of the Holy*. Oxford: Oxford University Press.

Partridge, C. (2004/2005). *The Re-Enchantment of the West: Alternative Spiritualities, Sacralization, Popular Culture, and Occulture. Volume I-II*. London: T&T Clark International.

Ryan Bengtsson, L., Braunerhielm, L., Gibson, L., Hoppstadius, F. and Kingsepp, E. (2022). 'Digital Media Innovations Through Participatory Action Research. Interventions for Digital Place-based Experiences.' *Nordicom Review*, 43 (2), pp. 134–151.

Saler, M. (2006). 'Modernity and Enchantment: A Historiographic Review.' *American Historical Review*, June 2006, pp. 692–716.

198　*Eva Kingsepp*

Saler, M. (2012). *As If: Modern Enchantment and the Literary Prehistory of Virtual Reality*. Oxford: Oxford University Press.

Sjödin, U. (2002). 'The Swedes and the Paranormal.' *Journal of Contemporary Religion*, 17 (1), pp. 75–85.

Smith, F. and Ironside, R. (2022). 'The Uncanny Place: A Critical Appraisal of Popular Paranormal TV Shows.' *The Journal of Popular Television*, 10 (1), pp. 95–108.

Thompson, R.C. (2010). '"Am I Going to See a Ghost Tonight?": Gettysburg Ghost Tours and the Performance of Belief.' *The Journal of American Culture*, 33 (2), pp. 79–91.

Thurfjell, D. (2019). *Det gudlösa folket: De postkristna svenskarna och religionen*. Stockholm: Norstedts.

Waskul, D. and Eaton, M. (eds.) (2018). *The Supernatural in Society, Culture, and History*. Philadelphia: Temple University Press.

Wijkmark, S. (2009). *Hemsökelser - Gotiken i sex berättelser av Selma Lagerlöf*. Diss. Karlstad: Karlstad University Studies.

Wright, D.W.M. (2020). 'Encountering UFOs and Aliens in the Tourism Industry.' *Journal of Tourism Futures*, 8 (1), pp. 7–23.

TV series

Det okända (2004–2019) TV4.

Websites

Visit Värmland, "Hemsökta platser i Värmland" ("Haunted places in Värmland"). Available Online: https://www.visitvarmland.se/sv/hemsokta-platser-i-varmland [Accessed 29 March 2018; no longer available].

14 Mythical Park

Reflections on Folklore, Its Natural Environment, and Tourism

Katja Hrobat Virloget

Introduction

This chapter analyses the exemplary case-study of "The Mythical Park" in Slovenia, which exemplifies a contemporary re-emerging of traditions, defined by researchers as the process of re-enchantment. Some researchers speak about inventing tradition, revitalisation, folklorisation, traditionalisation, commodification of traditions, past-presencing, and so on (see Clemente and Mugnaini, 2001; Testa, 2020; Testa and Isnart, 2020), while the term "enchantment" encompasses the more experiential and emotional aspects of these processes. Scholars have noted that the period of Enlightenment in Western societies was characterised by a lack of spirituality, loss of religion, and secularisation, while contemporary society is now inclined towards the "return" of traditions and their charm, resulting in new forms of religiosity (Testa and Isnart, 2020). As Alfred Gell (1992) has defined it, "enchantment" is the transformation of an object, place, person, or performance into something mysterious, fascinating, or magical, outside the rational perception of reality (Testa and Isnart, 2020). This chapter discusses an example of enchantment in the establishment of The Mythical Park, but in contrast to similar cases of traditionalisation, or re-traditionalisation and mythopoiesis (Testa, 2020), it did not happen "bottom-up," but "from above."

The Mythical Park in Rodik, located in the Karst region of Slovenia was, together with the village of Trebišća near Mošćenička Draga, on the Adriatic coast in Croatia, linked as a cross-border tourist destination based on the so-called mythical landscape or narrative tradition embedded in the local environment.[1] This chapter, building on decades of research on the narrative tradition of this place, was to present folklore in the place it originates – *in situ* with the local natural environment – to show the link between folklore and place-making. The Mythical Park of Rodik has received vast interest from the wider public and media. The upper part of The Mythical Park, the Lintver's route, was awarded second prize in 2021 by the Tourist Association of Slovenia in the category of "best thematic routes" (Visit Kras, 2022), and the whole Mythical Park received the honorary Valvasor award from the Slovenian Museum Society for the presentation of the mythical tradition

DOI: 10.4324/9781003374138-18

200   *Katja Hrobat Virloget*

(Bonin, Balkovec Debevec and Mlinar, 2022). The park was also selected as one of the best creative projects in small and remote places by the Urban Planning Institute of the Republic of Slovenia (Nikšič, Goršič and Seite, 2022). A year after the establishment of The Mythical Park in Rodik,[2] and having initiated the idea of using folklore in this way, I reflect on the positive and negative effects of presenting folklore in its natural environment for touristic purposes.

About the Project

My idea of presenting rich folklore embedded in the local landscape (Hrobat, 2011) was accepted with enthusiasm by the local community of Rodik. In cooperation with me as ethnologist, researching the folklore for decades, the local community of Rodik and surrounding places in the Karst region managed to get funds to establish The Mythical Park, perceived by them as a new economic opportunity in line with the contemporary trends of promoting heritage and green tourism. The people of Rodik are known for their hospitality and good sense of community, for their good restaurants and tourist farms, and for organising traditional festivities, such as celebrations for the local saint and a chestnut festival. Nowadays, local communities increasingly follow the contemporary trends of localisation by reviving past traditions to enrich the present (Fakin Bajec, 2011). I perceive the enthusiasm for The Mythical Park as part of contemporary trends for seeking "authentic" pre-Christian traditions, rooted in specific localities as a basis for the redefinition of local identity (Hrobat Virloget, 2019). This is in trend with the contemporary processes of localisation or revitalisation of local history and traditions as an answer to the processes of globalisation (Fakin Bajec, 2011). In small marginal communities in search of visibility and struggling to forge their identity, the return to specific local traditions can serve as a strong cultural glue against the disruptive social changes brought about by late-modern processes (Testa, 2020).

The common features of the parks on both sides of the Slovenian-Croatian border are the mythical traditions in the landscape presented *in situ*, in the form of narrative tradition and toponyms. Although the folklore in this project is not only associated with mythical elements, the non-professional writers of the project proposal insisted on calling it The Mythical Park to make it more attractive for the wider public. However, there are differences between these two parks. While in Trebišće the heritage route is based on mythical toponyms,[3] and the folklore narratives are almost non-existent, the latter is a fundamental feature of the park in Rodik, where folklore narratives are presented in the places from which they originate, and are explained. For example, narratives of the mythical pagan giant predecessors of Ajdi provide an explanation for the folk perception of the prehistoric settlement of Ajdovščina, now an archaeological site. Folklore about the devil riding a burning cart called "Šembilja" explains the folk perception of marks in the rock, identifying them as furrows created by his flaming wheels. Stories about certain caves explain them as entrances to the world beyond. Narratives of "supernatural"[4] beings, or deaths and killings from the cadastral border, mark the liminal space between the world of the living and the dead. There is a Christian legend about Jesus and St. Peter, which explains how certain caves in the Rodik environment were created. Folklore about the archaic mythological being Baba (English, Hag), who is embedded in a stone monolith, gives a symbolic meaning to the stone, which is also linked to weather rituals and beliefs. There are narratives about Lintver, the serpent-dragon from the Jezero (English, Lake), where Christian rituals of purification against the devil's forces were performed. This story explains the traditional perception of the unusual source of water on the top of the hill, and the storms as consequence of the anger of the serpent in this place, which is scientifically interpreted as a pre-Christian cult site (see Figure 14.1; Hrobat Virloget, 2007, 2021). In contrast with Rodik, in Trebišće a reconstructed (pre-) Slavic mythical story is presented (Belaj, 1998; Katičić, 2008). However, only two mythical toponyms are presented *in situ*, while in Rodik different folklore narratives are embedded in the local landscape (Hrobat, 2007, 2010). The two mythical beings, Perun above Trebišće and Baba from Rodik, the Slavic divine mythical couple (depicted in the project's logo), connect the two locations as a joint cross-border tourist destination.

Figure 14.1 Lintver.
(Picture by Author).

Figure 14.2 Mare's Head Cadastral Boundaries.
(Picture by Author).

The usual information boards are avoided in Rodik by presenting the mythical landscape locations via a GSM app, or in written form. Stone markers guide visitors along the mythical paths, and stories are interpreted in stone sculptures (see Figure 14.2). The youngest visitors can engage in fun games, and the solutions to riddles at different locations along the trail open interactive points in the visitor centres at Rodik[5] and Trebišće (Hrobat Virloget, 2021).

Folklore and Landscape in The Mythical Park

What is innovative in The Mythical Park is that the folklore is presented in its natural environment, and often provides explanations about specific locations in the landscape. As an expert Italian-English storyteller Giovanna Conforto reflected that all the narratives from Rodik, which have been published by the villagers in a book (Peršolja, 2000), do not make any sense if they are not related to the landscape from where they derive. Folklore gets its meaning only when it is told in the natural environment; therefore, the function of folklore for place-making is clear. The place does not have any sense without folklore, and, vice versa, the folklore does not have any sense without its relation to place. In the example of The Mythical Park, the stories about the Ajdi, the giants, do not have any sense if they are not heard in connection to the prehistoric and Roman hillfort of Ajdovščina. The legends of the

Mythical Park 203

Šembilja, the devil leaving the furrows behind his flaming cart, do not have any meaning if the visitor does not see the traces in the rock. The narratives about falling into certain caves and reaching the otherworld are just boring stories if you are not in front of these concrete Karstic abysses.

Anthropologists agree that space is a social construct; its conceptualis-ations arise from the changing historical contexts and cultural specificities of a given time (Descola and Pálson, 1996, p. 15). According to Gérard Lenclud (1995, pp. 4–7), landscape encompasses two levels of reality, the material, internal, and the mental, creative, which emerge from certain perspectives and conceptual schemes. Therefore, there is no "absolute" landscape because it should be perceived as a cultural process based on the relationship between place and space, inside and outside, and image and representation, all of which depend on the cultural and historical context (Hirsch, 1995). According to Pierre Bourdieu (1977, p. 14), space has no meaning apart from our prac-tice, or habitus, which constitutes and is constituted by an actors' movement through space. Therefore, meanings are not fixed in space but are activated by social practice. They are invoked by actors, who bring their own discursive knowledge and intentions to the interpretation of spatial meanings. Tim Ingold (2000) defines landscape by our experience of it through movement, action, and participation, and not as "space" or "land." Ways of functioning in an environment are levelled with ways of its perception, which disagrees with the opposition between naturalist and culturalist perspectives, between practical-technical interaction with the environment and its mythical-reli-gious, or cosmological, construction. Hunter-gatherers do not try to physi-cally reconstruct the environment to adapt it to their cosmological perceptions; rather, they conceptualise the environment as it is. The world becomes their home by living in it, by embodying its phenomena in everyday activities. This perception differs from the Western perception of nature as a material sub-strate that must be "humanised." For hunter-gatherers, life is in fact given by humanity's engagement with the environment, and not by approaching the world from a position outside of it. For instance, hunter-gatherers learn about their mythical ancestors and moral principles by perceiving and mov-ing through the landscape. Keith H. Basso calls this cultural activity the "sensing of place," with which he tries to focus the attention on "an ordinary way of engaging one's surroundings and finding them significant" (Basso, 2002 p. 143). The same can be argued also for the traditional perception of landscape in Europe (Hrobat, 2010).

There were several anthropological researchers of the so-called "native narrative traditions" outside of Europe (see Hirsch and O'Hanlon, 1995; Feld and Basso, 1996), but the connection of place to folklore entered into European folkloristics relatively late. Before the introduction of the concept of *place-lore* (Valk and Sävborg, 2018; Šrimpf Vendramin, 2021), the connec-tion between places, oral tradition, and toponyms was studied by researchers of Slavic mythology through the analysis of mythical landscapes as the rem-nants of the Slavic mythical worldview (see Belaj, 1998; Katičić, 2008; Hrobat, 2010; Belaj and Belaj, 2014; Pleterski, 2014). Folklorists realised later that it is folklore which gives meaning to places, because when it is narrated it changes the way people perceive and experience the natural environment around them (Šrimpf Vendramin, 2021). The narrative tradition, linked to its natural environment, provides the history, personality, and mysticism of a place and gives visitors an indication of how they should behave in the natural environment (Gunnell, 2018; Šrimpf Vendramin, 2021). An example from Rodik is the village boundaries, marked in the folklore narratives by liminal beings, deaths, killings, graves, and treasures, expressing dangerous liminal places in the landscape (Hrobat, 2010; Young, 2020; Hrobat Virloget, 2021). Places have their meaning only when linked to the communities who inhabit them, communities give meaning to them, and their embedded collective memories give meaning and form the basis for their communal identities (Halbwachs, 1971, 2001; Zonabend, 1993; Hrobat, 2010; Hrobat Virloget, 2020).

Reflections on Issues When Folklore and Landscape Meet with Tourism

Many researchers argue that the contemporary trends of presenting and marketing intangible heritage are influenced by the international politics of UNESCO and the states' registers of intangible heritage. Top-down approaches such as this can often have negative effects on heritage (Kirchenblatt-Giblett, 2006; Hafstein, 2007; Židov, 2019; Kropej Telban, 2021). However, in the case of The Mythical Park in Rodik positive consequences of the meeting of folklore, place, and tourism can be observed – for instance, the preservation of folklore which was linked to the landscape and rescued from extinction. Before my research folklore was relatively unnoticed by the people of Rodik, except for a book on local legends (Peršolja, 2000). However, it became a core interest of the community after the establishment of the park. It is interesting to note that one of the main mythical figures called Baba (English, Hag), whose stone prison was destroyed by workers building the water supply. It was only when the value of the mythical figure of Baba was researched and presented that villagers realised the loss of a part of their intangible landscape and made a re-evaluation of the significance of folklore, which had previously been perceived as fairly unimportant (Hrobat, 2010; Hrobat Virloget, 2019). Namely, in the time of the former Yugoslavia, when faith in modernity and progress dominated, the old local traditions together with the traditional architecture were neglected, and even destroyed as a sign of regression. It was in the search for new symbols of national identity in the 90s following the independence of Slovenia (as a former republic of Yugoslavia) that people started to rediscover their forgotten local roots and traditions (Fakin Bajec, 2011). Similar to other post-soviet countries, with decades of state atheism, a re-emergence of religiosity occurred after the fall of the communist regimes (Testa and Isnart, 2020). In the case of Rodik it was the ethnologist as a representative of power, with the mandate of heritage valuation (Muršič, 2005), that defined local folklore as heritage; therefore, the heritage was defined "from above" and it "returned" into the hands of people (Hrobat Virloget, 2019). It is up to local people now to evaluate what is meaningful for them. As Alessandro Testa and Cyril Isnart (2020) argue, heritage-making is a way of transforming traditional content per se, but at the same time also a way to think and build up peoples' own concepts, tools, and procedures on what they see as valuable.

Although The Mythical Park has rescued this folklore from extinction, it is important to question whether it is the same now as it was before? What happens to folklore once it is selected and transformed for tourist purposes?

There are also negative aspects to this kind of folklore preservation – firstly, the selection and "freezing" of local folklore. Among the hundreds of local tales, only 12 were selected for touristic presentation, only the ones that represent the most significant places in the mythical landscape were chosen. At each location the visitor can listen only to a single folktale, and to its ethnological interpretation. Although each location has more folktales attached to it, for the purposes of touristic presentation only one had to be selected. As an ethnologist I had to pick the folktales that are most representative of the meaning of the place, a choice that was not left to the public. For instance, for the Globoka cave (English, Deep cave) the local informant wanted to register on the mobile application a typical folk-tale of a fight between a hero and a dragon connected to the cave, which we can encounter in many collections of folk-tales all over Europe, but I decided to select a different folk-tale that expresses the specific significance of this particular cave as a place where local women committed suicide, believing that the dragon – sometimes a dwarf in variants of the story – from the cave would take them. This narrative was selected in order to present, together with other narratives from other caves in Rodik, the traditional perception of certain caves as the entrance to the world beyond; however, as a folklorist I am well aware other more typical and widespread folktales have also been attached to these symbolic places in the local landscape.

Another criterion in the selection of folklore narratives was the proximity of their place to the existing routes. These narratives were recorded in audio form for mobile applications, written down on paper for mailboxes at the 12 locations, and interpreted by the stone sculptures. It could be said that the local folklore was "petrified" for the needs of a tourist destination, not only in a symbolic sense. Can we still perceive these selected narratives of The Mythical Park as folklore or intangible heritage, now that they have been codified in this way? It has been suggested that intangible heritage does not have "authenticity," which is usually perceived as something fixed, unchanged over time, and "rooted" (Scounti, 2009). According to Ahmed Scounti, in order to create intangible heritage, we have to sacrifice something else that transforms a (living) tradition into heritage. These elements of tradition are no longer the same as before; they become something else, an "authentic illusion." A similar observation is made by Ulrich Kockel. The tradition is transformed into heritage when it is no longer in use in everyday life, when it is no longer transferred and when it is used outside of its historical context

(Kockel, 2008). It could be argued that in the process of commodification (Smith, Waterton and Watson, 2012; Weber, Hrobat Virloget and Gačnik, 2020) the tie of folklore to landscape was transformed into a successful touristic product. The selected folklore narrative in the park still maintains its original context, the place, but the milieu of the traditional storytelling has vanished – people no longer sit in front of the fire narrating local stories. The tradition has taken to other contemporary audio-visual forms, but through this it was also frozen in time and space. A question for the ethnologist is, how to maintain the living folklore, or how to return heritage to the living tradition?

One way of doing this is by organising storytelling events (see Figure 14.3), which according to the enthusiastic reception of organised storytelling events in the park is a big success with the wider public. It seems that storytelling is a good way of reviving narrative traditions by transforming the past into the future (Glassie, 2003 after Frlic, 2020, p. 28). As "in the old times," in a contemporary world storytelling events maintain a cohesive role in the traditions of community, in this case by providing a sense of the connectedness of participants to each other (Niles, 1999; Frlic, 2020). To avoid "freezing" the folklore the creators of the park also trained local tourist guides, teaching them how to narrate and interpret the folklore on their guided tours, in this way giving folklore back to its people and places. If the transmission of folklore before the creation of the park – even decades before – took place in the local community, the new form of transmission is through expert tourist-guides to target audiences, mostly transcending the local community to the pupils of

Figure 14.3 Storytelling Event.
(Picture by Author).

Mythical Park 207

local schools and visitors from Slovenia and beyond (Hrobat Virloget, 2019; Čebron Lipovec, 2021).

Most people do not engage with the landscape as they did previously through activities such as farming. Rather their main activity in the local landscape today is leisure. It is possible that people's connection with place and folklore will in the course of time be diminished to their own reduced paths, or those constructed by heritage organisations and created by the park. In this sense, The Mythic Park has managed to preserve only part of the folklore in its place of context. People no longer engage with the entire landscape as before, and it is possible that only the folklore selected for tourists will be known and (maybe) transferred to future generations.

The meeting of folklore, landscape, and tourism brings another danger, which is the trivialisation and banalisation of folklore. There is also the danger of "neo-paganistic" nationalistic interpretations (Hrobat Virloget, 2021). The danger is greater in cases where the experts do not have future control over the development of folklore-based tourism. This occurred in the Croatian part of The Mythical Park, where the mythical path existed before the international project.[6] In this location, the development of the tourist destination was left to the non-experts, non-ethnologists, and only to people from the tourist sector. With no ethnologist behind them, the accompanying activities were typical cases of "staged authenticity" (Goffman, 1959; Poljak Istenič, 2013, p. 106), or even worse, more comparable to "kitsch" activities.[7]

Folklore in tourism can also be misinterpreted. Such is the case of the nationalist discourses in the old interpretations in Trebišća, where the texts on the tables, written approximately three decades ago when the Mythical path was first established in Trebišća, linked the Slavic mythology to the "Old Croats" from the Early Middle Ages. However, Slavic mythology cannot be associated with the recently established nationalisation processes of the last two centuries. Looking now at the historical context of establishing the first mythical routes in Trebišća the nationalistic discourse was logical, since the routes were established right at the time of the national independence of Croatia from the former Yugoslavia, when these kinds of nationalistic discourses about rediscovering a national, Croatian identity were seen as progressive (Hrobat Virloget, 2021). From today's perspective it can be observed that this was a different historical context where folklore was one of the tools for creating the foundations of new national identities (Baycroft and Hopkin, 2012; Poljak Istenič, 2013). In any case, it can be observed that heritage is always the "present of the past" – a product of perceiving the past from the present which cannot avoid contemporary ideologies and political interests (Harvey, 2001; Slavec Gradišnik, 2014; Kropej Telban, 2021).

Misinterpretations were also frequent in the wider media. The newspapers often spoke about myths being presented in the park of Rodik, a misunderstanding that derived from the name of the park. However, it was strictly and repeatedly highlighted that the park is presenting the mythical landscape and mythical tradition as folklore containing some mythical elements, because

208   *Katja Hrobat Virloget*

myths as sacred texts with their accompanying rituals were not well preserved in Europe (Belaj, 1998; Mikhailov, 2002).

The danger of trivialisation, banalisation, and misinterpretation raise issues of control when folklore intersects with tourism. How much democracy can and should local communities and interested wider audiences be given in the interpretation of folklore if we would like to avoid the so-called authorised heritage discourse also including alternative discourses (Smith, 2006)? From this case study it could be said that ethnologists must maintain control over the interpretation and further development of these kinds of tourism products. However, this can only be successful when a trusting relationship between the ethnologist and the local community has been established, based on mutual collaboration, respect, and trust in the "authority" of science. In cases where the ethnologists are absent in the process of "heritage making" the interpretations can go in dangerous directions of exclusivist, nationalist, and autochthonistic ideas (Hrobat Virloget, 2019). In today's pluralistic democratic society, where science seems to have lost the role of the authoritative "truth-teller," as seen in the COVID-19 crisis, there is a need for critical engagement and the deconstruction of political myths by ethno-anthropologists (Rihtman Auguštin, 2001).

A reflection can be made on the educational aspects of The Mythical Park. Based on feedback from tourist guides and employees within the visitor centre in Rodik, the most frequent reaction of visitors is of self-reflection on their own local folklore or "intangible landscape," where folklore is embedded in the local landscape. By listening to the folklore narratives in Rodik, visitors often remember comparable folklore narratives from their childhood that they had almost forgotten. Their encounter with folklore and landscape in The Mythical Park encourages visitors to re-evaluate their own local folklore narratives and to find them relevant again, offering a different, mystical perspective of the world. However, as has been shown, the establishment of The Mythical Park has not only influenced visitors; it was the local community that was the first to re-evaluate the potential of their old folklore narratives and to recognise in them the possibility for new economic opportunities in the tourist sector. If the local narratives were more or less forgotten, after the establishment of the park they started to live again in the community to which they belong, although in a rather selective form, adapted for tourist purposes. The many restaurants and accommodation providers in the village gain profit from them, as do the villagers selling their local products in the visitor's centre; new events based on the narrative tradition are organised and the village was placed not only on the national, but international map of interesting tourist destinations, providing the villagers with pride. The encounter of folklore, landscape, and tourism opened up new opportunities for the local people, established a new foundation for collective identity and gave rise to a wider-self-reflection and re-evaluation of place-folklore narratives. It is true that the rich folklore embedded in the local landscape was fairly impoverished by adapting it for tourist purposes, but the positive side can be seen in its revival, or re-enchantment.

Conclusions on the Encounter of Folklore, Landscape, and Tourism in The Mythical Park

The encounter of folklore, landscape, and tourism in the case of The Mythical Park had a combination of positive and negative effects. The positive consequence of marketing folklore results in safeguarding it from extinction. As the old *milieus* of transgenerational transmission have disappeared, they have been substituted by new contemporary forms, such as audio-visual folklore interpretations in their natural environment, storytelling events, and other forms of touristic presentations (such as tourist guides, for example). Secondly, the meeting of folklore, landscape, and tourism in The Mythical Park has also resulted in a changing of the perception of landscape. Renewed links between folklore and place have resulted in the everyday landscape becoming something else, something more meaningful or even mystical, giving open space for creative imaginations. However, from the perspective of ethnology and the maintenance of scientific interpretations, there is a need to develop a trusting, long-term mutual collaboration between ethnologists and the local community for responsible tourism development.

From the perspective of heritage studies, it can be argued that with the encounter of folklore, landscape, and tourism nothing much has changed. Tradition, folklore, or heritage has always adapted to the needs of the present; it has always changed, been used and reused, and been selected, changing the contexts according to the needs of the present (Niles, 1999; Harvey, 2001; Hall, 2008; Frlic, 2020). As Ullrich Kockel argues, the notions of change and tradition as opposites derive from the Western perception, but in reality "change is a condition of continuity" (Kockel, 2008, p. 12). The same can be said for the folklore and landscape of The Mythical Park. It was almost extinguished, but a selection of it was preserved and transformed to adapt to the needs of the present, to create an attractive and unique tourist destination. Tourism has thus enabled the preservation of the once lost connection of folklore to its landscape, and transformed it into a new form that will probably live and adapt to the needs of the future. What was seen as lost has been revived and adapted to present and future needs, enabling in this way the entanglement of folklore and landscape to continue to live on under new contemporary circumstances. The tradition survives when it answers to the needs of the present. And the encounter of folklore, landscape, and tourism can be seen as an answer to the needs of the present, giving a way for its survival and new, maybe even unexpected, forms of living. From the establishment of the park, we can only observe "how people (will) write their own version of the past" (Isnart, 2020) through folklore, hopefully in mutual collaboration with ethnologists.

Notes

1 The park was established with the funds of the international project The Mythical Park. Joint cross-border tourist destination for the preservation, protection, and promotion of the heritage of the mythical area. Interreg V-A Slovenia – Croatia Co-operation Programme 2014 – 2020. The project was co-funded by the ERDF

210 *Katja Hrobat Virloget*

and led by the municipality of Hrpelje-Kozina, where the village of Rodik was located (Project duration: 1.9.2018–30.2.2021). The initial idea of the park was elaborated in a previous Interreg project with the title Living Landscape, led by University of Primorska.

2 Due to the Covid-19 measures the inauguration in April 2021 was online, but activities and visits were undertaken long before the inauguration.

3 Trebišća, deriving from the Slavic word "treba," denoting places of sacrifice; in this case, under the mountain called Perun, presenting the name of the Slavic god (Katičić, 2008, p. 306).

4 The term "supernatural" is in quotation marks, as it is frequently only a category of scientific discourse that does not necessarily coincide with the notions of the people, who often do not distinguish between "supernatural" and "natural" (Mencej, 2020, p. 144, 155).

5 In Rodik an info-centre with a museum was created with the exhibition entitled "Mythical and other world-makings" which presents different perceptions of the world through today's dominant scientific, and marginal mythical and artistic, discourses.

6 During the international project the interpretation on the path was only upgraded.

7 This is the case in the theatre performances in Trebišća enacting rituals of the ancient Slavs with the priest evoking the Slavic gods, where ancestors were presented as "rude, painted savages coming from the deep wilderness" (Hrobat Virloget, 2021, p. 39).

References

Basso, K. H. (2002). *Wisdom Sits in Places: Landscape and Language among the Western Apache*. Albuquerque: University of New Mexico Press.

Baycroft, T. and Hopkin, D. (eds.) (2012). *Folklore and Nationalism in Europe During the Long Nineteenth Century*. Leiden: Brill.

Belaj, V. (1998). *Hod kroz godinu. Mitska pozadina hrvatskih narodnih običaja i vjerovanja*. Zagreb: Golden marketing.

Belaj, V., and Belaj, J. (2014). *Sveti trokuti. Topografija hrvatske mitologije*. Zagreb: Institut za arheologiju, Matica hrvatska, Ibis grafika.

Bonin, F., Balkovec Debevec, M. and Mlinar, M. (2022). 'Valvasorjeva odličja za leto 2021.' Available Online: http://www.smd-drustvo.si/Arhiv%20dokumentov/3%20 Valvasor/2022/valvazor22press.pdf [Accessed 25 March 2022].

Bourdieu, P. (1977). *Outline of a Theory of Practice*. Cambridge: Cambridge University Press.

Čebron Lipovec, N. (2021). 'Poskus orisa izzivov v upravljanju Mitskega parka v Rodiku.' In K. Hrobat Virloget (ed.), *Mitska krajina: iz različnih perspektiv*. Koper: Založba Univerze na Primorskem, pp. 17–55.

Clemente, P. and Mugnaini, F. (eds.) (2001). *Oltre il folklore: Tradizioni popolari e antropologia nella società contemporanea*. Rome: Carocci.

Descola, P. and Pálson, G. (eds.) (1996). 'Introduction.' In *Nature and Society. Anthropological perspectives*. London: Routledge, pp. 1–22.

Fakin Bajec, J. (2011). *Procesi ustvarjanja kulturne dediščine. Kraševci med tradicijo in izzivi sodobne družbe*. Ljubljana: Založba ZRC, ZRC SAZU.

Feld, S. and Basso, K. H. (1996). *Senses of Place*. Santa Fe: New Mexico: School of American Research.

Frlic, Š. (2020). *"Zgodbe si jemljemo za svoje!" Za 2 groša fantazije in sodobno pripovedovanje na Slovenskem*. Ljubljana: Slovensko etnološko društvo.

Mythical Park 211

Gell, A. (1992). 'The Technology of Enchantment and the Enchantment of Technology.' In J. Coote and A. Shelton (eds.), *Anthropology, Art and Aesthetics.* Oxford: Clarendon Press, pp. 40–63.

Glassie, H. (2003). 'Tradition.' In B. Feintuch (ed.) *Eight Words for the Study of Expressive Culture.* Urbana: University of Illinois, pp. 176–197.

Goffman, E. (1959). *The Presentation of the Self in Everyday Life.* New York: Anchor Books.

Gunnell, T. (2018). 'The Power in the Place: Icelandic Álagablettir Legends in a Comparative Context.' In U. Valk and D. Sävborg (eds.), *Storied and Supernatural Places: Studies in Spatial and Social Dimensions of Folklore and Sagas.* Helsinki: Finnish Literature Society in SKS, pp. 27–41.

Hafstein, V. (2007). 'Laiming Culture: Intangible Heritage Inc., Folklore©, Traditional KnowledgeTM.' In D. Hemme, T. Tauschek and R. Bendix (eds.), *Prädikat "HERITAGE": Wertschöpfungen aus kulturellen Reourcen.* Berlin: LIT Verlag, pp. 75–100.

Halbwachs, M. (1971). *La topographie légendaire des évangelis en terre sainte. Etude de mémoire collective.* Paris: Presses Universitaires de France.

Halbwachs, M. (2001). *Kolektivni spomin.* Ljubljana: Studia Humanitatis.

Hall, S. (2008). 'Whose Heritage? Un-settling 'The Heritage,' Reimagining the Post-nation.' In R. Harrison, G. Fairclough, J.H.J. Jameson and J. Shofield (eds.), *The Heritage Reader.* London: Routledge, pp. 219–228.

Harvey, D.C. (2001). 'Heritage Pasts and Heritage Presents: Temporality, Meaning and the Scope of Heritage Studies.' *International Journal of Heritage Studies*, 7 (4), pp. 319–338.

Hirsch, E. (1995). 'Introduction. Landscape: Between Place and Space.' In E. Hirsch and M. O'Hanlon (eds.), *The Anthropology of Landscape. Perspectives on Place and Space.* Oxford: Clarendon Press, pp. 3–4, 22–23.

Hirsch, E. and O'Hanlon, M. (eds.) (1995). *The Anthropology of Landscape: Perspectives on Place and Space.* Oxford: Clarendon Press.

Hrobat, K. (2010). *Ko Baba dvigne krilo. Prostor in čas v folklori Krasa.* Ljubljana: Znanstvena založba Filozofske fakultete.

Hrobat, K. (2011). 'Mitično-arheološki parki: predlog kakovostnega dediščinskega turizma.' In S. Klaus and A. Kvartič (eds.), *Uporaba prostorov.* Ljubljana: Znanstvena založba Filozofske fakultete, pp. 7–12.

Hrobat Virloget, K. (2007). 'Use of oral tradition in archaeology: the case of Ajdovščina above Rodik, Slovenia.' *European journal of archaeology*, 10 (1), pp. 31–56.

Hrobat Virloget, K. (2019). 'O aktivni in pasivni vlogi stroke ter javnosti pri ustvar-janju nesnovne dediščine: primer Mitskega parka in starovercev.' In A. Svete and T. Petrović Leš (eds.), *Nesnovna dediščina med prakso in registri.* Ljubljana, Zagreb: Slovensko etnološko društvo, Hrvaško etnološko društvo, pp. 26–45.

Hrobat Virloget, K. (2021). 'Mitska krajina: razmisleki in smernice za Mitski park.' In K. Hrobat Virloget (ed.), *Mitska krajina: iz različnih perspektiv.* Koper: Založba Univerze na Primorskem, pp. 17–55.

Ingold, T. (2000). *The Perception of the Environment: Essays on Livelihood, Dwelling and Skill.* London: Routledge.

Isnart, C. (2020) 'The Enchantment of Local Religion: Tangling Cultural Heritage, Tradition and Religion in Southern Europe.' *Ethnologia Europaea*, 50 (1). Available Online: https://ee.openlibhums.org/article/id/1884/ [Accessed 28 June 2022].

212 *Katja Hrobat Virloget*

Katičić, R. (2008). *Božanski boj*. Zagreb, Mošćenićka draga: Ibis grafika, Odsjek za etnologiju i kulturnu antropologiju Filozofskog fakulteta Sveučilišta u Zagrebu, Katedra Čakavskog sabora Općine Mošćenička Draga.

Kirchenblatt-Giblett, B. (2006). 'World Heritage and Cultural Economics.' In I. Karp (ed.) *Museum Fictions: Public Cultures/Global Transformations*. Durham: Duke University Press, pp. 161–202.

Kockel, U. (2008). 'Putting the Folk in Their Place: Tradition, Ecology, and the Public Role of Ethnology.' *Anthropological Journal of European Cultures*, 17, pp. 5–23.

Kropej Telban, M. (2021). *Pripovedno izročilo, Razvoj in raziskovanje*. Založba ZRC, ZRC SAZU: Ljubljana.

Lenclud, G. (1995). 'L'ethnologie et le paysage.' In C. Voisenat (ed.), *Paysage au pluriel. Pour une approche ethnologique des paysages*. Paris: Éditions de la Maison des sciences de l'homme, pp. 3–18.

Mencej. M. (2020). 'Čarovništvo – diskurz ali praksa?' *Studia mythologica Slavica*, 23, pp. 137–158.

Mikhailov, N. (2002). *Mythologia slovenica: poskus rekonstrukcije slovenskega poganskega izročila*. Trst: Mladika, Knjižnica Dušana Černeta.

Muršič, R. (2005). 'Uvod. H kritiki ideologije dediščinstva ter slepega enačenja znanosti in stroke.' In J. Hudales and N. Visočnik (eds.), *Dediščina v očeh znanosti*. Ljubljana: Filozofska fakulteta, Oddelek za etnologijo in kulturno antropologijo, pp. 7–10.

Nikšič, M., Goršič, N. and Seite, G. (2022 – in print). '(Un)intruding acquaintances.' In M. Nikšič and N. Goršič (eds.) *Creative works in small and remote places: European best practices exploration*. Ljubljana: Urbanistični inštitut Republike Slovenije.

Niles, J. D. (1999). *Homo narrans*. Pennsylvania: University of Pennsylvania Press.

Peršolja, J. M. (2000). *Rodiške pravce in zgodbe*. Ljubljana: Mladika.

Pleterski, A. (2014). *Kulturni genom*. Ljubljana: Založba ZRC.

Poljak Istenič, S. (2013). *Tradicija v sodobnosti*. Ljubljana: Založba ZRC, ZRC SAZU.

Rihtman Auguštin, D. (2001). *Etnologija i etnomit*. Zagreb: Naklada Publica.

Scounti, A. (2009). 'The Authentic Illusion. Humanity's Intangible Cultural Heritage, the Moroccan Experience.' In S. Laurajane and A. Natsuko (eds.), *Intangible Heritage*. London: Routledge, pp. 74–92.

Slavec Gradišnik, I. (2014). 'V objemu dediščin.' In T. Dolžan Eržen, I. Slavec Gradišnik and N. Valentinčič Furlan (eds.), *Interpretacije dediščine*. Ljubljana: Slovensko etnološko društvo, pp. 8–24.

Smith, L. (2006). *Uses of Heritage*. London: Routledge.

Smith, L., Waterton, E. and Watson, S. (eds.) (2012). *The Cultural Moment in Tourism*. London: Routledge.

Šrimpf Vendramin, K. (2021). *Zgodbe in prostor*. Ljubljana: Založba ZRC, ZRC SAZU.

Testa, A. (2020). 'Intertwining Processes of Reconfiguring Tradition: Three European Case Studies.' *Ethnologia Europaea*, 50 (1). Available Online: https://ee.openlibhums.org/article/id/1888/ [Accessed 28 June 2022].

Testa, A. and Isnart, C. (2020). 'Reconfiguring Tradition(s) in Europe: An Introduction to the Special Issue.' *Ethnologia Europaea*, 50 (1) [online]. Available Online: https://ee.openlibhums.org/article/id/1917/ [Accessed 28 June 2022].

Valk, Ü. and Sävborg, D. (2018). 'Place-Lore, Liminal Storyworld and Ontology of the Supernatural. An Introduction.' In Ü. Valk and D. Sävborg (eds.), *Storied and*

Supernatural Places. Studies in Spatial and Social Dimensions of Folklore and Sagas. Helsinki: Finish Literature Society, SKS, pp. 7–24.

Visit Kras (2022). 'Mitski park Rodik.' Available Online: https://www.visitkras.info/mitski-park-rodik?p=kaj-poceti%2Fkras-pass-gourmet [Accessed 28 June 2022].

Weber, I., Hrobat Virloget, K. and Gačnik, A. (2020). 'Kulturni turizem.' In M. Lesjak, M. Sikošck and S. Kcrma (cds.), *Tematski turizem.* Koper: Založba Univerze na Primorskem, pp. 17–37.

Young, S. (2020). 'Public Bogies and Supernatural Landscapes in North-Western England in the 1800s.' *Time and Mind*, 14 (4), pp. 399–424.

Židov, N. (2019). 'Nacionalni in globalni seznami nesnovne kulturne dediščine in Unescova konvencija (2003).' In A. Svetel, and T. Petrović Leš (eds.), *Nesnovna dediščina med prakso in registri.* Ljubljana, Zagreb: Slovensko etnološko društvo, Hrvaško etnološko društvo, pp. 12–25.

Zonabend, F. (1993). *Dolgi spomin. Časi in zgodovina v vasi.* Ljubljana: ŠKUC, Filozofska fakulteta.

15 Virtually Haunted Places

Armchair Ghost Tours through Weird Space

Alicia Edwards-Boon

Armchair Tourism in the Digital Age

Ghost tourism saturates the modern-day English tourism industry. In towns and cities across the country, tourists gather to hear tour guides recount macabre and chilling histories of a place through tales of the supernatural. Ghost tours transform the city into a real-and-imagined space of supernatural possibility to convey hidden or obscured knowledge of the past and to illuminate often overlooked features of the cityscape. While in-person tours are a mainstay of modern-day supernatural placemaking, in the digital age it is also necessary to consider how virtual tours operate to define and create haunted place. An exploration of virtual ghost tourism becomes an even more pressing issue given the range of tours that have emerged in response to challenges and obstacles faced by the tourism industry in the wake of the global COVID-19 pandemic. The limitation on the physical and the "in-placeness" – through social distancing, highly restrictive travel, and ongoing lockdowns – implemented for public health and safety have occasioned a proliferation of creative and technology-inflected tourism activities and events by heritage sites and tour guide organisers to continue their programming and work.

This chapter offers a meditation on the role of virtual "armchair" ghost tourism and the formation of supernatural place, or what Jeannie Banks Thomas terms "weird space." Drawing on Edward Soja's notion of "Thirdspace," in which the boundaries between material realities and imagined space collapse – weird space is "both objective and subjective, concrete and abstract, real and imagined, of the moment and historical" (Thomas, 2015, p. 20). With specific reference to Flecky Bennett Productions' virtual Ghost Bus tours set in Chester, Manchester, and Liverpool, this chapter focuses on the intersections of what Thomas calls hyper-modern folklore – "the intermingling of folk, popular, consumer and digital cultures" – and ghost tourism (2015, p. 7). Far from a secondary, or "cheap"/inferior, method of constructing haunted spaces and producing heritage, I argue that supernatural stories relayed through digital ghost tours function equally to the act of storytelling *in situ* in the process of heritage production and supernatural placemaking.

DOI: 10.4324/9781003374138-19

Virtually Haunted Places   215

The ubiquity of digital media and communications in contemporary culture has influenced all aspects of travel. Kathryn N. McDaniel announces the need to expand existing definitions and theories of tourism proper in the twenty-first century in her introduction to the edited volume, *Virtual Dark Tourism: Ghost Roads* (2018). New media, such as computer technologies, have increased the availability of travel simulation, and virtual tourism is becoming the tourism of the next millennium (McDaniel, 2018). The internet is full of virtual tourism guides that combine textual descriptions with high-quality visual panorama images and videos (Byerly, 2013). Digital platforms such as YouTube enable tour guides, ghost-hunters, and paranormal enthusiasts to upload content and create immersive and engaging tourism experiences for people around the world. While scholars have explored in-person ghost tours through a range of themes and practices including Gothic tourism (McEvoy, 2010, 2016), dark tourism (Ironside, 2018), enchantment in the city (Holloway, 2010), and haunted heritage (Hanks, 2016), work on virtual forms of ghost tourism is scarce. Clearly, in the era of hypermediacy and ever-evolving technologies, we need to rethink and re-conceptualise our understanding of tourism (Lamerichs, 2019).

Contemporary theories of cyberspace insist upon Jean Baudrillard's paradigm of simulation as a "copy, always striving towards but never quite achieving mimetic replication of the real" (Crang et al., 1999, p. 6). However, to overvalue technology, or the virtual, for its ability to replicate is, in essence, to undervalue the possibilities of cyber-reality. A more fruitful understanding can be identified if we conceptualise the virtual in its original sense: not as a copy but as an alternative (Crang et al., 1999). From this perspective, we can avoid the errors that result when one positions virtual ghost tourism as a "cheap" and/or inferior method of tourist performance and exploring place, and appreciate and theorise it as an evolved cultural practice.

All travel begins in the imagination as a virtual experience because the texts and popular media we consume precede and influence our performance of and interactions with material space (McDaniel, 2018). However, we must consider the practice of travel that never culminates in physically visiting a particular place. "Armchair tourism" is the act of travelling to a place without physically going there, or rather, leaving the comfort of one's armchair. This form of travel is a strictly imaginative practice. This process of mental travel is enacted through reading texts, viewing visual and digital media, and participating in popular tourism simulations. In the twenty-first century, a variety of mental travel materials and simulations are available for tourists, but these technologies are simply the newest available possibilities in a long history of virtual travel texts and media. Innumerable works in a variety of media and forms have been produced with the intent of describing how places look and feel, or their significance (Ryden, 1993). For example, Alison Byerly outlines how imaginative travel was heavily commodified in the nineteenth century. From 360-degree panoramas to detailed travel narratives that recounted epic journeys across the globe, multiple efforts were made to replicate the "experience of going somewhere" (Byerly, 2013, p. 8). Physical travel,

216 *Alicia Edwards-Boon*

then, has been, and still remains, just one option within an ever-enlarging choice of touristic experiences.

From Face-to-Face to Screen-Based: Flecky Bennett's Virtual Ghost Bus Tours

The COVID-19 pandemic has shifted attention to digital opportunities and theories on tourism must adjust accordingly. Although the dominant narrative identifies the COVID pandemic as the catalyst for the reimagination and restructuring of how tourism can present, stage, and produce tourism destinations across the globe, virtual panoramas and YouTube recordings of in-person tours have been, for some time, available online. Nonetheless, there has been a causal increase in the amount of tour guides that have sought to utilise technology in intriguing ways to offer their patrons unique but equally thrilling ghost tour spectacles. Ian Waring, creator of Flecky Bennett Productions, for instance, is one tour guide who has sought to circumvent social distancing restrictions by offering a variety of online, virtual performances, through YouTube, Facebook Live, and Zoom. Designated as the "Manchester's ghost walker extraordinaire," Flecky Bennett is the costumed persona created and performed by Ian Waring (Oldfield, 2020). Since 2009, Waring has created over 15 in-person ghost walking performances in both the Greater Manchester area and London (Oldfield, 2020). With the onset of the pandemic and the postponement of all live performances, he says in an interview, "I was forced to think outside the box" (Durocher, 2021). In response to this need, Waring created over 18 original virtual ghost tour performances, set in a number of towns and cities in the United Kingdom, Europe, and America (Durocher, 2021). As a performer who draws upon his acting techniques in face-to-face tours, he is exceptionally well equipped to poach from his own work so as to transplatform his walks into fully online virtual tours.

Ghost tourism, by its very definition, already provides for the possibility of virtual forms. In her landmark work on ghost tourism and heritage, Michele Hanks defines ghost tourism as "any form of leisure or travel that involves encounters with or the pursuit of knowledge of the ghostly or haunted" (2016, p. 13). Her definition is inclusive and accounts for the practice of physical travel to haunted locations and extends the scope to include *any* act of leisure, or "the pursuit of knowledge," which includes mental and/or imaginary travel (Edwards, 2019, p. 1314). Further, "the pursuit of knowledge" aspect of ghost tourism may take the form of storytelling, an essential component that is readily trans-platformed to virtual experiences. Knowledge of ghosts sought after by tourists takes the form of stories of historical figures and/or stories of haunting experiences (Hanks, 2016). A popular form of ghost tourism, the ghost walk – and by extension, the ghost bus – is in essence a peregrination through ghostly stories and supernatural folklore. The shift from an in-person experience to an online tour is achieved with a high degree

Virtually Haunted Places 217

of success because storytelling remains at the core of the experience. Virtual ghost tourism is a change in style rather than substance.

In some of his performances, Ian Waring provides an interesting variation of virtual armchair ghost tourism. His virtual "bus tour" takes its inspiration from the in-person The Ghost Bus Tours, the "UK's ONLY comedy-horror theatre sightseeing experience on wheels" (Immersive Entertainments Ltd). The Ghost Bus Tours' in-person experience offers tourists the opportunity to ride in a 1960s black Routemaster bus, aptly named the Necrobus. The bus takes passengers on a tour of the city with the help of their tour guides, who are all classically trained actors (Immersive Entertainments Ltd). Each tour is immersive supernatural theatre showcasing a city's top attractions associated with haunting and macabre histories. Waring's virtual version functions in a similar vein. As part of his "Friday Fright Night" series, first broadcasted on Facebook Live and later uploaded to YouTube, Waring-as-Bennett takes tourists on a highly evocative virtual bus tour performance to landmarks and places of supernatural and occult significance in a variety of cities. Waring's virtual bus tours are not designed as exact replicas of the in-person bus tours, but are creative, virtual re-imaginings. Rather than a black Routemaster bus, at the beginning of each performance, viewers virtually board a uniquely designed bus: a hybrid between a wooden ship and a bus – sometimes with the addition of a top deck – complete with curtained windows, a giant skull and skeletal hands adorning its front, and a "The Ghost Bus" label branding its side. The virtual bus even comes complete with its own bus driver, performed by Waring's partner under the persona Buggerlugs. Whereas some online tours record the *in situ* event from the perspective of the tour-taker, or use static images on group Zoom-based platforms, Waring's tours are interactive, multimedia virtual spectacles that take tour-takers on a supernatural journey through a city.

The ease with which virtual tour-takers have been able to participate in the act of multimedia, intertextual performance negates critics like Yehuda E. Kalay, who asserts that a palpable connection to the past at physical heritage sites cannot be obtained through the mediation of a monitor. The assertion that the screen "acts as a barrier" that engenders "a sense of detachment" cannot be supported when one considers the success of Ian Waring's virtual tours (Kalay, 2008, p. 6). The virtual ghost bus tour echoes the movement and flow of its in-person counterpart by combining storytelling with a sense of movement through the use of multimedia footage and imagery. To create a connection with the specific city in question, virtual tourists are given the experience of "seeing" the city, in what feels to be real time, as the bus moves between checkpoints, or rather moments of storytelling. The camera gives the impression of a moving bus as it drives through the city, at street level, to each location on the itinerary. The camera becomes an extension of the tour-takers' body and transports the virtual ghost tourist to the places seen (Arthur and van Nuenen, 2019). The screen shows what the camera sees, and the camera mimics the gaze of an in-person tour taker looking out the front window of the bus when in motion. Sound effects of a moving bus

218   *Alicia Edwards-Boon*

accompany the movement of the camera to give the illusion of travel. Additionally, specific language and instructions used by Bennett complement the virtual gaze and situates the tour-taker within the virtual bus space. For instance, Bennett repeatedly requests for tour-takers to look out of their on-screen window to view a particular location. In this moment, a photographic image of the exterior of a specific building and/or site appears on the screen, framed by a curtained window. At certain checkpoints, travellers are brought "inside" the sites through photographic images of a building's interior spaces. Effort is taken to offer a sense of travel even when the tourist is displaced from the particular material environment. That being said, the tour is not just a series of framed images on a screen but a dynamic and theatrical tour that creates a seemingly palpable connection to the past through ghostly storytelling and multimedia. The bus ride is not from point A to point B, but driving into narrative.

Recycled Ghosts: Hypermodern Supernatural Folklore

Stories, according to Ken C. Ryden, are a chief way "by which people organise their physical surroundings" (1993, p. 56). For Ryden, "the sense of place achieves its clearest articulation through narrative" (Ryden, 1993, p. xiv). Supernatural narratives function to organise and memorialise the material landscape and have historically been used to do so. Karl Bell, in his study of the magical imagination from the late eighteenth century to the beginning of the First World War, documents the historical role of the supernatural within urban communities. With the ever-changing material conditions of a city, supernatural stories enable communities to preserve, maintain, or recuperate communal knowledge and/or histories without the need for a physical landmark to prompt the memory (Bell, 2012). The usefulness of supernatural folktales, particularly ghost stories, to recollect the past and convey specific place-based information of an area makes them an appealing device for the modern-day tourism and heritage industries. Ghosts are a form of communication to convey important cultural information to their audiences (Thomas, 2007). That is because, as Martyn Hudson argues, ghosts are the "visible exemplification of congealed histories and experiences" (2018, p. xiii). The presence of a ghost or haunting phenomenon proves to be a bridge between the past and the present, the living and the dead, the visible and invisible, offering a sense of continuity (Ackroyd, 2011).

Ghost tours are effectively an ambulatory compilation of supernatural folktales. In the traditional sense, a supernatural folktale is "an oral tale of supernatural creatures, events or activities that have been passed down through generations within a community" (Ironside and Massie, 2020, p. 228). In the age of popular consumption, hypermediacy, and digital communications, the transmission of supernatural folktales is no longer restricted within limited, intimate communities. As Frank de Caro suggests, in a modern context "folklore is not experienced in its usual performative contexts but through some sort of recycling," for example, through tourism (2013, p. 4).

Virtually Haunted Places 219

In other words, folklore continues to circulate, but its medium of transmission has been altered (Thomas, 2015). Ghost stories – and other supernatural stories more broadly – have been subject to recycling in multiple cultural forms, and, as such, mass culture ghosts and folk ghosts have entangled genealogies (Goldstein et al., 2007). Waring undertakes research from a variety of sources to gather supernatural stories for his tours. His tours then, both virtual and in-person, participate in, and are a product of, this form of folklore recycling. Supernatural folklore that was once restricted to community-based knowledge is extracted and isolated from its specific historical context and disseminated to a larger, public audience through digital revisions and re-imaginings. In other words, the tours recycle and recontextualise ghost stories to suit the purposes of the specific tour itinerary's narrative structure, route, and goals.

In the specific context of Bennett's virtual tour, the recycled supernatural folklore takes on a new form when integrated with digital culture. To account for the changes to folklore transmission, Jeannie Banks Thomas coined the term "hypermodern folklore": this "term recognizes the intermingling of folk, popular, consumer, and digital cultures" (2015, p. 7). Hypermodern folklore is a subset "that is distinguished by the impact, even to an excessive degree [...] of digital technology and other trends of our time" (Thomas, 2015, p. 7). As Thomas succinctly writes, "hypermodern folklore is lore that emerges from, deals with, or is significantly marked by contemporary technology and media (including the omnipresent Internet) or consumerism (with all the accessible excesses and its ability to generate pleasure mixed with anxiety)" (2015, pp. 7–8). The supernatural folklore transmitted in Bennett's tours is certainly marked by contemporary technology, media, and consumerism in more than one way. In terms of technology and media, as I will demonstrate later in this chapter, folktales expressed through digital media are altered in terms of how they can be re-imagined and conceptualised, particularly regarding their narrative and historical scope. In essence, folktales become recycled and repurposed into something new and modern because how they are interpreted and digested has changed with the emergence of new media and technologies. Ghost tours, in-person and virtual, are participatory and require an audience to thrive and survive, so there is always a level of consumerism at play. The specific folklore recorded within each tour is deliberately poached from various online and text materials and digitised through a fully multi-media performance, thus transforming individual folktales into a consumable new media product. That is not to suggest that the folktales are manufactured for the purpose of commercialism. The online tours are free for viewers to participate in as many times as they please. Instead, the tours have been part of Ian Waring's online supernatural tour branding and marketing strategy to maintain patron interest, mark various cities with his narrative flair, and expand his market, until his in-person tours resumed.

Some of Bennett's material derives explicitly from hypermodern folklore, making it a form that is both product *and* producer of new forms of supernatural folktale culture. For example, on his Manchester tour, tourists ride the virtual bus to the Manchester Museum which houses a collection of

220   *Alicia Edwards-Boon*

ancient Egyptian artefacts, such as mummies. However, it is not the mummies that harbour the ghosts, but a ten-inch-high statue. Bennett tells his patrons that "they believe he's got a curse of four thousand years, it's the pharaoh's curse [*sic*]" (2020a). A few years back, the statue was seen by staff to rotate in its glass case without any external interference. What makes this story interesting is the use of media material to legitimise the story. The tour includes a media clip of a television news report capturing the statue rotating over a period of time, to face the other direction. The folktale in this case is substantiated by recording technology. Although the method of transmission has changed over time, it does not detract from how ghost stories create a sense of supernatural place and heritage. In fact, the use of these technologies to convey a sense of reality to the stories helps to affirm the supernatural possibilities within the city.

Although the stories derive from a number of traditional and hypermodern sources, it is worth noting, however, that Bennett still deploys certain traditional methods of storytelling on the tour. If multimedia images are not in use to entice and coax the viewer's imagination, Bennett appears on screen to speak with his audience. He is sat against a completely pitch-black space, the only source light deriving from a small hand-held light that he shines on his face to add atmosphere. He uses narrative pacing, intonation, speech, and gestures in his storytelling practices to amplify narrative spectacle. However, it is not just the style of storytelling that mimics traditional forms. The relationship between storyteller and listener, and/or viewer, mirrors traditional forms of folklore transmission. The framework of stories told within an intimate group can be re-enacted if desired by the tour-taker. Bennett makes direct eye contact and speaks directly to the camera. This practice of storytelling gives the viewer the feeling of being directly spoken to. The experience provides the illusion of intimacy. Both Facebook Live streaming and the YouTube platforms enable the viewer to contribute to the affective, and ghost storytelling, experience of the tour. Tourists may dim the lights to add atmosphere and to concentrate their attention on the screen (Aldana Reyes, 2016). They can take the tour as an isolated, individual experience and thus enhance the intimacy, or participate in the spectacle and transform it into a group-watching event with family and friends. The framework exists for traditional storytelling, and it is up to the cyber-tourist to interact and engage with the tour in a manner that suits their desired viewing experience.

How to Create Weird Space or Virtually Touring Haunted Place

Much like on an in-person tour, to agree with Scott Brewster, the armchair cyber-tourist is invited to "step into," or rather drive through, "unfamiliar terrain" and explore "the ways in which the physical and social fabric" has been altered over time (2018, p. 313). A key aim of a haunted tour is to create new connections or to disturb habitualised links with a cityscape. The virtual tour deploys ghost stories from across different historical epochs at each checkpoint on the tour, in conjunction with supporting multimedia imagery

Virtually Haunted Places 221

and effects, disrupting the tour-takers' preconceptions and presumptions about its spaces. An example *par excellence* is the tale of haunting associated with Chester's The Old Boot Inn public house, which first opened in the 1640s. When they arrive at the checkpoint, viewers are first shown the exterior of the pub, and taken into the space by viewing a picture of its interior. Once "inside" Bennett initially conveys information about the pub and its peculiar culture. It is only after establishing its contemporary function that he reveals the building's past through a ghost story. According to Bennett, many years before the place was a pub, it was the largest brothel in Chester. The staff, after closing up at night, have "heard what sounds like women laughing and glasses clinking together." "Haunted by the previous ladies of the night," the building's historical function refuses to be erased (Flecky Bennett Productions, 2020b). He emphasises his story by embedding the phantasmal sounds of women laughing and glasses clinking together with a ghostly fine art image representing a prostitute. When Bennett informs his audience of the haunting, he deliberately extracts a particular layer from the building's historical palimpsest and brings it to the surface. This trace of social history rendered invisible by time is only made visible and reanimated through narration, and is emphasised using special audio effects. In this performative and imaginative process, different time-spaces can be toured and activated at each checkpoint.

By presenting the city through the lens of the supernatural, Waring's tours offer tour-takers a new interpretative strategy to understand and engage with the city and its material buildings. When Waring-as-Bennett portrays a city as haunted, he transforms it into what Jeannie Banks Thomas terms "weird space," an idea informed by Edward Soja's notion of "Thirdspace" (2015, p. 19). For Soja, first space is material space, "things that can be empirically mapped." Second space is imagined, conceived "in thoughtful re-presentations of human spatiality in mental or cognitive forms" (1996, p. 10). Third space is a theoretical designation to mark the collapse of these two polarities, a space of "the real and imagined" (Soja, 1996, p. 56). Third space is how place is understood and practised (Thomas, 2015). Put differently, cities are a collection of third spaces, a compilation of urban imaginaries that are projected onto, and practised in, a material environment. For Thomas, supernatural places "are everyday, third spaces that lean heavily towards the weird" (2015, p. 20). Waring's itineraries construct weird space, or more specifically, supernatural places, by suturing supernatural tales to a specific material site in the selected city. However, haunted place is only fully realised in the moment when the tour-taker's imagination collapses the supernatural narrative onto a location in the material environment. As the production of haunted place is an imaginative act, the tourist does not need to be in proximity to the material site. A photographic image provides enough of a visual prompt to clearly identify a landmark within the city and formulate a particular spatial imaginary. Even through fully online means Bennett still transforms abstract and unknown spaces into recognisable supernatural places.

The itinerary is part of a larger interpretative act to create the necessary connections between the time presence of the tour and the moment in the

222   *Alicia Edwards-Boon*

past that culminates in heritage meaning. Rodney Harrison's dialogical approach to heritage-making is the most suitable critical framework to understand the relationship between the supernatural and heritage place-making. For Harrison, heritage is "a particular set of relationships with the past in the present" that emerges "from the relationship between people, 'things' and their environments as part of a dialogue of collaborative process" (2013, p. 216). No one component in the dialogue is necessarily privileged as the origin of meaning-making, each element participates in this "dialogue" in different ways (Harrison, 2013, p. 217). For instance, heritage narratives are culturally sanctioned narratives projected onto material objects but remain subject to, and determined by, the material and historical realities of that object. Heritage places and/or objects are produced from social practices rather than a set of organic conditions. Phrased differently, historical objects do not have an intrinsic social value attached to them. Instead, heritage consists of learned associations and values deriving from the stories we, as a culture, tell about our past. How we connect with heritage objects is determined "not in its analytical precision, but in its psychological resonances," with some aspect of the past that emerges from this dialogical process (Davison, 2008, p. 33). Bennett deploys supernatural stories to initiate the dialogical process and entrench such resonances between the tour-taker and the historical landmark and/or place. To establish a supernatural place through historicised hauntings is to, intentionally or not, produce heritage.

To coax a strong and memorable relationship with the past and supernatural places, Waring uses his multimedia capabilities to visually corporealize and spatialise the ghosts of his stories. Rather than presenting the ghost as a disembodied abstract name, he incorporates historical photographs into his tour to humanise the ghost. This is not reserved for strictly "famous" historical persons, but also includes ordinary people that have become named and memorialised through hauntings. On his Liverpool tour, Bennett shares a story from 1866 about a woman named Elizabeth, who was killed in an unfortunate accident on stage when a fire curtain fell, and now haunts The Playhouse theatre. Upon revealing the name of the ghost, Bennett declares "we'll have a look at her," before showing his audience a historical photograph of the woman (Flecky Bennett Productions, 2021). Given the dated look of the image on the screen in conjunction with the clothing and hairstyle of the figure, the audience can only assume that this is a true photograph of Elizabeth. Once he gives the ghost not only an identity but a physical form, Bennett further prompts the imagination to construct the imaginative scene of the haunting through digital image manipulation. In a similar vein to The Old Boot Inn, Bennett takes the cyber-tourist "inside" the space of the building. At the Playhouse, Bennett takes this one step further and embeds the ghost in the building. It is said that Elizabeth's ghost always manifests in one specific seat in the theatre, "on the balcony, in the gallery area [...] in seat A5" (Flecky Bennett Productions 2021). At this point in the story, the cyber-tourist can see the interior of the theatre with Elizabeth situated in what appears to be seat A5. The imaginative cue allows the cyber-tourist to appreciate the ghost as a "real" person who has existed in time and heightens the tour-takers' imaginative association with the particular space. The transmission of the folkloric narrative is enhanced by the use of multimedia visual aids. It transforms the folktale from a tall-tale into a probable event in urban place and history.

Conclusion: The Future Possibilities of Ghost Tourism

The use of the supernatural to expand tourists' knowledge, understanding, and appreciation of local histories, heritage, and landmarks is a successful endeavour, even when practised through digital forms. In fact, the virtual tour plays an equal role in the creation and performance of supernatural or weird space, and this must be recognised. It cannot be emphasised strongly enough that online and digital forms of tourism are not a new phenomenon; they have existed since the dawn of hypermodernity. What is new is the urgency for developing a more inclusive critical framework for virtual ghost, and/or supernatural, tourism. Given its growing mainstream status, the compelling and popular imaginative activity shows no indication of decreasing in a post-COVID-19 era. Ghost tourism and its intersection with digital culture can offer the possibilities of global travel to supernatural places without the barriers of traditional travel. Supernatural spaces and places around the globe may soon be more easily available to the average ghost tourist with the simple click of a button.

References

Ackroyd, P. (2011). *The English Ghost: Spectres Through Time*. London: Vintage.

Aldana Reyes, X. (2016). *Horror Film and Affect: Towards a Corporeal Model of Viewership*. New York: Routledge.

Arthur, P.L. and van Nuenen T. (2019). 'Travel in the Digital Age.' In N. Das and T. Young (eds.), *The Cambridge History of Travel Writing*. Cambridge: Cambridge University Press, pp. 504–518.

Bell, K. (2012). *The Magical Imagination: Magic and Modernity in Urban England 1780–1914*. Cambridge: Cambridge University Press.

Brewster, S. (2018). 'Ghost Walking.' In S. Brewster and L. Thurston (eds.), *The Routledge Handbook to the Ghost Story*. London: Routledge, pp. 312–318.

Byerly, A. (2013). *Are We There Yet? Virtual Travel and Victorian Realism*. Ann Arbor: The University of Michigan Press.

Crang, M., Crang, P. and May, J. (1999). 'Introduction.' In *Virtual Geographies: Bodies, Space and Relations*. London: Routledge, pp. 1–20.

Davison, G. (2008). 'Heritage: From Patrimony to Pastiche.' In G. Fairclough, R. Harrison, J.H. Jameson, Jr., and J. Schofield (eds.), *The Heritage Reader*. London: Routledge, pp. 31–41.

de Caro, F. (2013). 'Introduction: Folklore's Messiness.' In F. de Carlo (ed.), *Folklore Recycled: Old Traditions in New Contexts*. Jackson: University Press of Mississippi, pp. 3–30.

224 *Alicia Edwards-Boon*

Durocher, A. (2021). 'Flecky Bennett's Ghost Walks Uncover Manchester's Ghosts in New Live Performances after Lockdown.' *Visit Manchester*, 28 October. Available Online: https://www.visitmanchester.com/ideas-and-inspiration/blog/read/2021/10/flecky-bennetts-ghost-walks-uncover-manchesters-ghosts-in-new-live-performances-after-lockdown-b1721 [Accessed 25 April 2022].

Edwards, A. (2019). '"Do the Ghosts Roam Along the Corridors Here at Ordsall Hall?" Paranormal Media, Haunted Heritage, and Investing Historical Capital.' *The Journal of Popular Culture*, 52 (6), pp. 1312–1333.

Flecky Bennett Productions. (2020a). *Flecky's Friday Fright Night...Episode 7...The "Virtual" Manchester Ghost Bus.* YouTube Video. Friday Fright Night. Available Online: https://www.youtube.com/watch?v=dqBNFp2CPK8 [Accessed 23 June 2022].

Flecky Bennett Productions. (2020b). *Flecky's Friday Fright Night Live... Episode Thirteen...The Chester "Virtual" Ghost Bus.* YouTube Video. Friday Fright Night. Available Online: https://www.youtube.com/watch?v=KFaSF2kdhAo&t=1839s [Accessed 3 July 2022].

Flecky Bennett Productions. (2021). *Flecky Bennett's Liverpool "Virtual" Ghost Bus.* YouTube Video. Friday Fright Night. Available Online: https://www.youtube.com/watch?v=Q0JcRuXG9BI [Accessed 23 June 2022].

Goldstein, D. Grider, S.A. and Thomas, J.B. (2007). 'Introduction: Old Spirits in New Bottles.' In D. Goldstein, S.A. Grider and J.B. Thomas (eds.), *Haunting Experiences: Ghosts in Contemporary Folklore.* Logan: Utah State University, pp. 1–22.

Hanks, M. (2016). *Haunted Heritage: The Cultural Politics of Ghost Tourism, Populism, and the Past.* London: Routledge.

Harrison, R. (2013). *Heritage: Critical Approaches.* London: Routledge.

Holloway, J. (2010). 'Legend-Tripping in Spooky Spaces: Ghost Tourism and Infrastructures of Enchantment.' *Environment and Planning D: Society and Space*, 28, pp. 618–37.

Hudson, M. (2018). *Ghosts, Landscapes and Social Memory.* London: Routledge.

Immersive Entertainments Ltd. (n.d.). 'About Us – The Ghost Bus Tours | Comedy-Horror Sightseeing Tours.' Available Online: https://www.theghostbustours.com/about/ [Accessed 23 June 2022].

Ironside, R. (2018). 'The Allure of Dark Tourism: Legend Tripping and Ghost Seeking.' In D. Waskul and M. Eaton (eds.), *The Supernatural in Society, Culture and History.* Philadelphia: Temple University Press, pp. 95–115.

Ironside, R. and Massie, S. (2020). 'The Folklore-Centric Gaze: A Relational Approach to Landscape, Folklore and Tourism.' *Time and Mind*, 13 (3), pp. 227–44.

Kalay, Y.E. (2008). 'Introduction: Preserving Cultural Heritage through Digital Media.' In Y.E. Kalay, T. Kvan and J. Affleck (eds.), *New Heritage: New Media and Cultural Heritage.* London: Routledge, pp. 1–10.

Lamerichs, N. (2019). 'Hunters, Climbers, Flâneurs: How Video Games Create and Design Tourism.' In C. Lundberg and V. Ziakas (eds.), *The Routledge Handbook of Popular Culture and Tourism.* London: Routledge, pp. 161–69.

McDaniel, K.N. (2018). 'Introduction to Virtual Dark Tourism: Disaster in the Space of the Imagination.' In K.N. McDaniel (ed.), *Virtual Dark Tourism: Ghost Roads.* Basingstoke: Palgrave Macmillan, pp. 1–18.

McEvoy, E. (2010). '"West End Ghosts and Southwark Horrors": London's Gothic Tourism.' In L. Phillips and A. Witchard (eds.), *London Gothic: Place, Space and the Gothic Imagination.* New York: Continuum, pp. 140–152.

McEvoy, E. (2016). *Gothic Tourism.* New York: Palgrave Macmillan.

Virtually Haunted Places   225

Oldfield, E. (2020). 'Meet Manchester's Ghost Walker Extraordinaire Flecky Bennett – and Pick from Guided Walks across the Boroughs and Beyond!' *Visit Manchester*, 2 March 2020. Available Online: https://www.visitmanchester.com/ideas-and-inspiration/blog/read/2020/03/meet-manchesters-ghost-walker-extraordinaire-flecky-bennett-and-pick-from-guided-walks-across-the-boroughs-and-beyond-b1103 [Accessed 15 July 2022].

Ryden, K.C. (1993). *Mapping the Invisible Landscape: Folklore, Writing and the Sense of Place*. Iowa City: University of Iowa Press.

Soja, E.W. (1996). *Thirdspace: Journeys to Los Angeles and Other Real-and-Imagined Places*. Cambridge: Blackwell Publishers Inc.

Thomas, J.B. (2007). 'On the Usefulness of Ghost Stories.' In D.E. Goldstein, S.A. Grider and J.B. Thomas (eds.), *Haunting Experiences: Ghosts in Contemporary Folklore*. Logan, Utah: Utah State University, pp. 25–59.

Thomas, J.B. (2015). 'Introduction.' In J.B. Thomas (ed.), *Putting the Supernatural in Its Place: Folklore, the Hypermodern, and the Ethereal*. Salt Lake City: University of Utah Press, pp. 1–23.

16 Concluding Remarks
Exploring Further

Rachael Ironside and Jack Hunter

The previous chapter – exploring virtual ghost tours in Manchester – feels like an appropriate place to end this collection. Accidentally, perhaps even serendipitously, the pages of this book have become their own virtual tour, and we, the readers, have become armchair tourists, investigating the relationship between folklore, people, and place in different regions throughout the world. As editors, we aimed in this collection to capture a multitude of international perspectives, to try and understand the role of folklore in an evolving, globalised world. We are conscious, however, that this book does not quite capture a truly global perspective – we are missing chapters examining the rich varieties of African, Asian, and Australian folklore traditions, for example. Nevertheless, we hope that this volume will make a useful contribution to this growing and important field of research, and that it will lead to opportunities for more inclusive studies in this area in the future – perhaps there may even be an opportunity to update this collection with chapters from other regions of the world. The chapters in this book, however, do provide some initial points of reflection, and it is to these that we now turn for our final concluding remarks.

This book has explored diverse case studies from urban and rural contexts around the world. In these places, folklore has been shown to connect people geographically, spatially, temporally, and socially with their environment. But they also point to a more subtle layer of the landscape, revealed by stories. The chapters in this book – whether considering the sacred springs of the Basque region, or the subterranean worlds of industry beneath Dudley in the United Kingdom – demonstrate the ways in which folkloric ideas and narratives reach through time to connect us with the emotional and psychical worlds of our ancestors – worlds of fairies, ghosts, fears, and "superstitions" that often seem distant and alien to the rational worldview that dominates much of contemporary Western society. This is likely part of their appeal to tourists.

For the indigenous peoples discussed in this book – Anishnaabe, indigenous Hawaiian, Chorotega and Sámi, amongst others – folklore and traditional ecological knowledge have connected people to the land for thousands of years, through many generations of colonial oppression, and in spite of enforced displacement from ancestral territories. The worldviews that emerge from this kind of long-term engagement with place begin from very different

DOI: 10.4324/9781003374138-20

Concluding Remarks 227

starting points to the broadly capitalist and materialist philosophy that underlies and motivates much mainstream tourism. As Linda Tuhiwai Smith reminds us, indigenous worldviews are often grounded in metaphysical notions that are difficult for Western perspectives to accommodate – ideas about the importance of establishing and maintaining reciprocal relationships with land, spirits, and a whole host of other-than-human persons through ceremony, for example (Tuhiwai Smith, 2012, p. 78). These are much more than just "different beliefs," they are different ways of *being* in the world. We might even say that there are deep-seated ontological differences between these perspectives (Carrithers et al., 2010; Holbraad, Pedersen and Viveiros de Castro, 2014; Holbraad and Pedersen, 2017). This raises all sorts of questions about the extent to which we can engage and participate in the other ontological perspectives we might encounter in folklore tourism. Is it possible to overcome ontological differences to find a common ground? How do we engage respectfully with other ontological perspectives? In his recent book *Ecologies of Participation* (2018), religious studies scholar Zayin Cabot explains his preference for the idea of "ecologies" over "ontologies," precisely for the reason that ecologies imply our own participation in the system, and its interconnectivity with other systems:

> I use the term ecologies to allow us to interact. Ontology by itself breeds conflict, implying that "I" am closer than "you." Ontologies, while provocative, remain useful paradoxes, but have little place in our lives. Ecologies are more useful and liveable if we are going to come together, and thus I argue for participation [...]
>
> (Cabot, 2018, p. 10)

Different ontologies may be porous, then, providing a means for us to pass into, out of, and between different modes of engaging with and understanding the world – what we might call "ontological tourism." Recent touristic developments, such as the proliferation of Ayahuasca tourism in the Peruvian Amazon (Prayag et al., 2016), for example, may be an instance of this kind of "ontological tourism," where tourists do more than simply observe cultural practices, but participate themselves by consuming the psychoactive concoction ayahuasca, even to the extent of experiencing "supernatural" figures from traditional indigenous folklore first-hand (Luke, 2011). This is not quite the place to engage in a complete discussion of the complexities and ethics of ayahuasca tourism, which can also have negative effects on both indigenous cultures and their ecosystems (Braczkowski et al., 2019). Done well, however, such experiences have a profound potential to provide deep and meaningful engagement with culture, tradition, and place through embodied experience, and can lead to powerful transformations in peoples' lives, including in the direction of an enhanced sense of connection to nature and a desire to work for its protection (Ruffell et al., 2022).

As the chapters in this book have highlighted, the relationship between folklore and tourism is complex. In all the places examined here, folklore brings

228   *Rachael Ironside and Jack Hunter*

opportunities for local and visiting communities. In revealing hidden histories and landscapes, stories can enliven and enrich spaces, bringing a new perspective that other, more traditional, forms of tourism may find difficult to achieve. In her chapter, Cortina Aracil demonstrates how layers of religious, mystical, and historical past are brought to life in Madrid through effective storytelling. The communicative value of folklore, bound to place and enmeshed in cultural tradition and belief, can provide an evocative tool to transmit knowledge and connect people to the natural and social environments that they visit. It may encourage people to *see* landscapes differently, even behave in ways that are more empathetic and respectful. For local communities, the attraction of folklore brings economic benefits – both directly and indirectly – providing unique attractions in areas where tourism infrastructure is sparse, or putting a destination "on the map" due to its folkloric association (a potential explored by both Macfarlane and Kingsepp in Dudley and Värmland, respectively). At a time when the challenges of tourism, environmentally and culturally, are being grappled with at an academic and governmental level, folklore could offer one pathway to a more sustainable tourism future.

However, despite the benefits of folklore tourism the challenges are equally acknowledged. The popularity of folklore can be both an opportunity and a burden for communities as the influx of new people raises questions about how best to promote and deliver tourist experiences in an authentic manner. These challenges are perhaps most visceral in natural environments that become damaged or vandalised by visitors, most often trying to recreate traditional customs in sacred spaces. In this respect, Colorado and Hurd echo the concerns of others (see Ironside and Massie, 2020) in relation to the environmental impact of people travelling to experience sites of folkloric significance. From a socio-cultural perspective, folklore may also be at risk of trivialisation and banalisation when commercialised as a tourism product. As Virloget explores in her chapter, it is important to navigate issues such as the authenticity, trivialisation, and the "freezing" of folklore, particularly when tourist experiences are created from the top-down. However, as she reflects, despite careful consideration the need to prioritise some areas of folklore over others to create an "experience" inevitably leads to the selective promotion of certain stories and the absence of others. As these decisions are often made by tourism providers, there is a risk that the true meaning and authenticity of folklore may become lost in its re-interpretation for new audiences. As such, in its effort to connect people with tradition and heritage, folklorisation can equally lead to a perception of place that may not be entirely accurate, or desirable, for communities.

Some of these arguments are not new (Goldstein, Grider, and Thomas, 2007; Light, 2007; Garcia, 2012), yet collectively they point to a growing need to achieve balance when storied places become sites of tourism. There is a delicate connection between physical place, communities, and folkloric knowledge, and this requires sensitivity when developing new tourism experiences. As others have acknowledged (George, 2010; Lőrincz, 2021), consultation with local communities is vitally important; arguably this should also extend

Concluding Remarks 229

to consultation about the ecological and physical environment. Folklore tourism is *experiential*, even *ontological*, in nature and this engenders particular practices and activities that may impact places and their people. Folklore is also a *living* heritage, where custom and tradition continue to bind the past to the present, while simultaneously informing new and evolving customs in our contemporary world. In White's chapter, he illustrates the important role that the dressing of trees played during the COVID-19 pandemic as communities sought out collective places for memorial and play. In Laurencekirk, a small town in the North-East of Scotland, a new fairy tree emerged over the course of the pandemic. It continues to be dressed with ribbons and beads, ornaments and colourful stones scattered around its base, all of which have been donated by members of the community. In 2021, a blue plaque emerged next to the tree, it reads:

> The Fairy Tree
> Est. a long time ago
> All Mythical Creatures & Pokémon Welcome
> Love
> The Squigglets.

The Fairy Tree, unknown until now, has become an enchanting feature of the local community. A living heritage that combines traditional folklore with contemporary cultural practices. Folklore, then, is not static; it dances through a multitude of voices, customs, and societal changes that shape the stories and heritage of a place. This is an opportunity and a responsibility for tourism to ensure that the people and places that inform storied landscapes are at the heart of decisions made about the use of folklore in contemporary tourist practices.

References

Braczkowski, A., Ruzo, A., Sanchez, F., Castagnino, R., Brown, C., Guynup, S., Winter, S., Gandy, D. and O'Bryan, C. (2019). 'The Ayahuasca Tourism Boom: An Undervalued Demand Driver for Jaguar Body Parts?' *Conservation Science and Practice*, 41 (3), pp. 314–325.

Cabot, Z. (2018). *Ecologies of Participation: Agents, Shamans, Mystics, and Diviners*. London: Rowman & Littlefield.

Carrithers, M., Candea, M., Sykes, K., Holbraad, M. and Venkatesan, S. (2010). 'Ontology is just another word for culture: Motion tabled at the 2008 Meeting of the Group for Debates in Anthropological Theory.' *Critique of Anthropology*, 30 (2): pp. 152–200.

Garcia, B.R. (2012). 'Management Issues in Dark Tourism Attractions: The case of Ghost Tours in Edinburgh and Toledo.' *Journal of Unconventional Parks, Tourism and Recreation Research*, 4(1), pp. 14–19.

George, E.W. (2010). 'Intangible Cultural Heritage, Ownership, Copyrights, and Tourism.' *International Journal of Culture, Tourism and Hospitality Research*, 4 (4), pp. 376–388.

230 *Rachael Ironside and Jack Hunter*

Goldstein, D., Grider, S. and Thomas, J.B. (2007). *Haunting Experiences: Ghosts in Contemporary Folklore*. University Press of Colorado.

Holbraad, M. and Pedersen, M.A. (2017). *The Ontological Turn: An Anthropological Exposition*. Cambridge: Cambridge University Press.

Holbraad, M., Pedersen, M.A. and Viveiros de Castro, E. (2014). 'The Politics of Ontology: Anthropological Positions.' Available Online: https://culanth.org/fieldsights/462-the-politics-of-ontology-anthropological-positions [Accessed 30th August 2022].

Ironside, R. and Massie, S. (2020). 'The Folklore-Centric Gaze: A Relational Approach to Landscape, Folklore and Tourism.' *Time and Mind*, 13 (3), pp. 227–244.

Light, D. (2007). 'Dracula Tourism in Romania Cultural Identity and the State.' *Annals of Tourism Research*, 34 (3), pp. 746–765.

Lőrincz, A. (2021). 'Intangible Heritage: The Change of Significance of Hungarian Embroidery over Time.' In T. Sádaba, N. Kalbaska, F. Cominelli, L. Cantoni, and M.T. Puig (eds.), *Fashion Communication*. Berlin: Springer, Cham, pp. 265–277.

Luke, D. (2011). 'Discarnate Entities and Dimethyltryptamine (DMT): Psychopharmacology, Phenomenology and Ontology.' *Journal of the Society for Psychical Research*, 75.1 (902), pp. 26–42.

Prayag, G., Mura, P., Hall, C.M. and Fontaine, J. (2016). 'Spirituality, Drugs, and Tourism: Tourists' and Shamans' Experiences of Ayahuasca in Iquitos, Peru.' *Tourism Recreation Research*, 41 (3), pp. 314–325.

Ruffell, S., Gandy, S., Tsang, W., Netzband, N., and Hollingdale, J. (2022). 'Participation in an Indigenous Amazonian Led Ayahuasca Retreat Associated with Increases in Nature Relatedness – A Pilot Study.' Available Online: https://doi.org/10.31234/osf.io/mytnf [Accessed 30th August 2022].

Tuhiwai Smith, L. (2012). *Decolonizing Methodologies: Research and Indigenous Peoples*. London: Zed Books.

Index

animism 5, 27
armchair tourism 15, 214–215, 220
Anishinaabeg 97–106
authenticity 12, 73, 145, 159, 164, 178,
  200, 205, 207, 228
Ayahuasca tourism 227

Black Country 169, 171, 173, 176

caves 28, 35, 125, 205
caverns 173, 175, 180
ceremony 14–15, 57–59, 61–62, 99–100,
  119, 227
cemetery 13, 162
cultural heritage 9, 28, 55, 58, 61, 64, 67,
  71, 73, 123, 146, 191–192, 194
custom 35, 40, 45, 48, 55–58, 163, 172

dark tourism 11, 215
devil 3, 33, 125, 137, 172, 200, 203
dialect 67, 69, 75
digital 76, 176, 190, 214–215
digital media 215, 219
digital cultures 219, 223
disenchantment 8, 160, 166, 188–189
Doric 68–70, 73, 75, 77–78
Dracula 9, 74
Dracula tourism 12
dreamtime 4
dressed trees 40; *see also* rag trees
Dudley attractions: Dudley canal 169–170,
  174; Dudley Tunnel 170, 174; Dudley
  Zoo 170; Dudley Castle 170, 175–176,
  179; Dudley Locust 173; Dudley Bug
  173–174; Dudley Fossils 173

ecology 5, 13, 97, 100, 104
ecological knowledge 4–5, 13–14, 226
economic 9–10, 12, 51, 72, 76, 111, 122,
  130, 144, 146, 148, 178, 192, 194,
  200, 208, 228

enchantment 11, 165, 176, 180, 189–190,
  199, 215
enchantment economy 11
environmental: charity 49; education
  13–14; impact 13, 27, 228; knowledge 4
extraterrestrials 186, 190, 193

festivals: Across the Grain festival 76;
  Chestnut festival 200; Doric festival
  76; Entierro de la Sardina (Burial of
  the Sardine) festival 163–164; Robin
  Hood Festival 8, 11; La Patum
  festival 58; Los Agüizotes 125;
  Marsden Imbolc Fire Festival 62–64;
  UFO festival 9
fairy-lore 67
folkloresque 50
folklore tourism 7–13, 18, 227–229
folkloristics 1, 59, 203
folklorisation 12, 199, 228
folklore-centric gaze 13–14, 36, 109, 151
food 8, 34, 77–78, 98–99, 143, 146
food tourism 144, 151
fossil 173–174, 178, 180

ghosts 29, 161, 175, 177, 188–189, 193,
  195, 218, 222
ghost stories 11, 161, 218–220
ghost tourism 8, 10–11, 186, 192, 194,
  214–216, 223
ghost tours and walks 8, 11–12, 161,
  175, 186–187, 193–194, 214, 216,
  218–219; ghost hunting 175–176,
  179, 186, 193, 215
GSM app 18, 202

Halloween 175–177, 193
hauntings 177, 189–191, 195, 216, 218,
  221–222
heritage tourism 122, 151
hypermodern folklore 219

232 *Index*

imp 172
indigenous 4–6, 14, 16–17, 68, 73, 76, 78, 97, 109, 112, 114–116, 118–119, 122–123, 131, 143–144, 147, 149–150, 226–227
industrial 129, 171, 173, 176, 178, 180

landscape 3–4, 13, 59, 71, 85–86, 88, 97, 110–111, 123–124, 127, 137, 139, 151, 159, 161–162, 169, 178–180, 200, 202, 204, 209, 218
language: Anishinaabeg 100; Nawat 124; Sámi 147–148; Scots 67–69; Irish 82–83, 86–90
language tourism 78
legend-tripping 10, 189, 195
limestone 170–174
Loch Ness Monster (Nessie) 10
lore 1, 31, 33, 48, 67, 84, 86, 90, 158, 161, 172–175, 178–179, 219

Madrid 157–159, 161–163
Manchester 216, 219
mining 4, 144, 170–174, 178
miracle 162–163
Most Haunted 175, 188, 195
Mothman 10
Museum: Black Country Living Museum 170, 176–177; Dudley Museum 173; International UFO Museum and Research Centre 9; Horniman Museum 50; House of Dun 75; Manchester Museum 219; Mothman Museum 10; Richard Jefferies Museum 50; Rural Life Living Museum 50; Saddleworth Museum 61; Weald and Downland Museum 50; Witches Museum 28
mythico-history 11, 178

nature 6, 13, 27–29, 34, 36, 62, 97, 119, 127, 135–136, 138, 141, 143, 149, 151, 164, 171, 203, 227
nature reserve 179
Nicaragua 122

offerings 30, 35, 42, 90, 99–100, 104, 124–125
Olowalu 109
omen 30, 33, 173
ontology 98, 186, 193, 227
ontological tourism 227
Okikendawt Island 101
oral tradition 85, 90, 114, 146, 164, 203

paranormal tourism 8, 11, 13, 186–189, 191, 194
park 49, 59, 109, 111, 124, 199
petroglyph 109–111, 113–115, 117
pilgrimage 3, 7–8, 27–28, 35, 84, 164
place lore 85–86, 203
placemaking 10, 12–13, 16, 41, 82, 157, 159, 173, 177–179, 214, 222
play 40, 47, 49, 58, 134, 179–180, 229
post-secular tourism 186

rag trees 40
reciprocity 14–15
re-enchantment 16, 157, 189–190, 195, 199, 208
relationality 104–105
revitalisation 27, 34, 112, 180, 199–200

saints 3, 35, 82, 157
sacred landscape 124
Sápmi 143
Satanic landscape 125
Slovenia 199, 204
Slow Food 145–146, 149
spirits 2–3, 27–31, 35, 102, 104, 109, 124–125, 127, 147, 172–174, 187, 227
socio-cultural 13, 17, 144, 146, 180, 228
spirituality 4, 28, 125, 129, 199
staged authenticity 207
subterranean 169, 178–180
superstition 1–2, 8, 67–68, 87, 160, 171–173, 178, 188, 194, 226
supernatural 2–3, 8, 10, 62, 74, 76, 118, 174–179, 188–189, 192, 201, 214, 221–223, 227
supernatural folklore 170, 216–220
Sweden 142, 186

The Mythical Park 199
Traditional Ecological Knowledge (TEK) 2, 4–7, 14, 226

UFOs 2, 186–187, 190–191, 193
uncanny 10, 180, 186, 188
underground 30, 126, 169, 171–172, 174, 176, 178
UNESCO 43, 55, 75, 128, 169, 204

vampires 19, 89, 191
virtual ghost tourism 214–215, 217

Wells 3, 15, 29–31, 34, 40–41, 51, 90
weird space 214, 220–221
wildness 134
witches 2, 137, 172, 177, 191